JOEL
AND THE TEMPLE CULT
OF JERUSALEM

SUPPLEMENTS

TO

VETUS TESTAMENTUM

EDITED BY

THE BOARD OF THE QUARTERLY

G. W. ANDERSON - P. A. H. DE BOER - G. R. CASTELLINO
HENRY CAZELLES - E. HAMMERSHAIMB - H. G. MAY
W. ZIMMERLI

VOLUME XXI

LEIDEN

E. J. BRILL

1971

JOEL
AND THE TEMPLE CULT
OF JERUSALEM

BY

G. W. AHLSTRÖM

LEIDEN
E. J. BRILL
1971

To RIE

CONTENTS

FOREWORD

This investigation is the result of many years of study of the book of Joel and of the many problems it presents to the modern scholar. There are still many things that remain unknown, but if some of the results of my work will lead the discussion in new directions, I will have accomplished my goal. A main thesis in the following discussion is that the prophet has not borrowed motifs and ideas from the Canaanite cultus, as has sometimes been advocated. Rather, the book of Joel describes what was going on in the Jerusalem temple cultus in his own time.

I wish to thank Reverend John R. Donahue, S.J., and Reverend John W. Brubaker for their help on the complexities of English composition and for retyping the manuscript.

A.S.O.R.
East Jerusalem, December 1969

G. W. AHLSTRÖM

ABBREVIATIONS

AASOR	The Annual of the American Schools of Oriental Research
ACUT	Acta et Commentationes Universitatis Tartuensis
AfO	Archiv für Orientforschung
AJSL	The American Journal of Semitic Languages and Literatures
ANET	Ancient Near Eastern Texts (ed. J. B. Pritchard)
ARM	Archives royales de Mari
ARW	Archiv für Religionswissenschaft
ATD	Das Alte Testament Deutsch
BA	Biblical Archaeologist
BASOR	Bulletin of the American Schools of Oriental Research
BK	Biblischer Kommentar (Altes Testament)
BWANT	Beiträge zur Wissenschaft vom Alten und Neuen Testament
BZ	Biblische Zeitschrift
BZAW	Beihefte zur Zeitschrift für die alttestamentliche Wissenschaft
CAD	The Assyrian Dictionary of the University of Chicago
CBQ	Catholic Biblical Quarterly
DTT	Dansk Teologisk Tidsskrift
EHAT	Exegetisches Handbuch zum Alten Testament
EphThL	Ephemerides Theologicae Lovanienses
FRLANT	Forschungen zur Religion und Literatur des Alten und Neuen Testaments
GHAT	Göttinger Handkommentar zum Alten Testament
HAT	Handbuch zum Alten Testament
HSAT	Die Heilige Schrift des Alten Testaments
HTR	The Harvard Theological Review
HUCA	Hebrew Union College Annual
ICC	The International Critical Commentary of the Holy Scriptures of the Old and New Testament
IDB	The Interpreter's Dictionary of the Bible
JAOS	Journal of the American Oriental Society
JBL	Journal of Biblical Literature
JJS	Journal of Jewish Studies
JNES	Journal of Near Eastern Studies
JSS	Journal of Semitic Studies
JThSt	The Journal of Theological Studies
KAI	Kanaanäische und Aramäische Inschriften (ed. H. Donner & W. Röllig)
LUÅ	Lunds Universitets Årsskrift
MRK	Myth, Ritual, and Kingship (ed. S. H. Hooke)
NTT	Norsk Teologisk Tidsskrift
OLZ	Orientalische Literaturzeitung
OTS	Oudtestamentische Studiën
RB	Revue Biblique internationale
RÉJ	Revue des études juives
RGG	Die Religion in Geschichte und Gegenwart
RHPhR	Revue d'histoire et de philosophie religieuses
RHR	Revue de l'histoire des religions
RoB	Religion och Bibel

SBU   Svenskt Bibliskt Uppsalgsverk
SEÅ   Svensk Exegetisk Årsbok
SKAT   Kommentar zum Alten Testament (ed. E. Sellin)
StTh   Studia Theologica
SVT   Supplements to Vetus Testamentum
ThLZ   Theologische Literaturzeitung
ThSt   Theological Studies
ThZ   Theologische Zeitschrift
UT   Ugaritic Textbook (ed. C. H. Gordon)
UUÅ   Uppsala Universitets Årsbok
VAB   Vorderasiatische Bibliothek
VT   Vetus Testamentum
WMANT   Wissenschaftliche Monographien zum Alten und Neuen Testament
ZAW   Zeitschrift für die alttestamentliche Wissenschaft
ZDMG   Zeitschrift der deutschen morgenländischen Gesellschaft
ZDPV   Zeitschfrift des deutschen Palästina-Vereins
ZfA   Zeitschrift für Assyriologie
ZThK   Zeitschrift für Theologie und Kirche

CHAPTER ONE

WORD STUDIES

The book of Joel does not give us any clear statement concerning
its time as is the case in most pre-exilic prophetical books. An investigation of Joel must, therefore, deal very much with the problem
of its time using all indications there are in the book as well as external
ones. Thus, the language of the book must be seriously taken into
consideration in order to see whether it can give us some hints about
the time Joel delivered his message.

Usually the phenomenon of Aramaisms has been cited as an
argument in favor of a late and post-exilic date of the book of Joel.
This argument is, however, a dubious one. It ought to be emphasized
that what has often been called Aramaisms can more often be understood as dialectical phenomena originally north-Canaanite-Israelite or
northwest-Semitic and therefore mostly of an early date.[1] To mention
a few examples we can begin with the form הנחת in 4:11 which one
has usually counted to the category of Aramaisms.[2] It should be noted
that the verb נחת, "go down", is found in such a text as Psalm 18:35
and its parallel in 2 Sam. 22:35.[3] This psalm is probably pre-exilic and
parts of it could indicate a north-Israelite provenance. Further
occurrences of the root נחת can be found in Pss. 38:3, 65:11, Job 21:13,
17:16, 2 Kings 6:8, Isa. 30:30. The stem is also found in Ugaritic,
UT 52:37, 68:11, 18. Thus it would be possible to conclude that this

---

[1] Cf. H. S. Nyberg, "Studien zum Religionskampf im Alten Testament",
ARW 35/38, p. 379, A. S. Kapelrud, *Joel Studies*, 1948, pp. 160 ff., Compare also
the discussion by A. M. van Dijk, "L'Ancien Testament et l'Orient", *Orientalia
et Biblica Lovaniensia* 1/57, pp. 25 ff., K. A. Kitchen, *Ancient Orient and Old Testament*, 1966, p. 145.

[2] Cf. H. Holzinger, "Sprachcharakter und Abfassungszeit des Buches Joel",
ZAW 9, 1889, pp. 95 f., K. Marti, *Der Prophet Joel* (HSAT³ II), 1910, p. 25. In
4:11 H. W. Wolff prefers to change the text saying that it is very improbable that
in this context we should find "eine Rede Jahwes", *Joel* (BK XIV:5), 1963, p. 88.
We are, however, not told why it is improbable.

[3] For the date of Psalm 18 see, among other, F. M. Cross, Jr. and D. N. Freed-
man, "A Royal Song of Thanksgiving", *JBL* 72/53, pp. 15 ff., W. F. Albright,
Archaeology and the Religion of Israel², 1946, p. 129, A. Weiser, *Die Psalmen* I (ATD
14), 1950, pp. 116 f., M. Dahood, *Psalms* I (The Anchor Bible 16), 1965, p. 104.
For נחת mostly occurring in poetry, cf. N. Snaith, *The Book of Job* (Studies in
Biblical Theology, Ser. 2, no 11), 1968, p. 107.

particular verb is rather old and cannot be used in a chain of indications for the language in Joel being typically post-exilic.

The same is true of the verb אנח, "to sigh", Joel 1:18, which also
occurs in an Ugaritic text, 2 Aqht 1:18.[1] In the Old Testament we
found it in Isa. 24:7, Jer. 22:23, Ezek. 9:4, 21:11 f., Prov. 29:2,
Lam. 1:4, 8, 11, 21, Ex. 2:23. From this stem we also find a noun,
אנחה, which occurs in Pss. 6:7, 31:11, 38:10, 102:6, Job 3:24,
23:2, Isa. 21:2, 35:10, 51:11, Jer. 45:3 and Lam. 1:22. It is evident
that not all of these texts can be assigned to the period after the Exile.

The designation of סוף as a late word of Aramaic origin, Joel 2:20,
is argued from its occurrance in 2 Chr. 20:16 and Ec. 3:11, 7:2,
12:13.[2] It occurs in the Aramaic part of Daniel in 4:8, 19, 6:27,
7:26, 28. It should be noted, however, that in the Hebrew part of
Daniel the term סוף does not occur at all which makes us understand
that סוף "was by no means pre-dominant in later times".[3] In place of
the assumed late סוף the Hebrew part of Daniel uses the term קץ,
8:17, 19, 9:25 f., 11:6, 13, 27, 35, 40, 45, 12:4, 6, 9, 13, 13:9. It is
doubtful whether, as has been maintained, סוף must always be understood as an Aramaism for קץ.[4] As a matter of fact the term קץ means
the end of something with the understanding that it will cease to
exist, a meaning which סוף also has in Aramaic. The phrase קץ כל־בשׂר
in Gen. 6:13 does not mean the physical limit of every person but the
end, the finish or termination of mankind. There will be no more
human beings. The same usage is found in Jer. 51:13—Babel will
cease to exist, cf. Ps. 39:5, Lam. 4:18. There is an aspect of time in
this term. It can designate the end of an epoch as is shown also by
Am. 8:2, Hab. 2:3 and Ezek 7:2 f. and by almost every other usage
in the Old Testament, as well as by its occurrences in the DSS and
in the Damascus Scroll.[5]

---

[1] Concerning אנח Holzinger considered it an old verb of Aramaic origin
which *via* poetry came into use in Hebrew in later times, *ZAW* 9/89, pp. 91 ff.

[2] Thus, for example, Holzinger, Bewer (*ICC* 26, p. 57), Sellin (*SKAT* XII:1,
p. 166), Wolff.

[3] Kapelrud, *Joel Studies*, p. 112.

[4] Cf. Gesenius-Buhl and Köhler-Baumgartner.

[5] N. Wieder, "The Term קץ in the Dead Sea Scrolls and in Hebrew Liturgical
Poetry", *JJS* 5/54, pp. 22 ff., G. Vermès, *Les manuscrits du désert de Juda*, 1953,
p. 47, F. Nötscher, *Zur Theologischen Terminologie der Qumran-Texte* (Bonner Bibl.
Beiträge 10), 1956, pp. 167 ff., M. Mansoor, *The Thanksgiving Hymns*, 1961, pp. 21,
99, n. 11., Cf. F. F. Hvidberg, *Menigheden af den nye Pagt i Damascus*, 1928, pp.
59 f., S. Holm-Nielsen, *Hodayot, Psalms from Qumran*, (Acta Theologica Danica II),
1960, p. 278. See also M. Wallenstein, "Some Lexical Material in the Judean
Scrolls", *VT* 4/54, pp. 211 ff.

In Joel 2:20 סֹפוֹ does not have this temporal nuance which would explain why קץ was avoided. The text speaks about the front side, פניו, of the Northerners as well as about their "rear guard",[1] i.e., the end of their troops, which makes the choice of סוף more adequate than קץ in this case. The occurrence of the verb סוף in Am. 3:15, Ps. 73:19,[2] Jer. 8:13 and Zeph 1:2 ff, is an indication that the root is not always or necessarily a late Aramaism.

Another phrase which, according to Wolff, is both rare and late is ואם in 1:2.[3] However, the context and style must be examined. Though almost every second half of the lines in vv. 2-7 begins with ו this does not make it *per se* a late style. The same pattern occurs in Job 21:2-6 where every second half-verse begins with ו and in v. 4 we find the same construction as in Joel 1:2 ה···ואם. This construction occurs sometimes in a double question, Gen. 17:17, Job 8:3, 11:2, 22:3, Isa. 49:24, Jer. 5:9, 14:22. Job 34:17 has האף···ואם and Gen. 18:21 has ה···ואם־לֹא while in 2 Sam. 24:13, we find ה···אם ואם. It can also be noted that the double question in Jer. 48:27 begins with ואם, cf. also Job 24:25, 40:8-9. One must conclude that ואם in such a construction does not necessarily indicate a post-exilic date, even though it can be considered a relatively late construction.

According to O. Procksch the apple, תפוח, Joel 1:12, was not cultivated in Palestine before the Persian period and Joel must therfore be of post-exilic origin.[4] However, it can be disputed whether the word תפוח should actually be translated "apple".[5] Whatever the translation, the occurrence of תפוח in some city names shows that the word has been known since the beginning of Israel's history in the land of Canaan.[6] Even if the apple or תפוח tree was not *cultivated* prior to the Persian period, it can be assumed that it had existed here and there in some forests, so that the thesis of Procksch is not conslusive.[7]

---

[1] Cf. E. König, *Einleitung in das Alte Testament*, 1893, p. 345.

[2] As for Ps. 73:19 סֹפוֹ may as well be a form of ספה, "sweep away", cf. M. Dahood, *Psalms* II (The Anchor Bible 17), 1968, p. 193.

[3] *Joel*, p. 21. Wolff refers here to Brockelmann, *Hebräische Syntax*, §. 169c, p. 161, but Brockelmann does not say anything about the time of this phenomenon.

[4] *Die kleinen prophetischen Schriften nach dem Exil*, 1916, p. 75.

[5] See for instance J. C. Trever, *IDB* I, pp. 175 ff.

[6] Bet Tappuah not far from Hebron, Josh. 15:33, Tappuah in Shephelah, Josh. 15:34, and Tappuah in Ephraim, Josh. 12:17, 16:8, 17:8. תפוח denoting a tree or its fruit occurs also in Song of Songs 2:3, 5, 7:8, 8:5 and in Prov. 25:11. The word *tph* in Ugaritic may be both a tree and a place name, cf. Gordon, *Ugaritic Textbook*, 1965, p. 499.

[7] "Sein vorkommen im Wald war eine beglückende Seltenheit", says G. Gerleman, *Ruth, Das Hohe Lied* (BK XVIII:2), 1963, p. 116.

In Joel 1:17 we find some *hapax legomena*—עבש, "shrink, shrivel", ממגרות, "pond, tank" (*sic* Köhler-Baumgartner; Kapelrud has "barns", and Wolff "Speicher"), מגרפות, "shovel" (cf. Syr. ܡܓܪܘܦܐ),[1] and פרדות, "grain of corn" (cf. Syr. ܦܪܝܕܐ, Jewish-Aram. פרידא). In 1:8 we find the imperative אלי fem. sg. of אלה which is supposed to be an Aramaism.[2] Wolff and others have classed all these terms as late which may be possible. אלה for example, occurs in non-biblical Hebrew (אליה).[3] It can, then, not be denied that this verb may indicate a relatively late time. On the other hand, we have no possibility of deciding what time such a *hapax legomenon* as עבש could point to.

In a study of Ps. 114/115 H. Lubscyzk has argued that רקד occurs only in late texts of which Joel 2:5 is an example.[4] Observation of the places where the stem רקד occurs throws doubt on such a thesis. The stem itself is of very old origin, found several times in Ugaritic proper names and once in the form, *mrqdm*, "dancers", (Rs 24.252),[5] cf. Akkadian *raqādu*, "to jump, to dance". In Hebrew we find the stem in Ps. 29:6; Ps. 114:4, Job 21:11, Nah. 3:2, Isa. 13:21, Eccl. 3:4, Joel 2:5, and 1 Chr. 15:29. Of these Ps. 29:6, Ps. 114:4, Job 21:11 [6] and Nah. 3:2 can be considered as pre-exilic. Many archaic features are found in Ps. 29, and H. Gunkel has judged it as a north-Israelite psalm because of the Phoenician use of the name Sirion for Hermon.[7] H. L. Ginsburg has maintained that the psalm is dependent upon a West-Semitic hymn (to Baal),[8] and W. F. Albright attributes the psalm to the 10th century calling it "a hymn to Baal which has been only

---

[1] Kapelrud takes תַּחַת in v. 17 as niph. תֵּחַת from חתת, *Joel*, p. 65, cf. H. Robinson, *HAT*³, p. 60.

[2] Robinson, *op. cit.*, p. 58, M. Wagner, *Die lexikalischen und grammatikalischen Aramaismen im alttestamentlichen Hebräisch* (BZAW 96), 1966, p. 24.

[3] For Wolff's view, cf. *Joel*, p. 4; on lateness of construction, cf. S. Gevirtz, *Patterns in the Early Poetry of Israel*, (Studies in Ancient Oriental Civilization, No. 32), 1963, p. 81, n. 34. Cf. M. Wagner, *op. cit.*, p. 24.

[4] "Einheit und heilsgeschichtliche Bedeutung von Ps. 114/115 (113)," *BZ* 11/67, p. 169.

[5] C. H. Gordon, *Ugaritic Textbook*, pp. 421, 485.

[6] For Job see the discussion by M. Pope, *Job* (The Anchor Bible 15), 1965, pp. XXX f.

[7] *Die Psalmen*, p. 125.

[8] *Atti del XIX Congresso Internazionale degli Orientalisti*, Rome, 1935, pp. 472 ff., *BA* 8/45, pp. 53 ff., cf. E. Pax, "Studien zur Theologie von Pslam 29", *BZ* 6/62, pp. 93 ff., W. Schmidt, *Königtum Gottes in Ugarit und Israel* (BZAW 80), 1961, pp. 45 ff., A. Weiser, *Die Psalmen* I (ATD 14), 1950, p. 166. H.-J. Kraus sees Psalm 29 as having taken over "Vorstellungen aus kanaanäischen Kultgesang", *Psalmen* I, p. 235.

slightly modified".[1] In the case of Ps. 114:4, we can agree with those who hold the opinion that there are so many archaic features in the psalm that it is most probable to ascribe it to the pre-exilic period.[2]

What then about Isa. 13:21? First of all, one can note that Isa. 13 must be older than 550 B.C. (cf. Jer. 51:11) because v. 17 mentions the danger of the Medes.[3] As in most other prophetic utterances, it is, however, difficult to decide what time this *maśśā'* refers to. Properly speaking an Isaiah oracle against Babel must not *a priori* be understood as not spoken by Isaiah of Jerusalem. It could very well have happened that Isaiah was concerned not only about Assur, but also about Babel. There is a period which could have caused Isaiah to prophecy against Babylon, the period of the reign of the Chaldean king Merodach-Baladan II (721-710, and 703). As we know Merodach-Baladan sought to stir up as many people as possible against Assyria and with this intent he sent messengers to king Hezekiah of Judah. Elam as a supporter of Merodach-Baladan belongs also to this picture, as do the Arabs mentioned in 13:20 since at this time they were Merodoch-Baladan's allies.[4] In light of Isaiah's appearence before Hezekiah after the visit of the Babylonian messengers to the Judean king, 2 Kings 20:14, Isa. 39, and his dissatisfaction with Hezekiah's friendly treatment of the Babylonians one could very well imagine that at some time during this period Isaiah uttered oracles of disaster against Babel, a disaster which, according to Isaiah, could well have been effected by the Medes who in the 8th century B.C. vere allies or vassals of Assyria.

It is also possible *apropros* of Isa. 13 that a disciple of Isaiah in a later period could have appropriated a prophecy of Isaiah. Such could have been the case in the beginning of the 7th century when the Medes and the Scythians attacked Assur, or in the time of Nabopolassar when the Babylonians in alliance with the Medes crushed the Assyrian

---

[1] *Archeology and the Religion of Israel*, 1953, p. 129, Cf. M. Dahood *Psalms I* (The Anchor Bible, 16), 1966, p. 178.

[2] Cf. Kraus, *Psalmen* II, p. 780, who thinks that the psalm received its present form in later Jerusalemite time. This may be true, but it does not mean that all the words used in it must be from the same late time.

[3] A. S. Kapelrud, *Joel Studies*, pp. 54 f.

[4] A. L. Oppenheim, *Ancient Mesopotamia*, p. 162, cf. *The Interpreter's Dictionary of the Bible* III, pp. 355 f., cf. J. A. Brinkman, "Elamite Military Aid to Merodach-Baladan", *JNES* 24/65, pp. 161 ff.

empire.[1] An Isaiah oracle could have been slightly modified to fit the historical situation and the expectations of that time.[2]

The result of this short investigation of the occurrences of רקד shows that the stem is of an old origin and that it occurs now and then in Israelite texts dating from the early monarchic period down to the post-exilic period. Since most of the texts belong to the latter half of the monarchic period, there is no way of telling exactly what period רקד in Joel 2:5 indicates.

The phrase, "Judah and Jerusalem," in Joel 4:1 (cf. vv 6 and 20), has been interpreted as a "stereotyped formula" referring to the post-exilic period and designating "the small community whose center was Jerusalem".[3] The statistics assembled by D. Jones show that the phrase belongs to the later writings of the Old Testament, namely, Jeremiah, Malachi, Chronicles, Ezra and Nehemiah, in addition to Joel. In the work of the Chronicler the phrase appears 20 times, but in the other books only one to three times. This indicates undoubtedly a late date and urges that Joel should be placed within the time span covered by these books, i.e. between c. 600 and 400 B.C. In Joel 4:1 the phrase may be a synonym for the ideal Israel, 4:2, 16. In 4:2 "Israel" could perhaps refer to the northern kingdom as well as to the two Israelite kingdoms, but in these passages as in 2:17 "Israel" refers primarily to the cult congregation of the Jerusalem temple, since people and cult congregation are often synonymous.[4]

The next phrase to be discussed, בני ציון in Joel 2:23, points to a period no earlier than the time of Jeremiah. We must first note an old composition technique in 2:21 ff. The admonition to rejoice and be glad is given first to the country, then to the beasts of the field, and finally in v. 23 to the בני ציון, the population and cult congregation of Jerusalem. The composition starts with the outer circle and

---

[1] Oppenheim, *op. cit.*, p. 170.

[2] Ahlström, "Oral and Written Transmission", *HTR* 59/66, p. 81.

[3] D. Jones, "The Tradition of the Oracles of Isaiah of Jerusalem", *ZAW* 67/55, p. 239. Cf. also G. A. Danell, *Studies in the Name of Israel in the Old Testament*, 1964, p. 268. H. Wildberger, *Jesaja* (BK X), 1965, p. 3.

[4] Cf. below p. 56. According to J. H. Grønbaek the term Judah never occurs with the meaning cult congregation, "Juda und Amalek. Überlieferungsgeschichtliche Erwägungen zu Exodus 17, 8-16", *StTh* 18/64, p. 31. This seems correct, cf. 3:5. However, the phrase Judah and Jerusalem in 4:1 may refer to the cult assembly as such because of the preceding phrase אשוב את שבות. For Joel there seems to be no difference.

proceeds to the inner circle, the center,[1] so that the בני ציון get an
assurance that what is necessary for life will be restored, namely the
life-giving rain which gives an abundant harvest. In this oracle we
find a close connection with nature and the cultic demand and com-
mand over the forces of nature—a phenomenon in agreement with
the inheritance from the pre-exilic Israelite religion in Canaan, but
which has not, at least for the early post-exilic period, been fully
acknowledged as part of the temple cult of Jerusalem. It is alleged
that the cult of the second temple severed the ties with nature and
the agrarian motivations of the festivals, so that a text like Joel 2:21 ff.
would be understood as referring to a time before the Exile.[2] However, this break with the agricultural ties did not occur immediately.
The first century after the return from Babylon witnessed the struggle
to establish a *modus vivendi* with the new cultural and political situation,
as well as to integrate old and new modes of interpreting Israel's
religion and history.[3] Thus we cannot draw any conclusion other than
that the temple of Zerubbabel was thought of as a symbol of the
re-establishment of the pre-exilic cult.[4]

The phrase בני ציון is very rare, occurring outside of Joel 2:23 only
in Lam. 4:2, Ps. 149:2, and in Zech, 9:13 with the 2nd person suffix.
The time of Lam. 4:2 will not be discussed here and we can turn our
attention to the more problematic Ps. 149. In verse 1 of the psalm we
find the phrase קהל חסידים "the congregation of the faithful, pious
ones", which does not occur anywhere else in the Hebrew bible.
This phrase is equivalent to the Greek συναγωγὴ 'Ασιδαίων in 1 Macc.
2:42. Another *hapax legomenon* is found in verse 9, משפט כתוב, "book
(writing) of judgement", which recalls the books of judgement
mentioned in Dan. 7:10.[5] E. Lipiński concludes on the basis of these
phrases that Psalm 149 derives from the Maccabean era.[6] This could
be correct even if a psalm like this contains many old and traditional

---

[1] Cf. Ps. 89:6-17 which begins with the cosmic aspects of the actions of Yahweh
and in vv. 15 ff. ends in the center, that is, with the cult congregation of Jerusalem,
the cultic procession and the people rejoicing over its god because of his deeds.
Cf. also Am. 1-2.

[2] Kapelrud, *Joel Studies*, p. 179.

[3] This could have been inspired by the experience of the Exile.

[4] Cf. J. M. Myers, *Ezra, Nehemiah* (The Anchor Bible 14), 1965, pp. 53 ff., cf.
also below pp. 122f. Cf. also Ezr. 3:4 f., 6:16 ff.

[5] Cf. Ecclus. 48:10.

[6] *La royauté de Yahwé dans la poésie et le culte de l'ancien Israel*, 1965, p. 269. H.
Gunkel says that קהל חסידים is here not the name of a party but "eine Ehrens-
bezeichnung Israels", *Die Psalmen*, 1925, p. 621.

motifs.[1] However the term, חסידים,[2] by its simple presence does not make a psalm late. In several other instances this term can stand for the cult congregation, Pss. 30:5, 31:24, 32:6, 37:28, 50:5, 132:9, 2 Chr. 6:41. Thus its occurence in Ps. 149 need not necessarily refer to the Hasideans of the Maccabean time. There is no proof that the designation קהל חסידים could not have originated earlier. However the conjunction of this phrase with the משפט כתוב in 149:9 along with the close association to Daniel 7:10 leads us to believe that we are dealing with a post-exilic psalm. Thus the three passages with בני ציון may point to a time after the fall of Jerusalem.[3]

The occurence of בניך ציון in Zech. 9:13 may somewhat complicate the picture. It is, namely, not quite indisputable that Zech. 9 must refer to a post-exilic period. If B. Otzen is correct, the parallel phrase בניך יון [4] in the same verse may point to a time after 660 B.C. and reflect military conditions in Egypt.[5] He views Zech. 9 and 10 as dealing with the return of the population of the northern kingdom and its joining with the still existing kingdom of Judah, so that the time of the utterances belong to the reign of king Josiah.[6] Therefore, בני ציון, does not decisively point to the post-exilic period. It seems, however, to belong to a later period in Israel's history.

S. R. Driver, among others, has maintained that אני which occurs in Joel 2:27 and 4:10, 17 is a term belonging to a late period.[7] Examination of the frequency of the terms אני and אנכי shows that both are used throughout the Old Testament, and, therefore, both may be considered old.[8] It is true, however, that אני is more common in books from later periods. In the books of Esther, Ezra, Nehemiah,

---

[1] This explains why, among others, S. Mowinckel (Psalmenstudien II, 1922, pp. 193 ff.), H. Schmidt (*Die Psalmen*, 1934, p. 149), and A. Weiser (*Die Psalmen* 2, ATD 15, 1950, p. 561) considered Psalm 149 as a pre-exilic psalm. H.-J. Kraus follows the same line of reasoning in maintaining that the psalm is an expression of the Jerusalemite cult tradition, but he is, however, uncertain about the date and feels that the psalm may well be from the time of Nehemiah, *Psalmen* (BK XV:2), 1961, pp. 966 f. Cf. H. Gunkel, *Die Psalmen*, pp. 620 f.

[2] It occurs also in vv. 5 and 9.

[3] It is possible that the phrase בני ציון was used for the whole population of the post-exilic Judah.

[4] Concerning the suggestion of reading בני יון, see Otzen, *Studien über Deuterosacharja*, 1964, p. 242. For the name יון which also occurs in Joel 4:6 see below pp. 116 ff.

[5] *Op. cit.*, p. 117.

[6] *Ibid.*, p. 218, cf. p. 223.

[7] *Joel and Amos*, 1915, p. 24.

[8] Cf. H. Bauer and P. Leander, *Historische Grammatik der Hebräischen Sprache des Alten Testaments*², 1962, § 29b, p. 260, § 28k, p. 249.

Daniel and I and II Chronicles אני occurs 76 times, while אנכי occurs only three times. In the books of Isaiah, Jeremiah and Ezechiel we find אני almost 300 times, but אנכי 64 times. In the book of the Twelve Prophets the figures are: אנכי 30 occurrences; אני 48 occurrences. It should be noted that the prophets Habbakuk and Zephaniah never use the form אנכי. In the Psalms אני occurs 68 times and אנכי 13 times. Another interesting phenomenon is that אנכי is more common in Deuteronomy than in the other books of the Pentateuch.[1] Also in Ruth אנכי is the more common pronoun (seven times). Here אני occurs only twice. It may be concluded, however, that אני is the form of the pronoun that, as time went on, became the more common one.[2]

In his investigation of the occurrences of these two forms U. Cassuto came to the conclusion that, as far as Genesis is concerned, they cannot be used in any way as indications for different sources. They are due "to general linguistic reasons only". In verbal clauses אנכי is always used, while in nominal clauses אני is found.[3] Though this may be true for prose narratives, the pattern does not hold for poetry. In Joel we find אני in nominal clauses in all three instances, 2:27, 4:10, 17. In Ps. 75:3 ff., on the other hand, אני is used in a verbal clause אני מישרים אשפט v. 3, as is אנכי in v. 4. Then again in v. 10 אני occurs in a verbal clause, cf. also Pss. 30:7, 31:23. In some Psalms אנכי is also found in nominal clauses, Pss. 39:13, 46:11, 50:7, 81:11, 109:22, 119:19, 141, 162. The example from Ps. 75 shows clearly that both forms of the pronoun can be used in one and the same text. A further argument against the possibility of using אני and אנכי to differentiate sources may be found in the Ugaritic usage of an and ank in one and the same text: UT 49:II:15, 21 f., 51:IV:59 f.,[4] 67:I:5 and II:12, 1 Aqht I:64:70 (an), 2 Aqht II:12 (ank), VI:32 (ank), 38 (an), 45 (ank), 3 Aqht, obv., 21 (ank), 26 (ank), 40 (ank).

Therefore, the form אני cannot *a priori* be taken as an indication

---

[1] P. Buis and J. Leclerq, *Le Deutéronome* (Sources Bibliques), 1963, p. 11.

[2] D. Barthélemy, *Les Devanciers d'Aquila* (SVT X), 1963, p. 69, J. Wijngaards, "הוציא and העלה, a twofold approach to the Exodus", *VT*, 15/65, p. 99, cf. M. Wagner, *BZAW* 96/66, p. 130.

[3] *The Documentary Hypothesis and the Composition of the Pentateuch*, 1961, pp. 43 ff., cf. pp. 50 f., 93.

[4] K. A. Kitchen, *Ancient Orient and the Old Testament*, 1966, p. 124 f., R. Mayer, *Einleitung in das Alte Testament* II, 1967, p. 46, M. Dahood, "Ugarit and the Old Testament", *Ephem. Theol. Lov.*, 44/68, p. 36, cf. also C. H. Gordon *Ugaritic Textbook*, 1965, § 6.2, p. 35.

for a late date. We should notice that in Joel 2:27 and 4:17 אני is part of a formula, and in formulas this form of the pronoun is the most common one. In these two passages of Joel, the formula reads אני יהוה אלהיכם[-ך]. The phrase אני יהוה announces the revelation and self-proclamation of the deity, and as such suggests a cultic *Sitz im Leben*.[1] According to K. Elliger, when this formula occurs in its extended form (with אלהיכם), as in Joel, it is a formula connected with the covenant and registers an objection to Israel's worship of other gods, Judg. 6:10, Ez. 20:7.[2] The *locus classicus* for the formula is the Decalogue, Ex. 20:2.[3] This is exactly in harmony with its use in Joel 2:27 and 4:17. This fact is emphasized in Joel by the addition of ואין עוד which occurs also in Isa. 45:5 f., 18, cf. v. 21 ff. where the phrase אני אל occurs.[4] There are also examples with the names אל, אלהים and אל שדי instead of Yahweh.[5] There are also passages where the name of the deity has been replaced by the pronoun הוא. According to Zimmermann, this phrase should be seen as the link between the Hebrew and the ἐγώ εἰμι of the LXX and the New Testament.[6]

The formula, in its totality, is not found often in the prophetical books. W. Zimmerli explains this phenomenon as due to the fact that, since it belongs to the old cult tradition of theophany, it is of a different character than the prophetic *Botschaftsempfang*, and hence rarely used by the prophets.[7] Such a view may explain its presence in Joel which is, for the most part, a composition using liturgical motifs

---

[1] W. Zimmerli, "Ich bin Jahwe", *Geschichte und Altes Testament*, 1953, pp. 186 ff., (= *Gottes Offenbarung*, 1963, pp. 17 ff., 34 ff.), H. Reventlow, *Wächter über Israel* (BZAW 82) 1962, p. 125, cf. E. Stauffer, "Probleme der Priestertradition", *ThLZ* 81/56, col. 148, K. Elliger, *Kleine Schriften zum Alten Testament*, 1966, pp. 226 f. For this phrase as equivalent to the NT ἐγώ εἰμι see, among others H. Zimmermann, "Das absolute 'Εγώ εἰμι als die neutestamentliche Offenbarungsformel", *BZ* 4/60, pp. 54 ff., 226 ff., cf. L. Hartman, *Prophecy Interpreted* (Coniectanea Biblica, New Test. Series 1), 1966, pp. 159 f. To the OT phrase see also W. Zimmerli, *Gottes Offenbarung*, pp. 11 ff., 72 ff.

[2] Elliger, *Kleine Schriften*, pp. 211 ff., 229.

[3] *Op. cit.*, p. 230.

[4] In a few instances אנכי יהוה occurs, Ex. 20:2, Isa. 43:11. and in Ps. 46:11 we find אנכי אלהים. In the first part of Isaiah, the so called proto-Isaiah, and in Amos and Micah the formula is not to be found. In Hosea it occurs in 12:10 and 13:4, both times with the addition of אלהיך מארץ מצרים, "your god from the land of Egypt".

[5] See the above mentioned works by Zimmermann and Zimmerli.

[6] *BZ* 4/60, pp. 64 f., "die LXX gibt an allen Stellen אני הוא mit ἐγώ εἰμι wieder", p. 65. אני הוא is found in Isa. 41:4, 43:10, 13, 25 (which has אנכי), 46:4, 48:12, 51:12 (also אנכי), 52:6, and Dt. 32:39.

[7] *Gottes Offenbarung*, p. 34.

and phrases. We may conclude, then, that Joel is in agreement with
the original form of the formula, and that the occurence of אני cannot,
of itself, point to any special period.

It should be noted, in this connection, that this kind of *Selbst-
praedikationsformula* has parallels outside the Old Testament,[1] which
indicates that the revelation idea is not unique to Israel. Finally, this
style is also found in connection with kings, "I, king N.",[2] a variation
of which is found in Ps. 116:16, אני עבדך, "I am your servant", i.e.
the king, who also calls himself בן אמתך the son of Yahweh's אמה.[3]

The phrase ואיש בדרכיו ילכון, 2:7, "everyone marches his way
(straight)" is followed by ולא יעבטון ארחותם which could be translated,
"and they do not change their battle order".[4] Then we have ואיש
אחיו לא ידחקון, "no one thrusts another", and finally לא יבצעו as the
last two words in v. 8, which is usually translated "they do not break
off (the ranks)". This can be questioned. We must remember that
the picture given in verses 7 and 8 is that of an army, so massive,
irresistible, and stern, that one might ask whether the traditional
translations of the verbs עבט (change), דחק (thrust), and בצע (break
off) give a meaning suitable to the context, even if they give a good
description of an army's approach. It should be kept in mind that the
aforementioned locusts serve as a background for the description of
the army. They are going through and over everything, and nothing
can stop them. The choice of דחק must, in this context, be said to be
very suitable, since this verb expresses the idea of very close ranks.
There is no space between the men; nobody can escape them;
everyone clings to the other.

The verb עבט may be a loan word from the Aramaic, ʿbṭ, "to seize,
hold", or from the Akkadian *ebēṭu*, "to tie, gird".[5] Thus, in their
march, they are coming in closed ranks, almost "tied" to each other.

---

[1] These need not be repeated here, see Zimmerli, *op. cit.*, pp. 26 ff.

[2] So already E. Norden who says that "die Formel einer Selbstpredikation mit
'Ich bin' und hinzugefügten Namen ursprünglich auf Götter beschränkt gewesen
und erst von diesen auf die Könige als ihre irdischen Repräsentanten übertragen
worden ist", *Agnostos Theos*, 1913, p. 214. Cf. A. Poebel, *Das appositionell bestimmte
Pronomen der 1. Pers. sing. in den westsemitischen Inschriften und im Alten Testament*, 1932.

[3] Cf. my book *Aspects of Syncretism in Israelite Religion*, pp. 76 f., M. Dahood,
Psalms II, p. 292.

[4] G. R. Driver, "Studies in the Vocabulary of the Old Testament", *JThSt* 34/33,
p. 378, cf. A. R. Hulst, *Old Testament Translation Problems*, 1960, p. 237.

[5] See J. C. Greenfield, "Studies in Aramaic Lexicography I", *JAOS* 82/62, pp.
295 f. Driver sees עבט as cognate to the Arabic عبط, "rend, change", *op. cit.* p. 378.

They are "steamrolling", their way.[1] The third verb under discussion, בצע, means "to cut off" and, therefore, the meaning "to break" could suit the context of Joel 2:8, but only if the preceeding לא is really a negation here. After the enemies have burst into the city through השלח, their action is described with the verb בצע. This root is sometimes used in connection with weaving or cutting of the woof, so that the idea of cutting (down the people) may be probable in Joel 2:8, cf. the Arabic بَضَعَ, "cut into pieces", and also Isa. 38:12. Therefore in all three instances we do not have the negative לא but the לא emphaticum, an equivalent of the Akkadian lû. We must reckon with two ways of expressing the emphatic particle, *la (or lu). It can occur as lamed emphaticum or as the independent plene לא or לו emphaticum. These latter forms have been misinterpreted by the later Massoretes as the negation לא and as the preposition and suffix לו, "to him", while the lamed emphaticum is usually mistaken for the preposition לְ.[2]

In Joel 2:7-8 עבט and שלח have been considered as indicative that Joel's language dates from a later period.[3] J. C. Greenfield has maintained that עבט must be seen as an Aramaic loanword.[4] This may be true and we should observe that besides our passage in Joel, the stem occurs only in Deuteronomy and Habakkuk.[5] The other word that has not only been understood as pointing to a late time,[6] but the meaning of which has been disputed is השלח in 2:8. This occurs in 2 Chr. 23:10, 32:5, Neh. 4:11, 17, Job 33:18, 36:12. Its presence in Job makes one doubt that it can be seen as belonging only to a later period.[7] If שלח means here spear or lance, then the word is an old

---

[1] The chiastic parallelism in vv. 7 f. should be noticed as supporting עבט and דחק giving almost the same idea:

ילכון—יעבטון
ידחקון—ילכון

[2] Cf. P. Haupt, "The Hebrew Stem NAHAL, to Rest", *AJSL* 22, 1905-06, p. 201, "Scripto plena des emphatischen la- im Hebräischen", *OLZ* 10/07, cols. 305 ff., I Eitan, "La particule emphatique 'La' dans la Bible", *RÉJ* 74/22, pp. 1 f., A. S. Kapelrud, *Joel Studies*, p. 175, H. S. Nyberg, *Hebreisk Grammatik*, 1952, § 28d, p. 53, F. Nötscher, "Zum emphatischen Lamed", *VT* 3/53, pp. 372 ff., M. Dahood, "Enclitic Mem and Emphatic Lamed in Psalm 85", *Biblica* 37/56, pp. 338 f., cf. *Psalms* I, p. 143.

[3] Wolff, *Joel*, p. 4.

[4] Greenfield, *JAOS* 82/62, pp. 295 f.

[5] Dt. 15:6, 8, 24:10-13, Hab. 2:6.

[6] A. Merx, *Die Prophetie des Joel und ihre Ausleger*, 1879, pp. 107 f., J. A. Bewer, *Obadiah and Joel (ICC 26)* 1911, p. 57, H. W. Wolff, *Joel*, p. 4.

[7] Cf. M. Pope, *Job*, (The Anchor Bible 15) 1965, pp. XXX ff.

West-Semitic one. It is found in Ugarit, I Krt, 20, as a designation for a weapon, cf. Akkad. *šelu*, "spear". There are, however, two other possible ways of rendering this term. First, it could be cognate to the Akkadian *šalḫu*, "frontwall", and then the meaning in Joel would be that the enemies are making a raid through the wall.[1] The preposition בעד suits this interpretation as well as the meaning "spear", but is perhaps better suited to the meaning "frontwall".[2] The meaning of frontwall is in accord with the parallelism in v. 9. The other possibility is to see השלח as referring to Siloah,[3] which also is in accord with the use of בעד. Isa. 8:6 and the mention of the "waters of Siloah, (מֵי הַשִּׁלֹחַ) which flow gently" might give a clue to Joel 2:8. According to Isaiah the people have despised the waters of Siloah, therefore disaster will come upon them. The waters of Siloah mean blessings. In Joel 2:8 we could have a picture of disaster coming this time through Siloah.[4] This interpretation would be in harmony with the whole passage.

Before leaving verses 7-8 of chapter two we should notice the accentuated 3rd person plural ending ־ין which occurs in v. 7 in the forms ירצון, ילכון and יעבטון; and in v. 8 in the forms ידחקון and ילכון. We are dealing here with the *nun paragogicum*, or perhaps the so-called *nun energicum*. This form of the ending is of an old date,[5] evidenced in other Semitic languages such as Ugaritic,[6] Akkadian(as an allative),[7] Aramaic[8] and Arabic. The question is whether it can be determined which aspect or rather which function the old ending has in Joel 2:7f. Both ירצון and ידחקון are followed by words beginning with a consonant. For this reason we could assume that the ending is *energicum*. The final two verbs in v. 8 do not have this kind of ending which

---

[1] Cf. Job 1:15.

[2] It should be noted that a word for "lance", רֹמַח, occurs (in pl.) in Joel 4:10, cf. Judg. 5:8, 1 Kings 18:28, The usual word for spear is חֲנִית.

[3] So W. Rudolph, "Wann wirkte Joel?", *Festschrift L. Rost*, 1967, p. 194.

[4] We can, of course, not be quite sure that we here should have to do with the name Siloah. It could as well be שֶׁלַח with the meaning of water-pipe, water conduit, as in Neh. 3:15, בְּרֵכַת הַשֶּׁלַח "the pool of the water conduit". השלח could then be compared with צִנּוֹר in 2 Sam. 5:6 ff.

[5] Cf. H. Bauer-P. Leander, *Historische Grammatik der Hebräischen Sprache des Alten Testaments*[2], 1962, § 40o, p. 300, P. Joüon, *Grammaire de l'hébreu biblique*, 1923, § 44e.

[6] Cf. E. Hammershaimb, *Das Verbum in Dialekt von Ras Schamra*, 1941, pp. 110 ff., 117 ff.

[7] Akkadian allative is used with verbs of motion.

[8] Cf. J. C. Greenfield, "Three Notes on the Sefire Inscription", *JSS* 11/66, pp. 103 f.

indicates that ־ין is something other than a pausal form here. The stress there is upon this ending and the movements these verbs describe make it possible to understand the verbs as having the *nun energicum* as the ending. If so, we have another indication for seeing לא as an emphatic particle.

One of the arguments used for assigning a post-exilic date to the book of Joel is the word pair מנחה and נסך in Joel 1:9, 13, 2:14. Nowack,[1] Sellin,[2] and Wolff[3] among others understand the terms as referring to the post-exilic *tāmīd* sacrifice. Even though Joel does not use the term *tāmīd* we cannot exclude the possibility of a reference to this sacrifice. The passages usually chosen in support of the identification of מנחה and נסך with the *tāmīd* sacrifice are Ex. 29:38-42, Lev. 23:13, 18, Nu. 6:15, 15:24, 28:3-9, 29:11, 16-39. However, in Lev. 23:13 only the *minḥāh* is mentioned, and instead of the *nesaek* we find the phrase וְנִסְכֹּה יַיִן. Thus the word pair, which according to Wolff occurs for the first time after the Exile,[4] is not found in Lev. 23:13 even if the phenomenon is there. Neh. 10:34 may serve as an indication of the weakness of Wolff's thesis. In this passage the phrases ומנחת התמיד and ולעולת התמיד ("the continual cereal offering" and "the continual burnt offering") occur.[5] Here *tāmīd* does not include the נסך.

Of a certain interest is another text which has not been considered by Wolff. Ezech. 45:17 mentions העולות והמנחה והנסך in a context dealing with the cultic role of the ruler, נשיא, in the temple which is to be built in Jerusalem after the Exile. We can ask here to what degree the prophet is building upon old phenomena. Has he invented something, or is he mentioning these kinds of sacrifices while talking of a cult practice which he knew was of an old date? When the prophet refers here to the cultic duties of the ruler—here called נשיא and not מלך [6]—he is at the same time in a way telling us about some

---

[1] W. Nowack, *Die kleinen Propheten* (GHAT III:4) 1922, p. 87.

[2] E. Sellin, *Das Zwölfprophetenbuch übersetz und erklärt* (SKAT XII:1) 1929, p. 148.

[3] H. W. Wolff, *Joel*, pp. 3, 35 f.

[4] *Op. cit.*, p. 36.

[5] *The Oxford Annotated Bible*, 1962. Perhaps it is not necessary to mention that *tāmīd* means regularly occuring sacrifices.

[6] For נשיא see E. Hammershaimb, "Ezechiel's View of the Monarchy", *Some Aspects of Old Testament Prophecy from Isaiah to Malachai*, 1966, pp. 54 ff., E. A. Speiser, "Background and Function of the Biblical *nāśi*'", *CBQ* 25/63, pp. 111 ff. One reason for Ezechiel's use of *nāśi*' could be that he recognized that Judah had to go on as a vassal state and therefore he would not use the term מלך which would mean something else, politically speaking. The prophet is here not speaking of the future ideal Davidic kingdom as in ch. 37 where we find the word מלך.

of the duties of the pre-exilic king. This means that the phenomenon, מנחה־נסך, must not necessarily be understood as a purely post-exilic "word pair" nor as always referring to the post exilic *tāmīd*. That both terms are old is shown by, for instance, 1 Kings 18:29 ff., Mic. 6:7 and Hos. 9:4, cf. 2 Kings 3:20, 16:15.[1] It seems somewhat dubious to make this word pair an argument for the late date of Joel. Its occurrence in Ez. 45:17 may as well argue for a late pre-exilic origin of such a word pair.

That מנחה is organically linked to offerings other than the cereal offerings is shown by Jer. 14:12 where we find it in combination with fasting. The phrase יעלו עלה ומנחה seems to take care of all kinds of sacrifices. It can be used as a general lerm for sacrifice, cf. Am. 5:22.[2] In Dan. 9:27 it stands for non-bloody offerings.

In discussing the *tāmīd*, one usually makes note of Joel 2:19. In this verse Yahweh answers his people and promises to give them wine and new grain and oil so that the people will be satisfied. He says, in addition, that he will no more make his people "to a reproach, a disgrace", חרפה, "among the nations". Commenting on this H. W. Wolff says that "merkwürdigerweise" (!) this passage does not mention the meal offerings and drink offerings as again possible,[3] in other words, the *tāmīd* should have been mentioned by Joel! This verse does not show a particular post-exilic "color", whatever that is. Meal-offerings and drink-offerings were given both in the pre-exilic time as well as in the post-exilic time. The divine oracle about the people no longer being given to חרפה among the nations can also suit the pre-exilic time as well as the time after the exile. Yahweh's intention is always to save his people, if it follows his commands and ways, his covenant and his cult. It is then not at all astonishing that the *tāmīd* is not mentioned here; it could be taken as evidence for the text dealing with either the pre-exilic or the early post-exilic time. As a reminder of how difficult it is to assign a definite date in such a case we should consider king Keret's sacrifice of lamb, bread and wine at one and the same occasion, I Krt 63 ff., 156 ff.[4]

---

[1] Kapelrud, *Joel Studies*, pp. 36 f.

[2] Cf. Holzinger, *ZAW* 9/89, p. 108, R. Rendtorff, *Studien zur Geschichte des Opfers im alten Israel* (WMANT 24), 1967, p. 195.

[3] *BK* XIV:5, p. 73. It is, of course, not astonishing if one approaches the text without presuppositions.

[4] R. de Vaux, *Studies in Old Testament Sacrifice*, 1964, p. 47, cf. W. Herrmann, "Götterspeise und Göttertrank in Ugarit und Israel", *ZAW* 72/60, pp. 205 ff.

Therefore, it can be said that the *tāmīd* had a long tradition even before the term תמיד came into use. When we discern some concern for the daily cult in the book of Joel, this does not necessarily point to a late date for the book. The mention of the עולת תמיד in Ez. 46:14f. may be understood as an indication of a pre-exilic phenomenon.[1] We can, in this connection, also mention 2 Kings 16:15. King Ahaz of Judah had a new altar made for the Solomonic temple, which was modeled after an altar at Damascus, and the priest Uriah is commanded by the king to burn the morning burnt offerings and the evening cereal offerings—among other sacrifices—at this new altar.[2] We must, therefore, reckon with the possibility that the phenomenon under discussion may go back far in time. When trying to reach the origin of the *tāmīd*, one should first examine the Canaanite-Hebrew tradition (cf. Hos. 9:4), rather than the influences from "Mesopotamian practices", as A. L. Oppenheim does.[3]

H. W. Wolff's opinion that we meet the *tāmīd* in the book of Joel in reference to the post-exilic time [4] cannot be supported by the textual evidence. It would be more accurate to say that what Joel is talking about in this respect became later on known as the *tāmīd*. If the book should be proven to be post-exilic, the conclusion may be that the *tāmīd* was not yet a technical term in the time of Joel.

Another question which should be discussed in dealing with the מנחה and the נסך is that the latter occurs in some prophets in connection with an illegitimate cultus, Isa. 57:6, Jer. 7:18, 19:13, 32:29, 44:17 ff., 25, Ez. 20:28, cf. Ps. 16:4.[5] In Isa. 57:6 both מנחה and נסך are sacrifices offered to the gods of the valley of death.[6] In Joel,

---

[1] Thus W. Zimmerli, *Ezechiel* (BK XIII), p. 1174.

[2] R. J. Thompson holds the view that "twice daily sacrifices were offered throughout the kingdom period", an opinion he builds on 1 Kings 18:29 (and 36) and 2 Kings 3:20, *Penitence and Sacrifice in early Israel outside the Levitical Law*, 1963, p. 130, cf. p. 129. See also H. H. Rowley, *Worship in Ancient Israel*, 1967, pp. 121 f.

[3] *Ancient Mesopotamia. Portrait of a Dead Civilization*, 1964, p. 188, cf. p. 365.

[4] *Joel*, pp. 3 and 35 f. Cf. R. de Vaux who maintains that the *tāmīd* "is certainly of post-exilic origin" in spite of the Chronicler's references to the monarchic time (1 Chr. 16:40, 2 Chr. 13:11, 31:3), *Ancient Israel*, p. 469.

[5] Cf. L. Kruse-Blinkenberg, "Offer", *Gads Danske Bibelleksikon* II, 1966, col. 369, R, Rendtorff, *Studien zur Geschichte des Opfers im alten Israel*, p. 171 f., 195.

[6] Cf. W. H. Irwin, " 'The Smooth Stones of the Wady?' Isaiah 57:6", *CBQ* 29/67, p. 39. Irwin, however, considers the sacrifices as food and drink offerings to the dead, rather than real sacrifices to gods, because the latter was a Canaanite rite and because of this the Judaeans could not have participated in it. This could be true, but the fact is also that the prophets very much opposed the Canaani-

however, their disappearence from the temple is lamented. The difference between Joel and the three other prophets may be of some importance. When Isaiah, Jeremiah and Ezechiel use נסך as a designation for sacrifices not being given to Yahweh, they are objecting to a certain rite that for them was too much associated with Canaanite cult practices.

Perhaps Joel is not of the same opinion here, in other words, he has not developed a special opinion about these offerings. He was not that kind of "reformer" or analyst. For him there were some kind of rituals that had to be fulfilled, but the disaster to the country did not permit any kind of sacrifices to Yahweh. We know that Joel objects to non-Yahwistic rites, but he does not seem to have connected נסך with such rites. Since the מנחה had long been connected with a libation offering, Joel does not seem to question the legitimacy of נסך. These two phenomena belong together. We may now ask the question whether מנחה and נסך in the book of Joel are terms for sacrifices in general or for what later on became known as the *tāmīd*? If Joel does include all kinds of sacrifices [1] here then the *tāmīd* is out of the picture. Though a satisfactory answer seems impossible, one way of discussing the problem would be to view the phrase מנחה ונסך ליהוה אלהיכם in 2:14 as telling the people that these sacrifices will be given to Yahweh, and not to other gods, in which case we might ask why else would the prophet mention ליהוה אלהיכם? [2] There is hope that these sacrifices will take place in the temple again, but they can be given only to Yahweh; he is their god, no one else. Such an interpretation would be in agreement with the tendency so far met in the book, namely, the opposition to "wrong" cult. This "wrong" cult is Joel's answer to the cause of the disaster.

In Joel 1:9, 13, 2:7 we come upon another phenomenon which has evoked some discussion regarding the time of the book, namely, the plural of משרת. Even though the verb שרת occurs in pre-exilic times in connection with cultic as well as individual service,[3] its

---

zation of the cult. It should be observed that מנחה is very rare in the prophetical writings of pre-exilic times, cf. R. Rendtorff, *op. cit.*, p. 61. In Isa. 43:23 it also stands for illegitimate offerings.

[1] Cf. Malachi for whom מנחה is a general term for sacrifices.

[2] Cf. Ezekiel's frequent use of כי אני יהוה which occurs several times in connection with utterances against idolatry, 6:7, 10, 13 f., 7:4, 9, 27, 20:42, 36:38, 37:28, 39:28.

[3] Cf. Holzinger, *ZAW* 9/89, pp. 102 ff., Chary *Les Prophètes et le culte*, p. 198, Kapelrud, *Joel Studies*, pp. 38 f.

usage as a designation for the cultic functions of the priests is considered as relatively late.[1] It is mainly as an apposition or a term in construction with priests and Levites that it has been understood as a post-exilic phenomenon.[2] Textual evidence shows that its usage in apposition to these groups cannot be considered as very old.[3] M Bič maintains, however, that Joel knows only the priests "ohne jede hierarchische Abstufung" and, therefore, this text gives us a picture of an old phenomenon.[4] The fact that this term is found in Joel in connection with the priests would suggest a contrary conclusion.[5] In the older usage of the Hebrew language משרתים does not occur in apposition either to the priests, or to the Levites. Thus its occurrence in Joel could point to a differentiation of the duties between the priests and Levites.[6]

In Joel the usual term for the temple is בית, 1:9, 13 f., 16 and 4:18. In 2:17 it is mentioned in the phrase האולם ולמזבח. These passages in connection with the mention of חומה, 2:7, 9 (the wall of Jerusalem?) have been used as arguments for a time after the second temple had been built and the wall would refer to the one built by Nehemiah.[7] Though this is a possibility, the wall referred to cannot be exactly specified since the text gives no information about what kind of wall is alluded to, so that a pre-exilic origin cannot *a priori* be excluded. Another possibility would be to see חומה as an expression for the remains of the city wall if Joel should turn out to be a post-exilic book.[8]

It should also be stressed that בית is not exclusively a post-exilic designation for temple. It occurs in pre-exilic times as a synonym for היכל, but in later writings בית does seem to be the more common word.[9]

---

[1] Holzinger, *op. cit.*, pp. 101 ff., Nowack, *GHAT* 111:4, p. 98, Chary, *op. cit.*, pp. 197 f., Deissler-Delcor, *La Sainte Bible* VIII, p. 149, Wolff, *Joel*, p. 36.

[2] Chary, *op. cit.*, p. 198.

[3] Cf. Holzinger, *op. cit.*, pp. 102 ff. For an opposite view, see Kapelrud, *op. cit.*, pp. 38 ff.

[4] Bič, *Das Buch Joel*, p. 27.

[5] One should also note here Isa. 61:6, Ez. 45:4, 5, Neh. 10:37, cf. also Ezek. 46:24, 2 Chr. 13:10, 23:6.

[6] For a discussion of משרת in this connection see W. Zimmerli, *Ezechiel* (BK XIII), pp. 131 f., cf. also A. H. J. Gunneweg, *Leviten und Priester* (FRLANT 89), 1965, p. 205.

[7] H. W. Wolff, Joel, pp. 2 f., A. Deissler and M. Delcor, *Les petits prophètes* (La Sainte Bible VIII), 1961, p. 138. cf. T. Henshaw, *The Latter Prophetes*, 1958, pp. 281 ff., H. H. Rowley, *The Growth of the Old Testament*, 1963, pp. 110 f.

[8] Cf. below pp. 114ff.

[9] See Th. Chary, *Les Prophètes et le culte a partir de l'exil*, 1955, p. 127. בית with

It is possible that the question "where is their god?" (2:17) announces to us that we have here some kind of liturgical formula which has been used by Joel. It occurs also in Pss. 79:10, 115:2, cf. 42:4, 11, Mic. 7:10. In Psalm 42 it is found in the second person singular and is preceeded by the phrase כל היום, the whole day,[1] which means that the speaker is in a particular liturgical situation.[2] In comparing Joel 2:17 to the psalms we find that the גוים have the same function in Joel as in the psalms. This may indicate that Joel is rooted in the cultic sphere. We need not emphasize that the question in 2:17 is of no use for the purpose of drawing any conclusions concerning the time of the book. It should be mentioned that we find a related idea in Dt. 9:26-28, as well as in Ex. 32:12, but this does not mean that Joel was necessarily influenced by these passages, as is maintained by H. W. Wolff.[3] One could argue with a high degree of probability that the passages in Deuteronomy and Exodus are dependent on cultic ideas or phenomena so that these books would be dependent on a common source along with the work of Joel.

At another place [4] in the present study, the phrase בין האולם ולמזבח 2:17, is discussed. The verse tells us that the priests should stand between the altar and the porch and there lament and weep, crying to Yahweh חוסה יהוה על־עמך,[5] "be compassionate for thy people

---

the meaning temple, sanctuary occurs in 2 Sam. 5:8, 7:5 f., 13, 1 Kings 6:25, 37 f., 7:12, 8:27, 29, 33, 38, 2 Kings 21:4, 23:11 f., 25:9, Pss. 23:6, 36:9, 42:5, 55:15, 69:10, 84:5, 11, 93:5, 122:1, 135:2, Isa. 2:2, Jer. 11:15, 23:11, 26:12, Hos. 9:15 Judg. 18:31. In Pss. 5:8 and 27:4 it occurs in parallelism with היכל. Ezechiel has in chapters 40-48 בית 50 times against 8 for היכל, see Chary, *op. cit.*, p. 127, n. 1. In this note Chary's statement about Zechariah is wrong. This prophet uses היכל 5 times (6:12, 13, 14, 15, 8:9) and בית 4 times (4:9, 7:3, 8:9, 11:13), then it occurs also in 5:11 referring to a temple for הרשעה.

[1] For this phrase see my *Psalm* 89, p. 90. On p. 135 the translation reads *täglich* which was a mistake.

[2] Chary understands these psalms as post-exilic, but gives no reason, *Les prophètes et le culte*, p. 205. Ps. 42 is, for instance, considered by H.-J. Kraus as probably pre-exilic, *Psalmen* I, p. 318. Several commentators assign Mic. 7:8-20 to the post-exilic time, *scil.* Sellin, Weiser, Robinson, cf. Chary, *op. cit.*, p. 205, n. 1, L. Rost, *Israel bei den Propheten*, 1937, p. 119, H. Birkeland, *Zum Hebräischen Traditionswesen*, 1938, p. 77. However, because of the mention of Assur (not Babel) and Egypt in 7:12 and Carmel and Gilead in v. 14, it could be possible to ascribe this part also to Micah, so O. Eissfeldt, *The Old Testament. An Introduction*, 1965, p. 412, A. S. Kapelrud, *SBU* II², col. 107 f., B. Reicke, "Liturgical Traditions in Mic. 7", *HTR* 60/67, pp. 349 ff., G. Östborn, *Yahweh's Words and Deeds*, 1951, pp. 47 f.

[3] Joel, p. 62.

[4] See pp. 53f.

[5] This form of the imperative occurs only here and in Neh. 13:22.

(spare thy people) Yahweh", that he would not give over his inheritance (property) [1] to disgrace, reproach (חרפה). The kind of
disgrace which would fall on them is expressed by the phrase למשל־בם
גוים, which must mean that the peoples will rule over them. Then
follows the question why one should say among the people איה אלהיהם,
"where is their god"? [2] If other nations or peoples should rule
over Yahweh's own inheritance the result would be such a question
as this. Its meaning is that Yahweh would be a god with no power;
he would be naught, and this is the חרפה which would come over
his people.

The phrase, למשל־בם, has sometimes been translated "saying a
mock-word against them". [3] This is the translation of Th. Chary who
thinks that the meaning "to rule over them" is impossible here
because no enemy other than the locusts has been mentioned in the
previous part of the book. [4] However, 1:6 seems already to have made
a connection between the locusts and a גוי. [5] Thus, Chary's argument
is not valid. Furthermore, it must be noted that משל II with ב always
means "to rule over"; see, for example, Gen. 1:18, 4:7, 45:8, 26,
Dt. 15:6, Josh. 12:5, Judg. 8:22 f., 14:4, 15:11, 2 Sam. 23:3,
1 Kings 5:1, Pss. 19:14, 22:29, 105:21, Isa. 3:4, 12, 19:4, Hab. 1:14,
Mic. 5:1, Jer. 22:30, cf. Ps. 136:8. The passage Joel 2:17 is the only
example Köhler-Baumgartner's dictionary lists under משל I, "be like,
say a mock-word". [6] The regular construction for this meaning is

---

[1] Cf. Mic. 7:14, 18, Jer. 3:18 f., 12:14 f., 16:18, Zeph. 2:9, Zech. 2:12, 8:12.
According to W. Holladay the term נחלה is an old jerusalemite one, "Prototypes
and Copies", *JBL* 79/60, p. 359.

[2] H.-J. Kraus finds it "bemerkenswert" that this question always is asked by
"den Heiden", *Psalmen* I, p. 319. With a right understanding of the original
cultic situation one will find that nobody else than the גוים (= the enemies or the
nonbelievers) can ask the question. Here it could be mentioned that E. Dalglish,
among others, considers verses 17 f. as part of a lamentation psalm, *Psalm Fifty-
One*, 1962, p. 242, n. 47.

[3] Thus von Orelli, Sellin, Th. H. Robinson, Weiser, Deissler and Delcor; see
also Lippl and Theis, *Die Heilige Schrift des Alten Testaments*, VIII, 3/1, 1937, p. 98.

[4] *Les prophètes est le culte*, p. 204. Bič is undecided, *Das Buch Joel*, pp. 61, 65.

[5] This led O. Procksch to see the locusts as a model for the enemies from the
North, *Die kleinen prophetischen Schriften nach dem Exil*, 1916, p. 81. We can mention
in this connection that the figure of locusts has been used in the Keret text from
Ugarit to describe the multitude of the people, Krt II:103 ff.

[6] For a discussion about משל as a single stem, with the meaning "rule" being
derived from the meaning "be like", see A. S. Herbert, "The 'Parable' (*māšāl*)
in the Old Testament", *Scottisch Journal of Theology* 7/54, pp. 180 f., cf. also A. R.
Johnson, *Sacral Kingship*[2], p. 102, G. Boström, *Paronomasi i den äldre hebreiska
maschallitteraturen* (LUÅ N. F. Avd. 1, 23:8), 1927, pp. 23 f., M. Dahood, *Biblica*
48/67, p. 434.

משל על. It seems that Köhler's listing of Joel 2:17 under משל I is
due to a special interpretation of the text and not to the construction
of the phrase.

Here we ought to note another aspect, namely, that the prayer in
2:17 can be seen in connection with the covenant idea. The reason
why Yahweh should intervene is not because the people here con-
fesses some sin.[1] At least nothing is said about that, even if the
chapter itself could be proof for the people's wrongdoing. What
should be observed here is that there exists a covenant between
Yahweh and his people, his נחלה. Because of this covenant Yahweh
is asked to intervene and not to give his people to חרפה. He and
not the גוים should rule over them. Thus the context also makes it
unnecessary to diverge from the usual meaning of משל ב.

There is in Joel one particular form which suggests that the book
would have been written down late rather than early, even if the
material of the first two chapters gives the impression of being old.
I am referring to the uncontracted מן־בני in 1:12 which occurs only
here among the prophets instead of the usual מִבְּנֵי. Bauer and
Leander's grammar considers this as an example of a *Neubildung*, and
as such, a late phenomenon in Hebrew.[2] It is rare in the older writings
of the Old Testament, but not uncommon in the later ones and in
the Dead Sea Scrolls. The uncontracted מן־בני is to be found in Lev.
1:14, 14:30, Judg. 10:11, 1 Chr. 4:42, 5:18, 9:3, 14, 32, 12:17, 26 f.,
21:26, 24:3, 26:10, 27:3, 10, 14, 2 Chr. 20:14, 19, 29:5, 34:3, 12,
cf. מן־בת in Lam. 1:6.[3] Thus it occurs only three times outside the
Chroniclers and Joel. This leads us to believe that this kind of usage
has become common in the time of the Chronicler or sometimes
before in the post-exilic period, and that the instances in Leviticus
and Judges are the custom of the final writer and not of the time these
passages refer to.

In conclusion, it must be clear that many of the words and phrases
having been used as arguments for a late date are not late at all. On
the other hand, the investigation thus far conducted shows several
phenomena which have to be understood as pointing to a late period

---

[1] Cf. M. Bič, *Das Buch Joel*, p. 65.

[2] *Historische Grammatik der hebräischen Sprache des Alten Testaments*, § 15, 1, p. 198.

[3] ומן־בני occurs in 1 Chr. 9:6, 7, 9:30, 32, 12:30, 15:17, 2 Chr. 8:9, 17:17,
29:13, 14. Other instances with the uncontracted מן can be found in Ex. 18:14,
Lev. 1:3, Judg. 5:20, 2 Sam 22:14, Jer. 44:28, Ps. 30:4, 73:19, 104:7, Prov.
27:8 (note the parallelism מִמְּקוֹמוֹ // מן קָנֶּה), Job 30:5, 1 Chr. 4:40, 2 Chr. 2:13,
8:8, Dan 9:25.

of the Biblical Hebrew. From this point of view, Joel cannot be from a time as early as Amos and Hosea or before, as has sometimes been advocated.[1] We would rather see it as belonging to a late pre-exilic or, perhaps with more probability, to an early post-exilic time.[2]

---

[1] K. A. Credner (870-65), *Das Buch Joel*, 1831, p. 41 ff. G. L. Robinson ("the closing years of the ninth century B.C."), *The Twelve Minor Prophets*, 1926, p. 43, G. Amon (the 9th cent.), *Die Abfassungszeit des Buches Joel* (Unpubl. diss. Würzburg), 1942, pp. 73, 93, M. Bič (9th cent.), *Das Buch Joel*, p. 9, H. Birkeland (a prophet of the 8th cent., but ch. 3-4 are post-exilic), *Zum Hebräischen Traditionswesen*, 1938, p. 66, J. Scharbert (pre-exilic), *Heilsmittler im Alten Testament und im Alten Orient*, 1964, p. 164. For a summary of the different opinions see also J. H. Kritzinger, *Die Profesie van Joël*, 1935, pp. III f., M. Bič, *Das Buch Joel*, p. 9.

[2] C. A. Keller (= 630-600 BC), *Commentaire de l'Ancien Testament*, 1965, so also Stocks, "Der 'Nördliche' und die Komposition des Buches Joel", *NKZ* 19/08, p. 741, E. König (the last years of king Josiah or immediately after his reign), *Einleitung in das Alte Testament*, 1893, p. 343, Kapelrud (the time of Jeremiah, around 600 BC), *Joel Studies*, pp. 191 f., B. Otzen (shortly before the exile), "Joelsbogen", *Gads Danske Bibelleksikon* I, 1965, cols. 989 f., A. Kuenen (the exile of 597 BC), *The Prophets and Prophecy in Israel*, p. 175 f., W. Rudolph (between 597-587 BC), "Wann wirkte Joel?", *Festschrift L. Rost* (BZAW 105), 1967, p. 195, A. Jepsen (from the exile), "Kleine Beiträge zum Zwölfprophetenbuch. 1. Joel", *ZAW* 56/38, pp. 90 ff., 93, L. Dennefeld (after 586 BC), "Les problèmes du livre de Joël", *Rev. des Sciences Religieuses* 6/26, pp. 32 f., L. Mariès (6th cent.), "A propos de récentes études sur Joël", *Recherches de Science Religieuse* 37/50, pp. 121 ff., W. Vatke (5th Cent.), *Historisch-kritische Einleitung in das Alte Testament*, (ed. H. G. S. Preiss), 1886, pp. 676 f. Th. Chary (before Malachi), *Les prophètes et le culte*, p. 183, O. Plöger (400-330), *Theokratie und Eschatologie*, 1959, p. 127, A. Merx (after Nehemiah), *Die Prophetie des Joel und ihre Ausleger*, 1879, p. 34, F. Nötscher (probably post-exilic), *Die Heilige Schrift in deutscher Übersetzung* III (Echter-Bibel), 1958, p. 702, E. Sellin (between Malachi and Alexander), *Einleitung in das Alte Testament*[8], 1950, pp. 125 ff., M. Treves (the time of Ptolemeus Soter), "The Date of Joel", *VT* 7/57, pp. 149 ff., K. Jensen (Maccabean time), "Indledningsspørgsmaal i Joels Bog", *DTT* 4/41, pp. 98 ff.

CHAPTER TWO

COVENANT PHRASEOLOGY

As one approaches the problem of covenant phraseology in the book of Joel he is immediately struck by the fact that the term ברית does not occur in the text of Joel. It should be noted that this is in harmony with the pre-exilic prophets who seldom mention the ברית.[1] However, the absence of the term ברית does not mean that the covenant idea is completely missing in Joel, for, as we have seen above, Joel 2:17 is an expression of this phenomenon. Joel stresses the phenomenon that Yahweh is the god of the people, i.e. the lord of the covenant, and Joel brings out the implications of this relationship. We must see the phrases שבו עדי, 2:12, and ושבו אל יהוה אלהיכם, 2:13, against this background.[2] In his discussion of Ez. 18:21 ff. H. Reventlow has argued that שוב belongs to the "sakral-rechtlichen Sprache", and that the idea is not a prophetic invention but has its root "in der Bundesverkündigung".[3] We find also in the book of Joel among the conceptions used in describing the character of Yahweh, conceptions connected with the covenant ideology. Therefore in both terminology and motifs Joel shows a familiarity with the covenant ideology, even while not using the term explicitly.

A prime example of the use of covenant terminology and motifs is found in 2:13, which follows close upon the *šûb*-idea of verse 12. In 2:13 Yahweh is described in the following terms:

[כי] חנון ורחום הוא
ארך אפים ורב חסד
ונחם על הרעה

[For] gracious and merciful is he,
'slow' in anger and great in loyalty (grace)
and sorry for evil.

---

[1] Cf. Joh. Lindblom, *Prophecy in Ancient Israel*, p. 329.

[2] For שוב in connection with the covenant see W. L. Holladay, *The Root šûbh in the Old Testament*, 1958, pp. 116 ff.

[3] *Wächter über Israel. Ezechiel und seine Tradition* (BZAW 82), 1962, pp. 118 f. According to Holladay the use of שוב in connection with the deity "would be as old as the verb itself, and as old as religion", *op. cit.*, p. 119. Cf. H. S. Nyberg, "Studien zum Religionskampf im Alten Testament", *ARW* 35/38, pp. 332 f., F. J. Helfmyer, *Die Nachfolge Gottes im Alten Testament* (Bonner Biblische Beiträge 29), 1968, pp. 167.

Exactly the same terminology is found in Jonah 4:2, with the exception that the motivation [כי] is there different כי אתה אל. We find almost the same wording, that is, as far as חסד, in the following passages: Ex. 34:6 (the Sinai covenant), Pss. 86:15, 103:8, 145:8, and Neh. 9:17 (where after חסד we have the phrase ולא עזבתם). Of these Ex. 34:6 and Ps. 86:15 are identical in having after חסד the word ואמת in place of ונחם על הרעה as found in Joel and Jonah. Ps. 145:8 differs in having וגדל חסד instead of the ורב חסד found in the other passages. This same verse inserts the name יהוה before ארך.[1] Thus we seem to be dealing with a special formula which in Ex. 34:6, Pss. 86:15, 103:8 has the order רחום וחנון ארך אפים ורב חסד, but in the other instances has reversed חנון and רחום.[2] D. R. Ap-Thomas understands the formula as an "official formula for the character of Yahweh".[3] What is the origin of such a formula? If it is an official formula—and let me say, even if it were not [4]— the only place where such a phraseology for describing the deity might have originated would be the center of the religion, that is, the sanctuary where the god lives and in a setting rooted in the covenant ritual. Already W. H. Bennett has suggested that "some description of Yahweh was part of the liturgy of some Israelite sanctuary before" anyone of these passages had been written,[5] while

---

[1] One should also note that instead of יהוה אל or אדני אל Joel 2:13 reads יהוה אלהיכם where the formula serves an explanatory function. Joel thus emphasizes that Yahweh is their god and nobody else, a theme which occurs several times in Joel.

[2] The phrase חנון ורחום is found in Pss. 111:4 and 112:4.

[3] "Some Aspects of the Root ḤNN in the OT", *JSS* 2/57, p. 141.

[4] Only in cultic circles can we find the origin of phrases and formulae connected with the deity. It is impossible to go behind the religious sphere and find how (if possible) the common man conceived of his god since the texts tell us nothing in this area. The views of the common man were certainly nurtured by what he saw, learned, and heard at the sanctuary.

[5] *Exodus* (The New Century Bible), 1908, p. 257, cf. J. Scharbert, "Form-geschichte und Exegese von Ex. 34, 6 f. und seine Parallelen", *Biblica* 38/57, pp. 131 ff., W. Beyerlin, *Origins and History of the Oldest Sinaitic Traditions*, 1965, pp. 137 f. Ap-Thomas views all the above mentioned passages, except Ex. 34, as post-exilic, *JSS* 2/57, pp. 139, n. 5, 145. When it concerns the Psalms as well as Jonah it is impossible to decide the time of origin with any certainty. Some psalms as well as Jonah may be pre-exilic. Such is the case with Ps. 86 which is a psalm for the "suffering servant", that is, the king, cf. my book *Psalm* 89, pp. 50 and 145. In verse 16, which I have discussed before (see *Aspects of Syncretism in Israelite Religion*, pp. 76 f.) the speaker, the king, talks about himself in the so-called servant style as well as about his mother as handmaiden (אמה) of Yahweh, cf. Ps. 116:16, and see C. Lindhagen, *The Servant Motif in the Old Testament*. 1950, p. 284, I. Engnell, *Studies*, p. 210, n. 2, cf. also K.-H. Bernhardt, *Das Problem der*

J. Scharbert has maintained that the formula has had its "Sitz im Leben" in liturgical invocations or in prayers.[1]

Even if it is true that the origin of this phrase is in the liturgical renewal of Israel's covenant, it should be pointed out that the description of the deity as "gracious" and "kind" is found also in Ugarit in the phrases ḥnn-'il, UT 107:6, and ḥnil, 2084:8 (PRU V, no. 84:8).[2] This is still another indication of how close the Israelites originally were to the Canaanites in ideology. In the Israelite religion the particular concept of the gracious deity has become more emphasized by its inclusion in a covenantal liturgical formula. This is a further indication that Joel uses cultic material and works very much with concepts and formulas which belonged to the renewal of the covenant, or could be associated with the covenant.

The phrase שוב עדי merits consideration here. It is a rare phrase with a somewhat stronger emphasis than שוב אל.[3] This construction is found also in Hos. 14:2, Am. 4:6, 8 ff., Isa. 9:12, 19:22, Job 22:23, Dt. 4:30, 30:2, Lam. 3:40. Of itself the phrase cannot be taken as

---

altorientalischen Königsideologie (SVT 8/61), p. 269, R. de Vaux, "Le roi d'Israël, vassal de Yahvé", *Mélanges E. Tisserant*, 1964, p. 121. In connection with Ps 86 M. Dahood, however, writes: "Modern scholars approach unanimity in classifying this psalm as the lament of an individual, but none seem to have noticed that this individual happens to be the Israelite king". *Psalms* II, 1968, p. 292. Dahood is thus inaccurate here. Concerning Ps. 145:8, one could discuss the possibility that it is a later psalm because the formula is somewhat altered. It reads חנון וגדל-חסד ורחום יהוה ארך אפים. As mentioned before the name יהוה has been inserted before ארך, and וגדל has replaced ורב,cf. Nah. 1:3. This may be seen as a disintegration of the formula.

[1] *Biblica*, 38/57, p. 132 "Die das Volk belehrenden Priester dürften beim Vortrag der Bundessatzungen solche Predigtartige und erzieherische Bemerkungen eingeflochten haben die aus den kultischen Gebetstexten den Vortragenden und dem zuhörenden Volk geläufig waren". *Ibid.*, p. 134. R. C. Dentan characterizes the formula as "patently liturgical" but says it is more natural to call it "a confession of faith", "The Literary Affinities of Exodus XXXIV 6 f", *VT* 13/63, p. 37.

[2] We could also note that the phrase *ltpn il dpid* describes El as a kind and merciful god. For this phrase see among others F. M. Cross, Jr., "Yahweh and the God of the Patriarchs", *HTR* 55/62, pp. 238 f. For *ḏ* and the Arabic *ḏu* being the same as the Phoenician ז and the Hebrew זו cf. H. Grimme, "Abriss der biblisch-hebräischen Metrik", *ZDMG* 50, 1896, p. 573, n. 1, W. F. Albright, "The Song of Deborah in the Light of Archeology", *BASOR* 62/36, p. 30. H. S. Nyberg, *Hebreisk Grammatik*, 1952, § 84j, Anm. 2, p. 253, "Deuteronomium 33:2-3", *ZDMG* 92/38, p. 338, E. Lipiński, "Judges 5, 4-5 et Psaume 68, 8-11", *Biblica* 48/67, pp. 198 f.

[3] Cf. H. W. Wolff, "Das Thema 'Umkehr' in der alttestamentlichen Prophetie", *ZThK* 48/51, p. 144, B. Albrektson, *Studies in the Text and Theology of the Book of Lamentations*, 1963, p. 154.

an indication for particularly late language in Joel. By the usage of
the phrase "turn to *me*", the oracle of Joel 2:12 stresses the fact that
the people must return to no other god than Yahweh. In their cult
the people have worshipped someone else, some other deity (or:
deities?), so that we must face the fact that Joel addresses a people
which has worshipped not only Yahweh, but also other gods and
that the people are Yahweh's own covenant people, the inhabitants
of Judah and Jerusalem. Such a situation would explain the stress
and importance as connoted by the phrase שוב עדי. As has been noted
above Joel 2:13 portrays Yahweh as a gracious and merciful god in
terms taken from the covenant ideology. If the people return to
Yahweh blessings will perhaps return and the מנחה and נסך will be
restored.[1] Thus we find here an emphasis on the right cult, that is,
cult according to Yahweh's *ṣĕdāqāh*, right cultic performances in connection with the "right heart", 2:12. If the cult has been wrong, this
means, according to the prophet, that the people practiced some other
cult, and this cult must necessarily have been directed to some other
god, because we have no right to believe that there was a godless cult
in the temple of Jerusalem. Thus the people had to turn back to
Yahweh, and the oracle of 2:13 shows that both the cult and the
directions of the people's hearts have been quite wrong. The importance of the oracle is that the demand for the people to turn back to
Yahweh is at the same time a demand for return to his cult, cf. Mal.
3:7. For Joel the temple is the center of the religion, 4:17, an idea
in accord with the semitic conception of the function of a temple,
namely the place where the god lives.[2] To serve Yahweh, according
to Joel, is to have a "right" cult in spirit and action which is in
accordance with צדקה and the covenant. This is what constitutes
religion for Joel.[3] Thus the question arises: is it possible that Joel is
addressing a post-exilic congregation? If it is true, as Wolff has
argued, that the use of שוב by the prophets often means a coming
back to something that existed before,[4] i.e. a restoration, then, what

---

[1] For the connection between covenant, *ṣĕdāqāh*, and fertility see for instance
Hos. 2:21 ff.

[2] Cf. p. 33.

[3] Thus Joel is not in harmony with what H. W. Wolff calls "der prophetischer
Ruf zum Umkehr", who understands it as something other "als die Hinwendung
zum Heiligtum", *ZThK* 48/51, p. 132., cf. also Wolff, "Das Kerygma des deutero-
nomistischen Geschichtswerk", *ZAW* 73/61, pp. 171 ff.

[4] *ZThK* 48/51, pp. 133 ff. Am. 5:25, Wolff maintains, is an example of the
desert time as an ideal epoch. שוב would then refer to this period as the be-

is to be restored in Joel is the Yahweh cult, as this prophet conceived of it. In light of Joel's admonition to the people to return to their *own* god, which can mean to leave some other god, the text could perhaps point to a pre-exilic time rather than to the time after the exile.[1]

It is too often taken for granted that in the post-exilic time there was no room for worship of any god other than Yahweh. Such an assumption represents a wrong view of Judaistic religion. We should refer here to the book of Malachi which is very much concerned about the cult of the second temple in the period presumably before Ezra and Nehemiah.[2] Malachi criticizes the temple cult saying that it is impure and worse than the ones of other peoples, 1:11. Judah has profaned the temple of Yahweh 2:11. Upon the altar of Yahweh, they have sacrificed "wrong" sacrifices, and they have covered the altar with tears, 2:13. This latter phenomenon points *de facto* to a ritual which the prophet considers as non-Yahwistic.[3] Therefore we must reckon with the possibility that the prophet considered it as directed to someone else. Since it is a rite of wailing and crying which Malachi condemns, it can be seen as a part of the pre-exilic cultic tradition which has been re-established in the temple of Jerusalem. It cannot of course be definitively proven whether Malachi saw the rite as dedicated to Yahweh or connected with some other deity, or whether he looked on it as a rite which for traditional reasons was part of the Jerusalem ritual and could be abrogated. The usual mode of designating a rite or phenomenon as non-Yahwistic, i.e. as belonging to another deity, is, in the prophetical books, to call it תועבה, as is

---

ginning of the people's history when Yahweh did not want cult or offerings, pp. 134 f. This is however a misinterpretation, cf. my article "Some Remarks on Prophets and Cult", *Essays in Divinity* VI 1968, pp. 113 ff. According to W. L. Holladay שוב with the meaning "turn back (from evil)" is not found "in the eight century prophets", *The Root šûbh in the Old Testament*, 1958, p. 147.

[1] Cf. E. König, *Einleitung in das Alte Testament*, p. 346., cf. J. Wellhausen, *Prolegomena*, New York, 1961, p. 111.

[2] Cf. O. Eissfeldt, *The Old Testament*, 1965, pp. 442 f., E. Sellin-G. Fohrer, *Einleitung in das Alte Testament*[10], 1965, pp. 516 f. Malachi's book is commonly supposed to belong to the time of king Artaxerxes I (464-424), and before Ezra and Nehemiah, cf. C. von Orelli, *The Twelve Minor Prophets*, 1893, p. 383 f., G. L. Robinson, *The Twelve Minor Prophets*, 1926, pp. 159 f., F. Horst, *HAT* 14, 1964, p. 263., Th. Chary advocates 470-450 B.C., *Les prophètes et le culte*, p. 161, and J. Klausner, c. 475 B.C., *The Messianic Idea in Israel*, 1956, pp. 206 ff. S. Dubnov, (495-450), *History of the Jews from the Beginning of Early Christianity* I, 1967, p. 345. See also A. Weiser, *ATD* 25, 1950, p. 178.

[3] Cf. below, p. 49.

done here in Malachi.[1] Therefore the mention of the altar of Yahweh
in Mal. 2:13 does not quite prove that the rite was Yahwistic from
the point of view of the prophet, but it could have been so from
the point of view of the priests. Here the prophet would have been
opposed to the priestly conception. The phrase ובעל בת־אל נכר[2]
Mat. 2:11, lends some support for the assumption that תועבה is a
rite not directed to Yahweh.[3] J. M. P. Smith may have been correct
in stating that "the contest of Yahwism with idolatry was by no means
brought to an end by the exile".[4]

We can thus say that Malachi in this matter is in harmony with the
pre-exilic prophets. The same may be said about Joel—without taking
any position here regarding its date. Joel is continuing the opposition
of the pre-exilic prophets and some other groups against "wrong"
cult, a cult that was not only dedicated to Yahweh, but also involved
worship of other deities. Such an opposition could also have been
feasible in the early post-exilic time after the completion of the second
temple. There is, then, no obstacle to assume that idolatry and
worship of, for example, Baal (or some other god) again had a place
in the temple worship. The choice of the verb שוב could be significant
in this context. When Joel in 2:17 proclaims that the people must
return to Yahweh, he could have equally said that they should no
longer worship any other god. His emphasis upon the phrase
אלהיכם, "your god", which occurs seven times in this book supports
this view.[5] If the people now returns, there is hope that Yahweh will
return and have pity on them;[6] the blessing will return making

---

[1] "Abomination, idolatry", cf. Dt. 7:25 f., 13:15, 20:15, 27:15, 32:16, 2 Kings
23:13, Isa. 1:13, 44:19, Jer. 6:15, 7:10, Ex. 7:20, 2 Chr. 28:3. See P. Humbert,
"Le substantif toʿēbā et le verbe tʿb dans l'Ancien Testament", *ZAW* 72/60, pp.
217 ff. and "L'étymologie du substantif toʿēbā", *Verbannung und Heimkehr* (Festschrift W. Rudolph), 1961, pp. 157 ff.

[2] Cf. J. M. Powis Smith, "A Critical and Exegetical Commentary on the Book
of Malachi", *ICC*, 1912, pp. 48 f. For a discussion of the phrase, see below
p. 49.

[3] Cf. Humbert, who says that in Lev. 17-26 "le grief de toʿēbā est donc formulé
sans référence directe à Yahvé, mais au cananéisme", p. 232. See also D. E.
Gowan who says that תועבה "always seems to refer to cultic irregularities",
"Prophets, Deuteronomy, and the syncretistic Cult in Israel", *Essays in Divinity*
VI, 1968, p. 107. Cf. R. P. Merendino, *Das deuteronomische Gesetz* (Bonner Bibl.
Beiträge 31), 1969, pp. 332 f.

[4] Malachi, *ICC*, p. 49.

[5] Cf. Hos. 5:4, Dt. 11:13 ff.

[6] For the phrase מי יודע ישוב ונחם note Jonah 3:9 and its usage there. In both
Jonah and Joel the phrase is connected with fasting.

possible the מנחה and נסך, 2:14, which, as far as we can deduce, Joel considered as necessary to a right covenant cult with Yahweh.

Another word which should be singled out as a term with covenant associations is חסד which is also found in the above mentioned liturgical description of Yahweh as a gracious god (2:13). This word is usually translated love, kindness, fidelity, devotion or loyalty—all terms which in some way express the Hebrew term. However, often and perhaps originally, חסד means firmness and strength,[1] so that we can understand how when it is used in connection with Yahweh's covenant relationship, it receives the connotations of loyalty and fidelity.[2] This kind of relationship may be precisely the one suggested by the use of the term in Joel 2:13.

The occurrence of the locusts in this book can be understood as the prophet's interpretation of the present disaster as due to the people's transgression of the covenant ordinances. They have turned away from Yahweh and therefore the curse has come upon them. Joel's description of the disaster is in accord with Dt. 28 and the curses listed there which result from breaking the covenant. Dt. 28 mentions for instance, drought (v. 23 f.), plagues (v. 27), slavery (v. 32), exile (v. 36), and locusts in v. 38.[3] According to D. J. McCarthy, these motifs when taken in conjunction with those of blessing "fit remarkably well into the picture of the whole as a covenant form".[4]

---

[1] L. J. Kuyper, "The Meaning of חסדו, Isa. XL 6f.", *VT* 13/63, pp. 489 ff.

[2] Cf. Ed. Jacob, *Theology of the Old Testament*, 1958, pp. 104 f., W. Harrelson, *Interpreting the Old Testament*, p. 329. For a discussion about חסד see also I. Elbogen, "Chesed, Verpflichtung, Verheissung, Bekräftigung", *Oriental Studies dedicated to Paul Haupt*, 1926, pp. 43 ff., N. Glueck, *Das Wort ḥesed im alttestamentlichen Sprachgebrauch*, (BZAW 47), 1927, pp. 35 ff., A. R. Johnson, "HESEḎ and HĀSÎḎ", *Interpretationes ad Vetus Testamentum pertinentes Sigmundo Mowinckel*, 1955, pp. 100 ff., H. J. Stoebe, "Die Bedeutung des Wortes HÄSÄD im Alten Testament", *VT* 2/52, pp. 244 ff., D. Cameron, *Songs of Sorrow and Praise*, 1924, p. 59 ff., S. Mowinckel, "Die Erkenntnis Gottes bei den alttestamentlichen Propheten", *NTT* 42/41 (tillegshefte), p. 34, N. Snaith, *The Distinctive Ideas of the Old Testament*, 1946, p. 122 ff., E. E. Flack, "The Concept of Grace in Biblical Thought", *Biblical Studies in Memory of H. C. Alleman*, 1960, pp. 140 ff., J. Coppens, "La doctrine biblique sur l'amour de dieu et du prochain", *EphThL* 40/64, pp. 259 ff. Cf. also M. Noth, *The Laws in the Pentateuch and other Studies*, Philadelphia 1967, p. 128.

[3] See D. J. McCarthy, *Treaty and Covenant* (Analecta Biblica 21) 1963, pp. 120 ff., Cf. M. Weinfeld, "Traces of Assyrian Treaty Formulae in Deuteronomy", *Biblica* 46/65, p. 424. Cf. also the occurrence of locusts in one of the Sefire inscriptions, Donner-Röllig, *KAI*, text 222A, line 27 f., J. A. Fitzmyer, *The Aramaic Inscriptions of Sefire* (Biblica et Orientalia 19), 1967, pp. 14 f., and 46.

[4] *Treaty and Covenant*, p. 124, cf. K. Baltzer, *Das Bundesformular*, pp. 158 f.,

The agreement of Joel with Dt. 28 is another suasive reason for holding that he thinks in terms of the covenant.

As has been mentioned above there is an emphasis on the idea that Yahweh and no one else is the god of the covenant and of the people, אלהיכם ואין עוד, cf. Dt. 4:35.[1] We have also discussed why Joel stressed this—the people did not really worship Yahweh, therefore Joel asks them to return (שוב) to *their* god, Yahweh. This in turn is rooted in an old concept of the Israelites that Yahweh had chosen them and made a covenant with them, so that only he is their god.[2] It should be noted here that Joel uses the same terminology as is used in the introduction to the Decalogue and which has been compared to the "preamble" of the Near Eastern treaties.[3] In the Decalogue this "preamble" is found in the concise formulation אנכי יהוה אלהיך, Ex. 20:2, Dt. 5:6.[4] This introductory formula occurs, also, in the pre-history of the covenant narrative in Dt. 29:5[5] with the slight change of having אני for אנכי and the 2nd person suffix in the plural. D. J. McCarthy has maintained that the version of the Decalogue in Dt. 5 "has much in common with the covenant form", but to characterize the Decalogue itself as a covenant or treaty form would be to go too far,[6] since the "fundamental elements of a covenant (treaty) form are lacking: there is no hint of a curse and/or blessing formula".[7]

D. R. Hillers, *Treaty Curses and the Old Testament Prophets* (Biblica et Orientalia 16), 1964, pp. 30 ff.

[1] Cf. C. Lindhagen, *The Servant Motif in the Old Testament*, 1950, pp. 122 ff.

[2] Compare also K. Elliger, "Ich bin der Herr — euer Gott", *Kleine Schriften zum AT*, 1966, pp. 211 ff., 228 f. Aa. Bentzen sees in 2:27 "a clearly defined monotheism", *Introduction* II², 1952, p. 137. However, the phrase ואין עוד clearly points out that this was not the case.

[3] G. E. Mendenhall, "Covenant Forms in Israelite Tradition", *BA* 17/54 p. 58. E. Nielsen maintains that it is only in the secondary form that the Decalogue can be said to resemble in some way the Hittite treaty formula, *De Ti Bud* (Festskrift udg. af Københavns Universitet, 11. Marts 1965), pp. 107 f. (Eng. ed. in *Studies in Biblical Theology*. Second Series 7, 1968, p. 131).

[4] G. E. Mendenhall, *IDB* I, p. 719. According to N. Lohfink this phrase is a reflex of the "Bundesformel", "Botschaft vom Bund. Das Deuteronomium", *Wort und Botschaft*, (ed. J. Schreiner), 1967, p. 171.

[5] For the text Dt. 28:69-30:20 see K. Baltzer, *Das Bundesformular*, pp. 43 ff. Cf. also 1 Sam. 12:14.

[6] As does W. Beyerlin, *Herkunft und Geschichte des ältesten Sinai-traditionen*, 1961, pp. 59 ff. (Engl. ed. *Origins and History of the Oldest Sinaitic Traditions*, 1965, pp. 49 ff.).

[7] McCarthy, *Treaty and Covenant*, p. 158, cf. E. Gerstenberger, "Covenant and Commandment", *JBL* 84/65, pp. 46 f.

It is impossible at this point to discuss the complex problem of the relationship between the Near Eastern treaty formulae and the Old Testament commandments as a part of the covenant,[1] nor whether the Decalogue was originally part of a cultic happening or secondarily became part of the Israelite liturgy.[2] What should be remembered is that in Dt. 5 the Decalogue is given in connection with Yahweh's theophany, as is the case in Ex. 19-20.[3] A theophany is very much a cultic phenomenon, cf. Ex. 29:43 ff., Ps. 50.[4] Presumably Joel's knowledge of the temple cult is in this respect reflecting the same kind of cultic setting as Dt. 5.[5]

Another motif closely associated with the covenant is found in 2:27 where Yahweh says that the people will know that he and no one else is their god. In Am. 3:2 Yahweh stresses that he has known, recognized (ידע), only Israel of all the clans of the earth,[6] and he will therefore "visit", i.e. punish (פקד), them because of their transgressions. The oracle is given here in the context of the covenant. The Northern kingdom has broken the covenant with their god, Yahweh (of Zion). Thus, when Joel uses the expression that the people will know only Yahweh, he refers to the re-establishment of the people as the people of Yahweh, and this can be done in keeping the covenant. According to the covenant Yahweh is *their* god, and only him will they recognize as their Lord, he who alone should live in the temple on Zion, 4:17.

The phrase בקרב ישראל also in 2:27 should be investigated in light of the above comments. The phrase occurs for the most part in Deuteronomy and Joshua, Dt. 17:20, Josh. 6:25, 13:13, cf. 7:13. Dt. 11:16 reads בקרב כל־ישראל and 21:8 has the phrase בקרב עמך ישראל, cf. also Zeph. 3:15, 17. It should be noted that this phrase does not occur in the other prophets, so that it is possible to consider it a

---

[1] McCarthy, *Treaty and Covenant*, pp. 152 ff., discusses this problem.

[2] So Gerstenberger, *JBL* 84/65, pp. 38 ff. One could argue that, even if some commandments and statutes could be shown to have originated in a secular setting, they are always ideologically the law of the god. The deity gives the law to his people. Cf. Hammurapi, Moses. For some Egyptian parallels to the Israelite commandments see S. Morenz, *Ägyptische Religion*, 1960, p. 62, n. 11.

[3] For the cultic character of Ex. 19:9 ff. see N. Lohfink, "Die Bundesurkunde des Königs Josias", *Biblica* 44/63, p. 489.

[4] Cf. below pp. 83ff. Cf. also K. Elliger, *Kleine Schriften*, p. 228.

[5] K. Koch, among others, assumes that the Decalogue was regularly recited to the whole people at a cult festival, *Was ist Formgeschichte²*, 1967, pp. 39 f.

[6] Cf. Hos. 8:2; 13:4. For ידע with this meaning, see H. B. Huffmon, "The Treaty Background of Hebrew *yāda'*", *BASOR* 181/66, pp. 31 ff.

Deuteronomistic phrase which Joel has used in alluding to the covenant.[1] Because it is almost a fixed formula the name Israel in it cannot have any real bearing on the question of the pre-exilic or post-exilic origin of the book of Joel.[2] The occurrence of the name Israel both here and in 4:2 can be nothing else than a reference to Israel as the people chosen by Yahweh.

At this point it should be noticed that the disaster which has come upon the people, has come according to the will of Yahweh, 2:25, cf. 2:11, 19. The locusts have been sent by Yahweh. The same kind of idea is expressed in Am. 3:6. The cult prophet Joel places this disaster in the framework of the covenant ideology, so that it is because of the broken covenant that Yahweh has punished the people. If they do not worship Yahweh who alone is their god, ואין עוד, 2:27, the punishment will be a catastrophe such as the one described in Joel 1-2. Amos and Joel are then in agreement with the basic religious idea expressed, for instance in Ps. 89:47 ff., that suffering is grounded in the will of Yahweh.[3]

The rooting of suffering in the will of Yahweh is expressed in another way, namely, that both blessings and disaster come from the place where the deity or deities dwell, from the mountain of the gods. Such a mountain is known from Ugarit, צפון, so that when we meet the term הצפוני in Joel 2:20 it recalls this concept in the same way as the image of Yahweh slaying his foes, his adversaries, the chaos power, expressed in several psalms, brings to mind the Ugaritic material.[4] In light of this background, the people from the North can be viewed not only as political powers,[5] but can, according to the original meaning of הצפוני, also be seen as of mythological significance, in the same manner as the term צפון in Israelite theology can be used in connection with the god mountain of Jerusalem, Zion, Ps. 48:3.[6]

---

[1] Cf. K. Baltzer, *Das Bundesformular*, p. 164.

[2] According to G. A. Danell "the cult congregation in the temple at Jerusalem had always been called Israel", *Studies in the Name Israel in the Old Testament*, 1946, p. 99. L. Rost understands the occurrence of the name Israel in this passage in Joel as referring to the exilic or post-exilic period, *Israel bei den Propheten* (BWANT 19), 1937, p. 124.

[3] Cf. my book, *Psalm* 89, p. 156.

[4] Pss. 68:31, 74:13 f., 89:10 f., 93:3 f., 104:5 ff., cf. Job. 26:12, Isa. 27:1, 51:9 f., Hab. 3:13 ff.

[5] In regard to the people from the North in Jer. 1:14, 4:61, 6:1, 22, A. S. Kapelrud says that Jeremiah "knew how to combine ancient mythological concepts with the accute, historical danger from the north", *Joel Studies*, p. 106. Cf. Th. H. Robinson, *HAT* 14³, 1964, p. 64.

[6] See among others H. Gressmann, *Der Messias*, p. 137, J. Morgenstern,

Thus we have an explanation of how צפון can be used as a designation for heaven in passages such as Job 26:7 and Isa. 14:13. In the former passage שמים and צפון are parallel terms. From an ideological point of view this is quite in order because the mountain of the gods is the place where the deity lives and meets his people, so that it is identical with heaven where a sky-god is thought to live. This identification of macrocosm with the microcosm is expressed in Psalm 11:4 there it says that "Yahweh is in his holy temple,[1] his throne is in heaven".[2] Thus the temple is heaven on earth.[3]

In 2:20 the term הצפוני in the singular form means "the one from the north, the northerner", referring to a single individual, but also used in reference to a collective, here, the enemies. H. Gressmann

---

"Psalm 48", *HUCA* 16/41, pp. 47 ff., A. Lauha, *Zaphon. Der Norden und die Nordvölker im Alten Testament*, 1943, pp. 43 ff., S. Mowinckel, *Der achtundsechzigste Psalm*, p. 43, Kapelrud, *Joel Studies*, pp. 93-108, 104 ff. P. L. Krinetzki, "Zur Poetik und Exegese von Ps. 48", *BZ* 4/60, pp. 86 ff., Jörg Jeremias, *Theophanie*, pp. 116 f., cf. J. Obermann, "An Antiphonal Psalm from Ras Shamra", *JBL* 55/36, p. 25, Ahlström, *Psalm* 89, p. 74. — For the Ugaritic phrase *ṣrrt ṣpn* compare G. R. Driver who sees *ṣrrt* as equivalent to Akkad. *ṣurru*, "inside, heart, center", *Cannanite Myths and Legends*, p. 501, n. 18. *CAD* explains center as "center (of an object)". M. Dahood, following Driver, translates ירכתי צפון as "the heart of Zaphon", *Psalm* I (Anchor Bible 16), p. 290. This could be possible because ירכה* means both the back side and the innermost part of something. However, using the term "heart" in connection with a mountain is not apt; "center" would be better, Cf. also E. Lipiński, *La royauté*, p. 395, n. 3.—The place name צרת השחר in Josh. 13:19 should be considered in this discussion. It may be that צרת here has the same meaning as Akkad. *ṣerretu* III, "sheen". Another possibility is the Phoenician צרת, "second wife, concubine", √צרר, (Donner-Röllig, *KAI* 27:17) which is the same as the Akkad. *ṣerretu* (fem. of *ṣerru*, "enemy") "second wife". צרת in Josh. 13:19 may be a Hebrew form comparable to the Ugaritic *ṣrrt* (√צרר). Thus צרת השחר can be translated as the sheen or brilliance of Shahar.

[1] This first sentence can also be translated: "Yahweh, his holy seat is in the temple", which gives a better parallelism with the following sentence. See M. Dahood, *Psalms* I, pp. 69 f. and compare E. Z. Melamed, "Break-Up of Stereotype Phrases as an Artistic Device in Biblical Poetry" *Studies in the Bible* (Scripta Hierosolymitana VIII), 1961, pp. 115 ff.

[2] Cf. Mic. 1:2-3. See also K. Yaron, "The Dirge of the King of Tyre", *Annual of the Swedish Theological Institute* III, 1964, p. 44, cf. R. Eissler, *Weltenmantel und Himmelzelt*, 1910, p. 607, G. Widengren, "Aspetti simbolici dei templi e luoghi di culto del vicino Oriente Antico", *Numen* 7/60, pp. 1 ff.

[3] This ideological-religious concept has not been fully understood by R. E. Clements, *God and Temple*, 1965. Cf. also, the criticism given by M. Haran who rightly emphasizes that every sanctuary and temple is a house of God, a בית, thus "the divine presence is itself already expressed" in the term בית יהוה, "Biblical Studies: The Idea of the Divine Presence in the Israelite Cult", *Tarbiz* 38/68, pp. 105-119, (Hebrew), cf. p. If., and the same author in *Biblica* 50/69, pp. 251 ff.

understood the term as a designation for a deity. He maintained that
not only is the mountain of the north a mountain of the gods, but that
the "northerner" is a definite divine being.[1] This is possible in light
of the Ras Shamra texts. Following the same line of reasoning as
Gressmann, S. Mowinckel has maintained that we must see in this
term a mythic being which in the final analysis must be connected
with the Ugaritic Baal Ṣaphon, and which in Joel 2:20 has become
"the king of the chaos powers".[2] Gressmann supports his view with
the argument that הצפוני cannot refer to the locusts because they
usually came from the east (the desert) and the south.[3] However, as
in many other instances, logic and mythology or logic and symbols
should not be played against each other. We can, for example, mention
the southern nations in Ez. 38, which in connection with the prophecy
of Gog are mentioned as coming from ירכתי צפון v. 15. To associate
such a people with the North is to use mythological language which
tells us that the people are as dangerous as the chaos power itself, or
as the god of death.[4] An association of the locusts, the enemies, with
the mythological term הצפוני is thus possible, since in Joel it has
been used as a personification of the hostile powers. When now
Yahweh turns the fate of his people in reestablishing the covenantal
relationship, the enemies will be completely annihilated.

---

[1] "So gut der Nordberg gleich dem Götterberg ist, so gut is der *Nördliche* ein
göttliches Wesen", *Der Ursprung der israelitisch-jüdischen Eschatologie* (FRLANT 6)
1905, p. 190.

[2] *NTT* 59/58, p. 13. It could be mentioned that C.C. Torrey saw a person in
this term, namely, Alexander the Great, "Alexander the Great in the Old Testament Prophecies", *BZAW* 41/25, p. 285.

[3] *Der Messias*, p. 137, Cf. Merx, *Die Prophetie des Joel*, pp. 64 f. According to
H. H. D. Stocks הצפוני referred to the Scythians, "Der 'Nördliche' und die
Komposition des Buches Joel", *Neue Kirchliche Zeitschrift*, 19/08, pp. 751 ff.

[4] Kapelrud, *Joel Studies*, pp. 103 f., B. S. Childs, "The Enemey from the North
and the Chaos Tradition", *JBL* 78/59, p. 197. Cf. J. Z. Smith, "Earth and Gods",
Journal of Religion 49/69, p. 111.

CHAPTER THREE

CULT TERMS AND CULT PRACTICES

The Near Eastern phenomenon of "elders" as an institution of government can be traced back to the Hittite Kingdom in Asia Minor and northwestern Syria as well as to ancient Mesopotamia. H. Klengel sees a connection between the old tribal organization and the elders. He believes that in Asia Minor the elders were part of the original "Verfassungsform" with political functions in the government of a tribe or city. They were responsible for legal and juridical problems and seemed to have exercised some supervisory role over the cult.[1]

In Israel we find a parallel institution and similar roles attributed to the elders. They had juridical functions, Dt. 19:21; and decided cases at the city gate, Dt. 25:7. Their political functions are evident in Judges 9:2 and 1 Kings 12:6, where they act as counsellors, and in 1 Sam. 8:4, 2 Sam. 5:3, 1 Kings 12:1 ff., they elect kings. In the cult they represent the people, Ex. 18:12, 1 Kings 8:3, Joel 1:14, 2:16,[2] and were responsible for convoking the cult congregation, 1 Kings 21:8 f., Ezra 10:8. It is clear from 1 Kings 20:7 ff. that they could have played some part in the decision to wage war, cf. 1 Sam. 11:1, 2 Sam. 17:4, 2 Chr. 25:17.[3] The elders still played some role in the late monarchic time, 2 Kings 23:1 f. When Josiah called together the people of Judah and Jerusalem to listen to the reading of the newly discovered "law book" and to make a new covenant he called first upon the elders as the representatives of the people. This was an official gathering at the temple, and thus a religious occasion with important consequences for the life of the whole country, so it

---

[1] H. Klengel, "Die Rolle der 'Ältesten' (LÚᴹᴱˢˢᵁ.GI) im Kleinasien der Hethiterzeit," *ZfA* 57/65, pp. 235 f., and *Orientalia*, N.S. 29/60, pp. 357 ff. Cf. O. R. Gurney, *The Hittites*, 1952, pp. 68 f., A. Malamat, "Kingship and Council in Israel and Sumer", *JNES*, 22/63, pp. 247 ff. Th. Jacobsen prefers to call this "Verfassungsform" a "primitive democracy" which, however, is not an adequate term, "Primitive Democracy in Ancient Mesopotamia", *JNES*, 2/43, pp. 159 ff., 166.

[2] "The Elders have an important functional role to play in a covenant rite involving all the people", A. Cody, "Ex. 18:22", *Biblica*, 49/68, p. 164.

[3] For the elders in Israel, see J. L. McKenzie, "The elders in the OT", *Analecta Biblica*, 10/59, pp. 388 ff., R. de Vaux, *Ancient Israel*, 1961, pp. 8, 137 f., 152 f., cf. M. Noth, *Geschichte Israels*³, 1956, p. 104.

is noteworthy that the elders, the leaders or the clans or the cities, are called first. This argues that the system of elders was so deeply rooted in the Israelite-Judahite society that it could not be neglected or "dismissed" even in well-organized kingdoms. It was a phenomenon older than the Israelite nation itself which perhaps explains why it survived the disaster of Judah and re-appears as the natural mode of representation of the people in the post-exilic period, Ezra 10:8, 14. It is clear from Isa. 3:1 ff. that the elders are seen as one of the pillars of Israelite society,[1] and the natural representatives of the people.[2]

In the light of what has been said, it is quite in order that Joel asks the priests to call upon the elders in summoning the people to a fast, 1:14, 2:16. He follows here an old custom.[3] We should note in this context that the whole message of the book of Joel is directed to the elders, הזקנים, and the inhabitants of the country, 1:2. This illustrates the importance of the elders and their responsibilities in the cultic sphere.

The term שׂשׂוֹן in 1:12 is one of the many indications that Joel not only uses cultic motifs, but actually describes cult practices. The passage, Joel 1:8-12, must be seen against the background of the Canaanite cult and its characteristics. It begins with an imperative, אֱלִי, lament, v. 8, and then there follows a statement that both meal and drink offerings are cut off [4] from the temple, therefore the priests are to mourn, v. 9. The fields are laid waste, wine and fruit and barley have perished, vv. 10 f., cf. Isa. 16. It is noteworthy that there is no hostility to sacrifices in Joel. They are part of the right Yahweh cult. We should also note that the priests do not mourn or lament because of any wrong they have done. Rather, because of the catastrophe there is no longer any reason for or possibility of the joyous cultic celebrations of the ingathering of the fruit, the wine or the crops. There can be no שׂשׂון, because the fields are laid waste, שֻׁדַּד, the grain is destroyed, the wine is dried up, v. 10. The farm laborers or tillers of the soil, אכרים, and the wine dressers כרמים are confounded and wail because there is no harvest, v. 11. When all this

---

[1] Cf. Johs. Perdersen who considers the זקן as belonging to the king's counsel, *Israel* III-IV, pp. 72 f.

[2] J. L. McKenzie, *op. cit.*, p. 400 f.

[3] Cf. Kapelrud, *Joel Studies*, pp. 48 f. Wolff's conclusion that the mention of the elders in 1:14 shows "die Kleinheit der nachexilischen Gemeinde von Jerusalem und Juda" (*Joel*, BK XIV, 5, p. 38) is thus meaningless.

[4] Cf. 1:5. For the religious usage of the verb כרת, cf. Kapelrud, *Joel Studies*, pp. 25 ff., 35.

is absent the joy of men fades away. In such a situation the priests had to mourn.

The picture Joel gives of the Jerusalem temple cult is one which is very much rooted in old Canaanite phenomena.[1] Joy and lament played an important role in both religions.[2] The picture given in Joel 1:8 ff. deals with a situation which is not only a catastrophe for the harvest, but as such, "cuts off" the sacrifices in the temple, which were necessary, and the joy of the "sons of men", v. 12, so that the time is one of lamentation. It is in this connection that we meet another term of cultic importance, namely אִכָּר.

The term אכרים in Joel 1:11 is a loan-word from the Akkadian *ikkaru* (Sum. engar)[3] with the meaning, plowman, farm laborer, husbandman. It occurs in Am. 5:16 in the same context as in Joel. H. Gese maintains, as does M. Bič, that אכר has been used to mark some kind of non-Israelite phenomenon, and Gese holds that the אכרים occur in Israel first in connection with the introduction of the "Domänenwesen".[4] In both the above passages the *'ikkārīm* are connected with the "shame", sorrow and lamentation due to crop failure, cf. Jer. 14:4. In Am. 5:16 the *'ikkārīm* together with those skilled in lamentation are called upon for lamentations. In Joel 1:11 they are mentioned in company with the כרמים, the winedressers,[5] who lament the failure of the vine.[6] Without the harvest there will be no joy, ששון, cf. Isa. 16:10. One gets the impression that it is no mere accident that Joel tells us that these people are lamenting. When we find in Am. 5:16 a call to lament then there is reason to assume that these classes of laborers were the logical ones to express the joy or the laments connected with the old harvest rituals.[7] When Gese asks: "Was soll die Klage in den Weingärten,"[8] he has not observed that these were the natural places for laments when the harvest of the

---

[1] F. F. Hvidberg, *Weeping and Laughter in the Old Testament*, Copenhagen and Leiden, 1962.

[2] In regard to Israel, one can compare two such different texts as Isa. 22:12 f., and Dt. 16:13 ff.

[3] H. Gese, "Kleine Beiträge zum Verständnis des Amosbuches", *VT* 12/62, p. 432, cf. H. W. Wolff, *Joel*, p. 37, A. Jepsen, *ZAW* 56/38, pp. 89 f.

[4] Gese, *op. cit.*, p. 432 f., M. Bič, *Das Buch Joel*, p. 31.

[5] Compare also Isa. 61:5, 2 Chr. 26:10.

[6] Note the associations of the withered wine, הוביש תירוש, Joel 1:11, and the אכר being הוביש, v. 11, cf. Jer. 14:4.

[7] Cf. Kapelrud, *Joel Studies*, p. 42, H. Reventlow, *Liturgie und prophetisches Ich bei Jeremia*, 1963, p. 156.

[8] *VT* 12/62, p. 433.

vine failed. Behind this custom we can find old Canaanite fertility
rites which have become part of the Israelite cult. Much of the
prophetic polemic against the so-called non-Israelite rituals at the
different sanctuaries is part of their struggle against old Canaanite
features which had in a natural way been taken over by the Israelites
in process of their assimilation to the Canaanite culture.[1] In his
comments on Am. 5:16 Gese is correct in saying that the lament
over a dead person was held in a house,[2] but it must be remembered
that the lament here and in Joel does not concern a private person.
Rather we must posit some connection with cultic lamentations behind
which originally were laments over the dead god. This provides the
inspiration for Amos' laments over Israel in ch. 5, and provided a
matrix of language and ideas which the people understood. Therefore,
it is not necessary to see in Joel 1:11 the use of foreign cultic rites
connected with the term אכר which would have been incorporated
into the Yahweh cult.

Apropos of the term ששׂון [3] it should be noted that in Isa. 12:3,
the term can be connected with a waterdrawing rite. Furthermore,
as Mowinckel maintains, the whole chapter can be seen from the
viewpoint of such a relationship.[4] In other instances the term describes
the joy connected with the sacrifices and the cultic winedrinking,[5]
which is a typical Canaanite feature,[6] cf. Isa. 22:13.

In the case of Joel 1:12 W. L. Holladay, following A. Heschel,[7]

---

[1] Cf. my book, *Aspects*, pp. 9 ff.

[2] *VT* 12/62, p. 434.

[3] Pss. 45:8, 51:10, 14, 105:43, 119:111, Isa. 12:3, 22:13, 35:10, 51:3, 11, 61:3, Jer. 7:34, 15:16, 16:9, 25:10, 31:13, 33:9, 11, Joel, 1:12, Zech. 8:19, Esth. 8:16 f.

[4] *Tronstigningssalmerne*, 1917, p. 61, n. 5, cf. *Psalmenstudien* II, pp. 36, 100 ff. If Mowinckel is right then we have no way of determining the age of Ch. 12. It should also be noted that Mowinckel is opposed to the theory that the two psalm quotations in Isa. 12 should be "late Jewish innovations in the temple cult", *The Psalms in Israel's Worship* I, p. 123, n. 58. For the water-drawing rite, cf. 1 Sam. 7:6, and G. Widengren, *Psalm* 110, pp. 22 ff., H. Riesenfeld, *Jésus Transfiguré*, 1947, p. 25. Kapelrud draws attention here to the Ugaritic text *'nt* II:38-42, *Joel Studies*, p. 44, cf. also H.-J. Kraus, *Psalmen*, p. 762. For a different opinion see C. Schedl, "Aus dem Bache am Wege", *ZAW* 73/61, pp. 291-294.

[5] Cf. Isa. 22:13 f. and Kapelrud, *op. cit.*, p. 43.

[6] For the impact of these customs and rituals on Israelite life and religion see, for instance, Am. 6:14 ff., Jer. 16:9-13. It may be that in Jer. 7:34 the prophet has borrowed his motif from something which happened on the *bāmōt* because the preceding verses mention Yahweh destroying the cult places were the people of Judah and Jerusalem "sinned", cf. Jer. 31:12 f.

[7] A. Heschel, *The Prophets*, pp. 114 f.

has argued that the terms joy and delight refer to the "delights of marriage". Holladay notes that the ששון and שמחה occur as a word-pair 13 times in the Old Testament, and concludes that such usage implies the "joy of marriage and wedding" since "their antithesis" is mourning.[1] Such an opinion is at the same time too restrictive of the meaning of the terms, and impossible to apply to every usage in the Old Testament. There are, for example, other instances of joy than the joys of marriage, and in Joel 1:12, ששון, cannot be limited to married couples. Since we do not find the word-pair here ששון may have been used in some other way. In line with other motifs and phenomena mentioned in the first chapter of Joel, the term may here, as suggested before, refer to the cultic joy, the antithesis of which is the cultic mourning and lamentation, Joel 1:5, 9. Thus ששון stands for the joy which follows the rites of fertility, so that one can say that Holladay's view has some validity since one of the important features of the Canaanite cultus is the sacred marriage.[2]

In the book of Jeremiah the phrase קול ששון וקול שמחה קול חתן וקול כלה, "the voice of mirth and the voice of gladness, the voice of the bridegroom and the voice of the bride", occurs several times, Jer. 7:34, 16:9, 25:10, 33:11. This phrase refers usually to the ordinary marriage customs, but it could conceivably also be used in a ritual associated with fertility at the annual autumnal festival, as Kapelrud has suggested.[3] Since there is no way of establishing the contrary, we must reckon with this possibility, especially since Ez. 26:31 and Hos. 2:11 may be indications for such a possibility. In these passages we find Yahweh's utterances that he will put an end to the people's joy and their cultic festivals.

Jer. 31:13 and 33:9 cannot be seen as expressions for this kind of joy, but for the joy which comes because of Yahweh's action in a not too distant future which also could be a reason for cultic celebra-

---

[1] "Jeremiah and Moses: Further Observations", *JBL* 85/66, p. 23. Zech. 8:19 or Isa. 51:3 cannot be used in support of this theory.

[2] J. Pedersen says that even if there had existed a *hieros gamos* ritual in Israel "every trace of it has disappeared", *Israel* III-IV p. 471. Cf., however, H.-J. Kraus who finds the *hieros gamos* motif is still reflected in Ps. 110, *Psalmen* (BK XV), p. LXIX, cf. p. 759, "vielleicht ist im Bereich des Mythos ein *hieros gamos* vorauszusetzen". H. Ringgren has maintained that the metaphorical language in Prov. 7:4f, 4:68, as well as in such texts as Hos. 2, Isa. 62:4 f, must be seen against the background of an original *hieros gamos* rite to which certain groups have been opposed, *Word and Wisdom*, pp. 106, 111 f., 133 f., "Hieros gamos i Egypten, Sumer och Israel", *RoB* 18/59, pp. 46 ff.

[3] *Joel Studies*, p. 43.

tions and thus joy. In Jer. 15:16 it is said that Yahweh's words are for the prophet his joy.[1] Such examples show that in the time of Jeremiah, the term שֹׂשׂ could be used both as a general word for joy as well as still being an expression for the old "Canaanite" phenomenon of cultic joy in connection with some special fertility rites.

Another term for joy used by Joel is גיל, which means "to shout for joy, to rejoice, *exultare*",[2] a meaning occuring as well in Ugaritic, II Krt. 15:99. We find in Arabic the noun جِيل, "circular course", and the verb جَال, "go around (in a circle)"[3] a meaning connoted also by the Hebrew root, Ps. 89:17,[4] cf. Ps. 118:24, where it stands for the cultic joy expressed in the procession. J. Pedersen, F. F. Hvidberg,[5] P. Humbert,[6] H. W. Wolff,[7] and Dorothea W. Harvey,[8] among others, have connected גיל with ritual performances in the Canaanite fertility cult. This may be the case, for example, in Hos. 10:5 which has always been a stumbling block.[9] Pedersen thinks that יגילו is here an expression for the cultic joy which he connects with the resurrection of the deity.[10] This could be the case, since the meaning of the verb גיל is closely connected with the joy over a good harvest and the lifegiving powers in Canaan. It is also noteworthy that גיל does not occur in the Pentateuch, nor in the historical books, exept for 1 Chr. 16:31, which is a psalm. The word is at home in poetry and is found

---

[1] It could be possible that Jer. 15:15-18 is a "quotation" from an old lamentation, cf. A. Weiser, *Der Prophet Jermia* (ATD 20-21), p. 132. Compare also E. Gerstenberger, "Jeremiah's complaints: Observations on Jer. 15, 10-21", *JBL* 82/63, p. 401, H. Reventlow, *Liturgie und prophetisches Ich bei Jeremia*, pp. 219 ff.

[2] Mandelkern, *Concordantiae, s.v.*

[3] Cf. W. W. Müller, *ZAW* 75/63, p. 308. Ps. 2:11, וגילו ברעדה, M. Dahood sees this גיל as another root and translates the phrase as "live in trembling", *Psalms* I (The Anchor Bible 16), p. 13.

[4] Verse 16 shows that the text deals with the procession, cf. my book *Psalm 89*, pp. 90 f.

[5] *Weeping and Laughter*, pp. 100 f., 109 f., Cf. W. C. Graham, *AJSL* 45/29, pp. 174 f.

[6] "'Laetari et exultare' dans la vocabulaire religieuse de l'AT", *RHPhR* 22/42, pp. 204 ff., 208.

[7] *Hosea* (BK XIV :1), p. 197.

[8] "Rejoice not, O Israel", *Israel's Prophetic Heritage* (ed. B. W. Anderson — W. Harrelson), 1962, pp. 116 ff.

[9] There is no need to correct יגילו to ייללו or יחילו. J. Johansson understood גיל as a *didd*-word, here having the meaning be frightened, *Profeten Hosea*, Uppsala 1899, p. 200. H. S. Nyberg renders, "Denn in Trauer sind עם und seine Gemeinde gefallen — während seine Priester über ihn jauchzen — wegen seiner Herrlichkeit, weil sie ihm entschwunden", *Studien zum Hoseabuche*, p. 74.

[10] *Israel* III-IV, p. 470, n. 3 (= p. 713).

also in Proverbs and some prophetic writings. However, Amos, Micah and Ezechiel do not use it. This pattern of usage suggests that circles responsible for the picture of the religion of Israel and Judah which is handed down in the historical books avoided the term, גִיל, because it was too closely associated with particular fertility rites which they opposed. This is, however, not to say as D. W. Harvey that "*ṣāḥaq* and *gîl* do not seem to be used officially for any legitimate forms of public rejoicing in the Israelite cult", while at the same time she states that "the term was in popular use in the cult", and cites evidence from the psalms for this view.[1] The use of *gîl* in such psalms as 89:16 ff. and 118:24 f. contradicts her view about the official usage of the verb and her implicit distinction between public official and popular use is invalid since it must be stressed that if a term or phrase is used in the cult, in a liturgy, then this means we are dealing with the official sphere and no other. The cultus is an official matter; the temples and sanctuaries are the religious centers of the collective, be it tribe, city, village, or capital of the kingdom. The cult at such sanctuaries is not a private matter. Psalms such as 89 and 118 were in all probability used in the temple cult.[2] The former describes the liturgical features connected with the Davidic king-ritual, his enthronement and Yahweh's covenant with him and his dynasty. Such a psalm surely reflects official conceptions.[3] We should, in regard to Ps. 118:24, notice the following:

זה־היום עשה יהוה

This is the day Yahweh acts (takes action)

---

[1] Harvey, *op. cit.*, pp. 118, 120.

[2] H. S. May considers Ps. 118 as having been used and composed at the temple of Arad, "Psalm 118: The Song of the Citadel", *Religion in Antiquity* (Suppl. to Numen XIV), 1968, pp. 97 ff. E. Lipiński maintains that Ps. 89 originated in court circles in Jerusalem as a piece of literature and not as a cultic oracle. It "tend à accréditer l'idée de la permanence de la dynastie davidique" in a time when its position was weak, *Le poème royal du Psaume LXXXIX* 1-5. 20-38 (Cahiers de la Revue Biblique 6), 1967, p. 86. How then were the ideas of the psalm advocated among the people? Who heard the psalm? Would not the best place for such a "propaganda" have been the temple?

[3] When Miss Harvey says that "the prophetical and the official attitude in Israel seems to differ from the usual attitude toward cultic joy in the Near East" (*op. cit.*, p. 25), it must be stated that she has not proven her hypothesis. It should also be streesed that the prophetic attitude can in no way be equated with the official one, and Miss Harvey has not established the nature of the official attitude. The official attitude toward religion in the kingdom of Judah is, of course, to be sought at the royal temple of Jerusalem.

and then follows the cohortative:

נגילה ונשמחה בו

Let us rejoice and be glad on it.[1]

This shows that we are dealing with a special cult day, presumably the יום יהוה,[2] on which the people rejoice because of Yahweh's saving deeds. Verses 26 f. relate more liturgical phenomena: [3]

ברוך הבא בשם יהוה

Blessed be he who enters with [4] the name of Yahweh.

There follows the priestly blessing, "we bless you from [5] the house of Yahweh" (מבית יהיה), and the admonition to bind the חג, which presumably is the festal sacrifice,[6] to the horns of the

---

[1] As in this verse, שמח and גיל often occur as a wordpair or in parallelism with each other, Pss. 14:7, 16:9, 21:2, 31:8, 32:11, 48:12, 53:7, 96:11, 97:1, 8, 149:2, Prov. 23:24 f., 24:17, Isa. 9:2, 16:10, 25:9, 66:10, Hos. 9:1, Hab. 1:15, Jer. 48:33, Zeph. 3:17, etc. This phenomenon can also be traced back to Ugarit, II Krt I-II (= UT 125), 99, cf. also Lipiński, *La royauté de Yahwé dans la poésie et le culte de l'ancien Israël*, 1966, pp. 258 f.

[2] For יום יהוה as the special day on which Yahweh acts (עשׂה), see below pp. 65ff.

[3] Cf. H.-J. Kraus, *Psalmen* (BK XV), pp. 808 f., Ahlström, *Psalm* 89, p. 144. See also J. J. Petuchowski, *VT* 5/55, p. 267.

[4] Cf. 1 Sam. 17:45. ב could here be what is called in Arabic *bā' et-ta'dije*, cf. H. S. Nyberg, *Studien zum Hoseabuche*, pp. 40, 60, 82.

[5] J. Meysing omits מן and gives the translation: "We bless you, House of Yahweh", "A Text-Reconstruction of Ps. CXVII (CXVIII) 27, ", *VT* 10/60, p. 133. This may be due to a misunderstanding of the liturgical situation. From the house of Yahweh, the temple, the blessings go out. The same author thinks that Ps. 118:27 is so strange in its construction that it is doubtful whether it is an original part of the psalm, pp. 130 f. Granting that the construction is rare or strange does not necessarily mean that it is impossible or is some sort of addition. Because of a comparison with Nu. 6:25 (יאר יהוה פניו אליך) Meysing comes to the conclusion that something is missing in Ps. 118:27. However, there is in fact no real difference between saying that Yahweh will shine upon them or that Yahweh's face will shine upon (or enlighten) the people. (The *waw* in ויאר, v. 27, may be *waw emphaticum*, for this see M. Pope, *JAOS* 73/53, p. 98, P. Wernberg-Møller, "'Pleonastic' *Waw* in Classical Hebrew", *JSS* 3/58, pp. 321 ff., M. Dahood, "Ugaritic Studies and the Bible", *Gregorianum* 43/62, pp. 66 f.) For the coming of Yahweh desribed in solar categories see Dt. 33:2, Pss. 50:2, 80:2, 94: 1, cf. Ps. 27:1, Isa. 10:17, 60:1, 3, Ezek. 10:4, Mic. 7:8; in Ps. 84:12 Yahweh is called שמשׁ.

[6] For חג as signifying not only the festival but sometimes also the sacrificial animal see B. Gärtner", טליא als Messiasbezeichnung", *SEA* 18-19/53-54, pp. 102 ff., and W. Robertson Smith, *The Religion of the Semites*, p. 341, n. 2, Fr. Delitzsch, *Biblischer Commentar über die Psalmen*³, 1874, pp. 232 f., Meysing, *VT* 10/60, p. 133, cf. also N. Füglister, *Die Heilsbedeutung des Pascha*, 1963, pp. 54 f. חג as "sacrifice" may also be supported by the parallelism in Ex. 23:18. Here M. Noth

altar.[1] The sacrifice may have taken place in close connection with Yahweh's epiphany in v. 27.

The one who is coming with the name of Yahweh may be none other than the king, perhaps riding up to Jerusalem on an ass—the animal used for sacral processions [2]—after the humiliation and symbolic suffering, death and resurrection had been liturgically performed "in the valley". He comes forth as צדיק and נושע (saved),[3] and he is blessed from the temple of Yahweh. The whole ritual is thus the basic reason for the joy of the people.[4]

Such a text cannot be called a popular text, but we are rather dealing with a text the origin and natural setting of which is to be sought in the official sphere, the temple cult. Therefore גיל and שמח cannot be singled out as belonging to some kind of popular cult alone.[5] It has been noted above that גיל does not occur in the Pentateuch or in the historical books, and is absent from some of the prophetic books. However, since not all prophets avoid the term, we must reckon with different views among them concerning the Israelite religion and its rituals. According to Wolff the prophet Joel would have a different conception of cult from, for example, Amos, Hosea, Jeremiah and Ezechiel who do not use the word גיל.[6] The

---

gives the meaning "festal sacrifice", *Exodus* (The Old Testament Library), p. 192 (= *ATD* 5, p. 155), cf. also H. Schmidt, *Die Psalmen* (HAT 15), 1934, pp. 212, 214.

[1] The idea in v. 27b may be as Gärtner has expressed it (following the Targum): "Bindet das Festopfer mit Seilen und bringt es (sein Blut) an die Hörner des Altars", op. cit., p. 102. For binding the sacrificial animal with cords, compare Gen. 22:9.

[2] Cf. Gen. 49:10 f., 1 Kings 1:33, 38, Zech. 9:9.

[3] Cf. Zech. 9:9. Another indication for seeing the king in Ps. 118 is the term אלי, "my God". This way of addressing the deity is originally a royal prerogative, see my book *Psalm* 89, pp. 114 f.

[4] The problem with a cult psalm is always whether, in its present form, it re-presents an original liturgical text, or, because of a later and somewhat changed setting, has been "reworked". To the present writer it is clear that Ps. 118 as we now have it reflects a liturgical context. Therefore it is impossible to agree with R. Preuss who says about vv. 19 ff. that we do not find here a cultic procession but the actual experienced realization of the eschatological expectation as this was at hand at the time of the Exile, "Der Gottesknecht im Alten Testament", *ZAW* 67/55, p. 90. Even if the "psalmist" was going to Jerusalem dreaming of the "new Jerusalem" such a text as this one may have been used, but it is hard to believe and much harder to prove that it has originated at this particular time. Given the way people act a man such as the one Preuss envisions would probably have used an old psalm to express his expectations.

[5] Speaking of popular cult it should be noted that no one has attempted to define what it means.

[6] It occurs in Hos. 9:1 about the joy of other peoples, cf. also Hos. 10:5.

Jerusalem cult would not be seen by Joel as a security for or guarantee
of the final fortune, salvation.[1] All the above mentioned prophets
share in common the struggle to eliminate fertility rites from the
religion of Yahweh. This struggle is also present in Joel even if the
so-called hatred toward the "Canaanite phenomena" which can be
seen in other prophetical utterances is not that pronounced in Joel
since he uses more liturgical phrases. But, in the same vein as an Amos
or Hosea, Isaiah or Jeremiah, Joel also emphasizes that the people
must turn back to Yahweh, *their* god, 2:14, and thus abandon the
worship of other gods. Joel stresses the idea that only Yahweh is the
giver of life, rain, fertility and blessings, so that it is in the cult where
salvation is assured. It may be true that Joel can not be put on the
same level as the above mentioned prophets, since he, or rather, his
book shows more of the Canaanite heritage, as would be expected
in a "cult prophet". This indicates that the cult in the time of Joel is
not very much different from the cult of pre-exilic times. In his choice
of גיל and שמח, 1:16, 2:21, 23, Joel uses a terminology which has
been used for a long time in the Jerusalem cult. He does not indicate
how he reacted to the customs which were connected with these
terms. In this manner he is in agreement with Isaiah who also uses
these terms in his prophecy about the "prince of peace", 9:2. Both
גיל and שמח are here connected with the joy of the harvest with
which these words have long been associated. P. Humbert considers
the phrase שמחו לפניך in Isa. 9:2 as referring to a specific rite connected
with the enthronement ritual.[2] Thus, both Isaiah and Joel use this
word with the same understanding, and neither has connected it
with non-Israelite customs and rites. This makes it difficult to weave
the occurrence of גיל and שמח in Joel into a pattern of indications
which must point to a post-exilic origin of the book.

We have already remarked that ששן and the context of its usage is
seen against the background or the firmly established fertility cult
in Canaan. The same view is maintained about גיל as well as about
the word-pair שמח־גיל. The problem evoked by such terms is how
much of the old customs and rites taken over from Canaan has been
preserved in the Israelite religion and how much of it is reflected in

---

[1] *Joel*, p. 40. Here I must disagree which will be shown by this whole study.
[2] *RHPhR* 22/42, p. 199. "Bref, tout le passage Es. 9, 1 suiv. est calqué sur
le schéma de la fête d'intronisation en automme et les prédicats divins attribués
au Messie dans le v. 5 suiv. sont le pendant de l'octroi des titres royaux au mo-
narque à l'instant de l'investiture", p. 200.

Joel. Before attempting an answer to such a question—which I have tentatively done in another context—[1] one must be more specific and ask: what form of Israelite religion? For example, from the polemics of Amos we can see that the Northern kingdom, Israel, did not have exactly the same kind of cultic performances or theological ideas as were common in Judah. From Hosea we get a definite picture of how the deity was conceived in Israel. Here Yahweh has been "baalized", but in Judah and Jerusalem, the development seems to have been along different lines.[2] As far as is known, in Jerusalem Yahweh has not at all been identified with Baal since in Jerusalem he is known as Yahweh El Eljon. In the temple of Jerusalem Baal was distinguished from Yahweh, and both were worshipped there in company with a third diety, the goddess, Ashera, 2 Kings 23:4 ff.[3]

A second specification of Israelite religion which is true of every other religion is that we must distinguish in Judah and Israel between the official religion of the royal temples and the forms of religion carried out in temples and sanctuaries other than Jerusalem and Bethel. Since the religion of the Northern kingdom is not the topic of the present study, our main concern is with the form of religion which was at home in the official temple cult of Jerusalem at the time of Joel, whenever that is. In discussing the first two chapters of the book of Joel, one has to raise the question of the Canaanite and Jebusite heritage and how much of this was still alive as part of the Jerusalem temple cult at the time of Joel. The whole investigation here will, in a certain sense, be an answer to that kind of question.[4]

---

[1] *Aspects of Syncretism in Israelite Religion*, 1963.

[2] Cf. my article "Some Remarks on Prophets and Cult", *Transitions in Biblical Scholarship* (Essays in Divinity VI), ed. J. C. Rylaarsdam, 1968, pp. 117 ff.

[3] For these problems cf. *Aspects of Syncretism*, pp. 50 f., 58 ff. 87. In this connection one could also mention such a text as Zeph. 1:9 which speaks about those who climb, עַל־הַמִּפְתָּן, which has been understood as Baal's podium or postament, cf. G. Gerleman, *Zephanja*, 1942, pp. 8 f., S. Mowinckel, "Jahves dag", *NTT* 59/58, p. 24, F. Horst in Th. H. Robinson and F. Horst, *Die Zwölf kleinen Propheten* (HAT 14), 1964, pp. 190, 192. H. Donner translates מִפְתָּן with "Schwelle", which seems to be more adequate, "Die Schwellenhüpfer: Beobachtungen zu Zephanja 1,8 f.", *JSS* XV/70, pp. 42 ff. In this connection one should note that nearly "every excavation of sites from periods before the Babylonian Exile shows that the majority of the Judeans practiced idolatry", F. Bamberger, "The Mind of Nelson Glueck", *Near Eastern Archaeology in the Twentieth Century*. Essays in Honor of Nelson Glueck, ed. J. A. Sanders, 1970, p. XX.

[4] The easy answer, often repeated almost as a slogan, that Israel according to its faith had changed the content of the forms it inherited from the Canaanite religion cannot be taken seriously. Such an affirmation has to be proven in every

In addressing ourselves to the phenomena connected with גיל and
שמח it was noted above that J. Pedersen, among others, sees these
terms in Hos. 10:5 as connected with the fertility cult and the priests'
rejoicing over the deity "when they announce its resurrection".[1] Even
were this a correct interpretation of Hosea, we would still have to
ask whether the same applies to Joel. There is no clear text which
gives an indisputable answer. However if we recall Joel's emphasis
on Yahweh as *the god* of the people to whom they should return, we
may rightly suspect that the vegetation rites in the temple may have
been associated by Joel with a deity of vegetation.[2] The above in-
quiry into the meaning of גיל and שמח showed clearly that these terms
are connected closely with the harvest and its customs which would
be cultic rites, cf. Isa. 16:10 ff. In Joel 1:16 this word-pair is found
in parallelism to אכל, food, which is cut off from the people as the
rites of גיל and שמחה are cut off from the temple. Joel 2:21, 23 shows
a more direct reference to the harvest and because of this passage we
must ask whether the book of Joel can be seen as an expression of the
old Canaanite-Israelite rites of harvest and joy which were still in
force in the temple of Jerusalem at the time of Joel.

Such a situation may be indicated by Joel 2:18 ff, 24 ff. Even
1:8-12 may be understood as connected in some way with the old
fertility rites,[3] as was indicated above in dealing with the terms אכרים
and כרמים, 1:11. In Joel 2:19 it is clearly said that Yahweh is the
giver of wine and oil. The statement in v. 24 that "the threshing floors
shall be full of grain and the winepresses shall give abundance of
wine and oil" refers to old Canaanite phenomena which have become
an integral part of Israelite life. "Threshing floor", גרן and "wine-
press", יקב, are intimately connected with Canaanite harvest rites

---

single case—and that has not yet been done. The process of changing the contents may in several instances be seen as a rather slow process.

[1] *Israel* III-IV, p. 713. Sellin understood גיל in Hos. 10:5 as "*sie tanzen seinet-
wegen* . . . sie veranstalten einen Bittgottesdienst mit Springprozession", *SKAT*
XII:1, p. 104.

[2] We should notice that in 1:19 f. the prophet says that he will cry to Yahweh
and that even the animals are longing for Yahweh, not for anyone else. The
prophet and the animals know who is the giver of rain and fertility, but obviously
not the people. Joel has here somewhat changed the picture of Ps. 42:2.

[3] Cf. H. Reventlow who says that we here meet with motifs "die aus dem
Bereich des kanaanäischen Naturkults übernommen ist", *Liturgie und prophetisches
Ich bei Jeremia*, pp. 157 ff. For דגן and תירוש (v. 10) as originally being deities, see
Albright, *BASOR* 139/55, p. 18, Dahood, *Ephem. Theol. Lovaniensis* 44/68, pp.
53 f. This may still be the case in Hos. 7:14.

and the two words are often used as actual synonyms for a cult place.[1] As has been noted, the oracle in v. 24 ascribes to Yahweh the result of the harvest. If the people follow the right cultic way, the *mišpāṭ* and *ṣĕdāqāh* of Yahweh, he will give them an abundant harvest. This is the blessing, ברכה, 2:14. The people will eat and be satisfied, cf. Ps. 22:27, and praise the name of Yahweh, their god, v. 26, and thus they will know that Yahweh is in the midst of Israel. Then follows the formula אני יהוה, here with the addition אלהיכם ואין עוד, v. 27, which stresses again that no one other than Yahweh is their god. According to W. Zimmerli, this phrase belongs to an old cult tradition connected with the theophany.[2] The verb, הלל, in v. 26, which often expresses cultic praise, suggests a cultic setting.[3] The verb אכל in the same verse, as well as אָכֵל in 1:16, may include the sacrificial meal. Verses 26 f. again stress that Yahweh is the giver of all these material goods, he is their god and no one else. The wonder is his, therefore, they should worship him only. If so, they will always know that Yahweh will be in their midst, and they will never again be put to חרפה. The "right" cult guarantees all this.

Thus, the kinds of blessings which usually come from Baal are said here to be given by Yahweh alone. In reality this goes against the "law" of the country, Canaan, and at the same time is the main argument used by the prophets in their struggle for a "pure" Israelite cult, so that Joel is in agreement with the other prophets. In a country where the only right thing in this sphere was to consider the fertility gods as the givers of rain and all the subsequent blessings of the earth, these prophets carried on a bitter struggle to make Israel and Judah see these phenomena in another perspective. For them it is Yahweh alone who has life giving powers.[4] This statement took on the guise of an almost impossible ideal since, as the continual prophetic polemics against the people's "apostasy" indicate, this kind of thought did not penetrate deeply to the people.

Analysis of Joel 1:5 ff. shows that there are here motifs which had their original setting in the Canaanite culture and religion,[5] as is the

---

[1] See further my article in *VT* 11/61 pp. 115 ff.

[2] *Gottes Offenbarung*, pp. 17 ff., 34 ff. See also above p. 30.

[3] Cf. Pss. 69:31, 74:21, 113:1, 3, 135:1, 145:2, 148:5, 13 149:3, 1 Chr. 29:13, cf. O. Grether, *Name und Wort Gottes im AT* (BZAW 64), 1934, p. 37 f.

[4] Cf. K.-H. Bernhardt, *Das Problem der altorientalischen Königsideologie im Alten Testament* (SVT 8), 1961, p. 107, n. 1.

[5] Cf. F. F. Hvidberg, *Weeping and Laughter*, pp. 140 ff., A. S. Kapelrud, *Joel Studies*, p. 17 ff., G. Widengren, "Early Hebrew Myths and their Interpretation",

case, for example, with a similar passage in Isaiah 24:7 ff. We might
therefore ask whether the admonition in Joel 1:8 can be seen against
this background. H. W. Wolff claims that in this verse there is a motif
of devastation and calamity from the post-exilic period.[1] This still
does not exclude the possibility that Joel used an old phenomenon.
As is the case with Am. 5:16 ff., this passage of Joel must be seen in
connections with the sayings about the day of Yahweh,[2] and in such
sayings old mythological motifs come very much to the fore. Apropos
of Joel 1:8, we should recall F. F. Hvidberg's opinion that we can
recognize here a "proverbial simile" rooted in the Canaanite cult, the
model of which was the weeping of the goddess 'Anat over Baal,[3] UT
67, IV:26 ff.[4] The admonition in Joel 1:8 reads as follows:

אלי כבתולה חגרת־שׂק
על בעל נעוריה

Lament like a virgin girded with sack (cloth)
over the lord of her youth!

For Hvidberg the phrase בעל נעוריה "is remarkable because *ba'al*,
which usually means 'husband', does not agree very well with בתולה
'virgin'. " He further maintains that it is difficult to understand how
the sorrow and grief of the virgin "for her dead betrothed may have
been of such a character in Israel that it might be proverbial".[5] This
could scarcely have been the case were the "virgin" an ordinary
woman. Thus, when the origin of this motif is considered, Wolff's
argument that the *bĕtūlāh* refers to a bride to be, is less probable. He
maintains that the old Canaanite myth was no longer known in the
days of Joel, so that an allusion to it would have been unintelligible.[6]
Even Hvidberg is of the opinion that even when we trace the meaning
and background of the phrase back to 'Anat's weeping over Baal,
"any memory of the proverb at the time of the Prophet was lost long
ago".[7] Such views are difficult either to prove or disprove. We must

---

Myth, Ritual, and Kingship, p. 190, M. Bič, *Das Buch Joel*, pp. 18 f., H. Reventlow,
Liturgie und Prophetisches Ich bei Jeremia, pp. 157 f.

[1] *Joel* (BK XIV:5), p. 33.

[2] Reventlow, *op. cit.*, p. 157.

[3] *Weeping and Laughter*, pp. 141 f.

[4] Cf. G. R. Driver, *Canaanite Myths and Legends*, 1956, p. 109, J. Aistleitner,
Die mythologischen und kultischen Texte aus Ras Schamra, 1964, p. 17, J. Gray, *The
Legacy of Canaan*[2] (SVT V), 1965. pp. 63, 65.

[5] *Weeping and Laughter*, p. 142.

[6] *Joel*, p. 34.

[7] *Weeping and Laughter*, p. 142.

remember, however, that the people of the post-exilic community of Judah and Jerusalem could be reproached, as in Malachi, for participation in an impure Yahweh cultus. The cultic weeping could thus have been part of a fertility rite still being performed in the second temple. We could therefore assume that reminiscences and survivals of pre-exilic rituals associated with a goddess (Asherah) had played a certain role, even after the Exile.[1] Support for this view comes from Mal. 2:10 ff. where the prophet mentions בת־אל נכר, "daughter of a foreign god", as well as the weeping which covers the altar of Yahweh. Perhaps the expression "daughter of a foreign god" (v. 11) is parallel to the phrase בני אלים "gods," and we could assume a goddess behind this phrase, a goddess that Judah is said to have married,[2] so that their cult is not directed to Yahweh. If by the phrase the prophet had meant simply to designate foreign women, he would have used the phrase נשים נכריות, (1 Kings 11:1, 8, Ezr. 10:2, Neh. 13:26) since an ordinary woman is never called a daughter of a god. The latter expression connotes something special. In Malachi 2:10 ff. we find that the people has profaned Yahweh's temple, קדש,[3] and has covered his altar with tears, v. 13, and has thus broken the covenant, v. 10.[4] The tears covering the altar cannot be anything other than an allusion to a rite of which the prophet disapproves.[5] Since women are not allowed to approach Yahweh's altar,[6] it cannot be the divorced wives who are weeping in sorrow and grief at the altar of Yahweh. Therefore, by using the word תועבה, in v. 11, the prophet is registering his disaproval of a non-Yahwistic ritual.[7]

According to A. Isaksson the covenant mentioned in v. 14 "must be the same as in v. 10, viz. the covenant between Yahweh and his chosen people", and he further says that the whole passage is "a sharp condemnation of apostasy to a heathen cult in Jerusalem."[8]

---

[1] For the discussion about a goddess in the Israelite religion, see Ahlström, *Aspects of Syncretism*, pp. 50 ff., R. Patai, *The Hebrew Goddess*, 1967, pp. 29 ff.

[2] Hvidberg, *op. cit.*, pp. 121 f. אל נכר, "foreign god", occurs in Dt. 32:12, Ps. 81:10, Mal. 2:11, cf. Dan. 11:39 (אלוה נכר), and the plural אלהי נכר in Gen. 35:2, 4, Dt. 31:16, Josh. 24:20, 23, Judg. 10:16, 1 Sam. 7:3, Jer. 5:19.

[3] Cf. K. Elliger, *ATD* 25, p. 189.

[4] ברית does not refer to a marriage contract.

[5] Cf. H. Ringgren, *Israelite Religion*, p. 197.

[6] Cf. J. M. Powis Smith, *ICC* 27, 1912, p. 51.

[7] Thus C. C. Torrey, "The Prophecy of Malachi", *JBL* 17/98, pp. 4 f., 8 ff., cf. Hvidberg, *Weeping* and *Laughter*, pp. 120 ff.

[8] *Marriage and Ministry in the New Temple*, 1965, p. 31. Verse 12 supports this interpretation. The terms עֵר וְעֹנֶה, "he who arouses himself and [he who] ans-

Malachi is always interested primarily in what he himself considers to be a pure and right Yahweh cult,[1] and the social and moral problems are not his main concern here. In this passage his concern is the cult, and according to him, worship was not being directed to Yahweh alone. The metaphorical expression, "a daughter of a foreign god", is an indication of the real situation, and may have been used to direct our attention to the phenomenon we are concerned with. According to Mal. 2:10 ff., the post-exilic Judah of his time did not have a true Yahweh worship, and had in effect embraced some other kind of religion which could be called illegitimate, i.e. תועבה.[2]

Returning to the *bĕtūlāh* motif we can perhaps hold that in Joel 1:8 it is part of a quotation formula with religious connotations.[3] Its position in the first chapter of the book may be an indication of this because in this section there are many traditional expressions, the origin of which is associated with Canaanite-Israelite syncretistic phenomena.[4] One might object that we are simply dealing with the

---

wers" (or "sings a lament"), may have something to do with rituals which the prophet did not accept as Yahwistic. The one who at the same time does this and brings an offering to Yahweh will be "cut off". Malachai is thus opposing syncretistic phenomena in the temple of Yahweh.

[1] The passage in Mal. 3:1 ff. has been associated by A. Haldar with the ritual of "the dead god being sought, and here his return to the temple is foretold. As in the analogous rites in Mesopotamia a messenger goes first, and prepares the way", *Associations of Cult Prophets among the Ancient Semites*, 1945, p. 129. Neglecting the context in which this verse stands, Haldar may be said to be right. However, the context deals with the coming of the god of justice and his judgment, 2:17, 3:2 ff. For this purpose Malachi has used a terminology which originally may have been connected with the liturgy of a dying god (i.e. Baal of Jerusalem). Now the prophet may have used this idea in another way predicting the coming of a "prophet", a "messenger of the covenant" who will prepare the way for Yahweh. (cf. J. Lindblom, *Prophecy in Ancient Israel*, p. 421). This may be the idea with which 3:23 and the mention of Elijah has been associated, cf. O. Eissfeldt, *The Old Testament. An Introduction*, 1965, p. 442. Also E. Lipiński considers the text in Mal. 3:1 having been built up according to a "tradition liturgique qu'il utilise remonte au moins au VIIᵉ siecle". It is here a "prélude à l'épiphanie cultuelle de Yahwé", *La royauté de Yahvé dans la poésie et le culte de l'ancien Israël*, p. 377, cf. p. 262.

[2] S. Segert has maintained that in the post-exilic time "the cult of different idols was not completely abandoned" but he sees its influence as "very limited" because it was "no longer a substantial threat to the Judean religion", "Surviving of Canaanite Elements in Israelite Religion", in *Studi sull'Oriente e la Bibbia* (Festschrift P. G. Rinaldi), 1967, p. 159. This may in some way be right, but the "threat" was not completely eliminated during the first century after the return which may be clear from the book of Malachi and the reforms of Ezra and Nehemiah.

[3] For בתולה used in connection with sexual initiation rites, see L. Rost, "Erwägungen zu Hosea 4, 13 f." *Festschrift A. Bertholet*, 1950, 454 ff.

[4] Cf. H. Reventlow, *Liturgie und prophetisches Ich bei Jeremia*, p. 157.

description of a locust plague and its consequences. This is true, but the categories used in describing the plague are those which were already present from the beginning of the life of Israel in Canaan, and these categories are at home in the mythological-theological sphere.

In this context we should recall that the *bĕtūlāh* motif has been used as a personification for the land, for the people and for Jerusalem, 2 Kings 19:21, Isa. 37:22, Jer. 14:17, 18:13, 31:4, 21, Am. 5:2, Lam. 1:15, 2:13, cf. Isa. 23:12 (Sidon), Isa. 47:1 (Babel), Ps. 137:8 (Babel), Jer. 46:11 (Egypt). Such personification explains why Joel 1:8 begins with an imperative in the 2nd person fem. singular. The question might be raised as to why the people is pictured as Yahweh's virgin when it is more often symbolized as the son of Yahweh. One possible explanation is an allusion to the very common Canaanite idea of the deity having a virgin deity at his side, an idea which lived on in Israelite mythology. In the course of time some circles reacted negatively to this conception, and the phrase was used instead in connection with the people,[1] probably as an interpretation of the covenant relationship.[2] In this connection we might mention the metaphor of the two wives of Yahweh, Oholah and Oholibah, Ezek. 23:4 ff., as was also the case with the Ugaritic El (UT 52). Ezechiel used this motif for his religio-political purpose.[3]

Joel 1:19-20 is made up of traditional lamentation material, cf. Ps. 65:13, Jer. 9:9, 23:10. The reference to a drought in these verses cannot be in harmony with the damaging ravages of the locusts. The fire, אש, which destroys the pastures, refers rather to a picture of the burning summer heat.[4] Hvidberg has distinguished this

---

[1] For the Old Testament censure of some old Canaanite myths, cf. H. Gunkel, *Genesis*, 2nd ed., p. 134, I. Engnell, *Studies*, p. 174, G. Widengren in *Myth, Ritual, and Kingship*, p. 158, C. H. Gordon, *Greek and Hebrew Civilizations*, 1965, passim, Ahlström, *Aspects of Syncretism*, pp. 80 ff.

[2] Already as early as in the eighth century the old mythological concept of the deity having a *paredros* at his side had met with strong opposition from the prophet Hosea, who uses the idea but changes it so that Israel is the wife of Yahweh. This is due to the fact that the strong polemics in Hosea show that the cult, according to this prophet, was more Canaanite than Israelite. Therefore, the "wife" Yahweh had chosen was an apostate.

[3] We can also add Ezek. 16:7 ff. with its "erotische Symbolsprache" (Widengren, *Sakrales Königtum*, p. 77) which has its root in the same mythological conception of the deity having a wife or a "virgin" at his side. For Ezek. 23 cf. also Gordon, *op. cit.*, p. 176, n. 1.

[4] For the parallelism להט//אכל see, among others, E. Lipiński, *La royauté de Yahwé*, p. 223. Cf. also Joel 2:3.

passage from the context where "the season which forms the background" of Joel's utterances "is the beginning of the harvest", so
we have here, as in Jer. 22:18, traditional material which originally
had no association with locusts.[1] The prophet seems to be picking
and choosing phrases and motifs from his vast knowledge of cultic
material, in the present case, material associated with lamentations.
For this reason his composition mirrors many old features from rites
of weeping and lamentation, of death and devastation, as well as from
hymns of joy and restoration.

In reference to the motif of weeping, we might consider the roots
אבל, 1:9 f.,[2] and בכה, 2:12, 17, as originally suggesting lamentation
rites and cultic weeping for the deity.[3] The suggestion that this kind
of weeping and sorrow could have had a place in the ritual of the
Jerusalem temple at the time of Joel, appears initially out of the
question. When 1:9 mentions the mourning of the priests one could
understand this as if they were weeping before Yahweh. The text,
however, does not state this, so that the question may be raised: "are
they performing a rite of mourning here?" It is stated that the priests
are mourning, and this may be a special rite which the prophet
mentions. Is the prophet insinuating that the Yahweh priests are
performing some mourning rite which they should not? Or are they
simply sorry in general over the lack of מנחה and נסך?[4] This latter
alternative is out of place here since Joel is talking about cultic
happenings and cultic wrongdoings in the temple. The word, אבל,[5]
means usually to mourn (for somebody), to observe the rites of
mourning. Perhaps Joel is alluding to this idea in 1:9, and, as support
for this hypothesis, one should notice that in 1:13 f. the prophet asks
the priests to gird themselves in sackcloth and to lament, to sanctify
a fast and to cry unto Yahweh, cf. 2:15 ff. Therefore, the term אבל
in 1:9 may well refer to a non-Yahwistic ritual. Instead of continuing
their mourning rites, they are to begin a fast and lament and cry to

---

[1] *Weeping and Laughter*, p. 141.

[2] To read imperative אִבְלוּ in v. 9b (so W. Baumgartner, "Joel 1 und 2", *BZAW*
34/20, pp. 10 ff.) instead of MT's אָבְלוּ is according to E. Kutsch "unnötig",
"Heuschreckenplage und Tag Jahwes in Joel 1 und 2", *ThZ* 18/62, p. 82 n.

[3] Cf. Hos. 10:5, and see, for instance, H. W. Wolff, *Hosea*, p. 228, F. F. Hvid-
berg, *Weeping and Laughter*, pp. 99 f., 114, A. S. Kapelrud, *Joel Studies*, pp. 37 f.,
G. Widengren, *Sakrales Königtum*, p. 63, H. Reventlow *Liturgie und prophetisches
Ich bei Jeremia*, p. 157.

[4] Thus. H. W. Wolff, *Joel*, p. 36.

[5] For אבל see, among others, Kapelrud, *Joel Studies*, pp. 37 f., M. Weiss,
"Methodologisches über die Behandlung der Metapher", *ThZ* 23/67, pp. 16 ff.

Yahweh that he may change the situation. If such an interpretation is correct, it will be impossible to agree with M. Bič that we are dealing here with motifs "borrowed" from the Canaanite cultus.[1] It would be more true to say that the Canaanite heritage in the Jerusalem cultus is still strong,[2] and that the prophetic polemic could still find a target.

Of particular interest from a liturgical point of view is the rare phrase, בין האולם ולמזבח, 2:17, which should be compared to Ez. 8:16 where we find בין···בין instead of בין···ול in Joel. It should be noted that the second בין can be replaced with the preposition ל because of a contamination with מן···ל,[3] cf. 2 Sam. 19:36, so that it seems impossible to use this construction in Joel as an argument about the time of the work. In the case of Ezechiel, he is in 8:16 describing a special ritual that presumably not only existed in his vision, but—as most visions are built upon some realities—had also existed in the Solomonic temple. We should recall that the prophetic books and the psalms, as a rule, do not give detailed information on how and where the priests should stand and act. Therefore the presence of such rare information in Joel 2:17 [4] should be indicative of something, cf. also 1:13. It has at times been suggested that Joel is an actual liturgy,[5] but in the light of the phenomenon of a prophet exhorting the priests to take their positions at a certain location in the sanctuary, it seems that we have here a reflection of a *manuale* rather than an actual liturgy. The space between the altar and the porch (אולם) is the place where the priests perform some of their functions. According to Ez. 8:16, the priests waited at this very place for the rising of the sun [6] which was seen as an expression for the epiphany of Yahweh.[7] Although in Ezechiel and Joel we find the

---

[1] *Das Buch Joel*, p. 22. Cf. Th. Chary who says, that "Joël, en effet, ne lutte pas contre l'idolatrie: il en utilise seulement le vocabulaire", *Les prophètes et le culte*, p. 208. Why should Joel use this kind of vocabulary if he had no need of fighting idolatry?

[2] Cf. H. Reventlow who says that for this "ist die prophetische Polemik der sicherste Beweis", *Liturgie und prophetisches Ich bei Jeremia*, p. 157.

[3] Cf. Carl Brockelmann, *Hebräische Syntax*, § 112, p. 111.

[4] Cf. O. Eissfeldt, *The Old Testament. An Introduction*, 1965, p. 112.

[5] See below, pp. 74, 132 ff.

[6] Jer. 2:27 could refer to the same liturgical position.

[7] Several other texts support a conclusion that Yahweh had solar characteristics, cf. above p. 42, n. 5. In Ps. 84:12 Yahweh is called שמש, "sun". Cf. my book *Psalm* 89, pp. 85 ff. W. Zimmerli maintains that "diese Ritualelemente im Verständnis derer, die sie übten, nicht als Verrat am Jahwehglauben, sondern als Elemente einer

priests performing their functions in the same location, the situation in the two prophetic books is different. According to Joel 2:17 the priests will not see the splendor of Yahweh as in Ezechiel. Instead they must first weep and cry so that he may come and answer them. Then the גוים would not be able to ask the question "where is their god?", a question which in effect says that Yahweh should be considered as naught.[1]

As a designation for those worshipping Yahweh, Joel 3:5 has the common phrase, יקרא בשם יהוה, cf. Dt. 18:5, Ps. 116:4.[2] It has a parallel at the end of verse 5 with those whom Yahweh calls, יהוה קרא, i.e., the ones who will survive the disaster, the פליטה, and who will worship Yahweh on his holy mountain, Zion, in Jerusalem, when the right cultus is restored. It should also be observed that Judah is not even mentioned which clearly shows that we are dealing with a time when it is acknowledged that Yahweh can have only one temple, that of Jerusalem.

To call upon the name of Yahweh—which, of course, must be done in a "right" way, i.e. the right cultic way—has as its result the saving deeds of Yahweh. The pouring out of the *rūaḥ*, 3:1 f., is connected with this phenomenon.[3] Joel is here prophecying about the ideal status of the cultus without which there can be no right religion.

---

möglichen solaren Interpretation Jahwes verstanden worden sind". It cannot be determined whether this goes back to the time of Solomon or the time of the Assyrian domination, *Ezechiel* (BK XIII), p. 221. Even though Ezechiel castigates the solar interpretation, he cannot fully free himself from it.

[1] Compare the irony in Elijah's similar question to the prophet-priests of Baal, 1 Kings 18:27. Cf. also Ps. 79:10, 115:2 and S. Talmon, "Synonymous Readings in the Textual Traditions of the Old Testament", *Studies in the Bible* (Scripta Hierosolymitana VIII), 1961, p. 342.

[2] Cf. E. Lipiński, *La royauté de Yahwé dans la poésie et le culte de l'Ancien Israël*, p. 321 ff. S. Mowinckel calls it a phrase of "cultic supplication" used "especially by the one who is performing the cult, a task in the first instance belonging to the priests", *The Psalms in Israel's Worship* I, p. 117. Cf. H. Brongers, "Die Wendung bešem jhwh im Alten Testament", *ZAW* 77/65, pp. 1 ff., A. R. Johnson, *The Cultic Prophet in Ancient Israel*[2], 1962, p. 54 f. For קרא שם על as an act of possession, see J. Schreiner, *Sion-Jerusalem*, p. 41, R. A. Carlson, *David, the Chosen King*, p. 74.

[3] Cf. O. Plöger, *Theokratie und Eschatologie*, p. 125. For an Akkadian parallel to the deity saving a remnant, see the Irra Epic IV: 130 ff. Cf. P. F. Gössmann, *Das Era-Epos*, 1955, pp. 83 f.; for a review of Gössmann, see B. Kienast, *ZfA* 54/61, pp. 244-49. This epic deals with a special political situation in which Babylon is in great calamity. The epic shows that a small remnant due to divine grace will survive and it will grow to a powerful people, cf. B. Albrektson, *History and the Gods*, 1967, p. 90. Worthy of note is that the epic ends with an oracle of blessing. According to A. L. Oppenheim the Irra epic "is a late and poetic concoction", *Ancient Mesopotamia*, 1964, p. 267.

Therefore, this part of the text of Joel cannot be characterized as a liturgy, even though it is very much influenced by and concerned with liturgical and cultic phenomena.[1]

In regard to the verb, קרא, H. S. Nyberg, among others,[2] has maintained that it belongs very much to the cultic sphere, in reference to the summoning to cultic performances. Such is the case, for example, in Joel 1:14 and 2:15, קראו עצרה. Usually the עצרה,[3] a solemn assembly gathered together for a festival, 2 Kings 10:20, Am. 5:21, Isa. 1:13, "is carried out after an official proclamation".[4] The מקראי קדש in Lev. 23:2 Nyberg views as a synonym for מועד. The calling of an assembly, קרא מקרא, in Isa. 1:13 is the calling of the people to a cult festival, and קריאי העדה, Num. 1:16 (in 26:9 קרואי, cf. 16:2), Nyberg considers as the ones in a particular meaning called to a cult assembly.[5] To this we can add the phrase קרא צום in 1 Kings 21:9, 12, 2 Chr. 20:3, Isa. 58:5, Jer. 36:9, Jon. 3:5, and Ezr. 8:21.

A parallel to this latter phrase is קדשו צום, which occurs in Joel 1:14 and 2:15, which are the only instances of קדש used in connection with the noun צום. In both passages it is followed by קרא עצרה, and in 2:16 we find the phrase קדשו קהל, "make a holy congregation, sanctify a congregation", so that קרא and קדש are in parallel position;[6] קרא concerns the summoning to cult actions and קדש emphasizes the ritual holiness. It should also be noted that קדש can be connected with עצרה, 2 Kings 10:20, and three times it occurs with מלחמה, Mic. 3:5, Jer. 6:4 and in Joel 4:9. Concerning the term קהל, H. W. Wolff maintains that in post-exilic times this designated the people

---

[1] For קרא שם as a liturgical phrase (Ps. 99:6, Lam. 3:55, cf. Dt. 32:3), see, for example, E. Lipiński, *La royauté*, p. 321. According to J. Bourke the שם theology is a deuteronomistic phenomenon, *RB*, 66/59, p. 201. See also J. Schreiner who says that Dtn has not created this idea, which should be seen as rooted in the tradition of the Amphictyony and the Ark. It has been especially exploited by Dt and Dtn, *Sion-Jerusalem*, pp. 158 ff., Cf. R. A. Carlson, *David, the Chosen* King, pp. 110-113. See also below pp. 124 f.

[2] "Korah's upprör (Num. 16 f.)", *SEÅ* 12/47, pp. 230 f., cf. Wolff, *Joel*, pp. 37 f., cf. also Zeph. 1:7.

[3] For the stem עצר see. E. Kutsch, "Die Wurzel עצר im Hebräischen", *VT* 2/52, pp. 57 ff., Ahlström, "Notes to Isaiah 53:8 f.", *BZ* 13/69, pp. 95 f.

[4] J. B. Segal, *The Hebrew Passover*, p. 209.

[5] Nyberg, *op. cit.*, pp. 230 f. For קראי מועד in Num. 16:2, 26:9, 27:3 see J. M. Grintz who translates, "The Ones Called (*vocati* not *electi*) for (the) Meeting (Council)" saying that the term מועד originally meant "meeting, council...and hence any established time for meeting...and so especially the Holidays", "The Treaty of Joshua and the Gibeonites", *JAOS* 86/66, pp. 118, n. 20.

[6] Cf. Wolff ("die Anordnung einer kultischen Handlung"), *Joel*, p. 37.

coming together "zum Gottesdienst" [1] which cannot be denied, but it should be remembered that this was also the case in pre-exilic times. Nyberg has maintained that קהל in the Old Testament has a strict religious significance: people constituted as a cult assembly, gathered for cultic action, for holy war,[2] Gen. 49:6, Ex. 12:6, 16:3, Lev. 4:13, 20:4, Num. 10:7, 15:15, 17:12, 20:6, Dt. 9:10, 31:30, Jos. 8:35, Judg. 20:2, 21:5,8, 1 Kings 8:65, 12:3, and further Dt. 5:22, 10:4, Pss. 22:23, 26, 35:18, 40:10 f., Prov. 5:14 (קהל ועדה), Jer. 44:15, 50:9. We should also note that the divine assembly can be called a קהל, Ps. 89:6.[3]

When a cult assembly, עצרה, is called, and a holy fast proclaimed, קדשו צום, the שופר trumpet [4] must sound from Zion to call the whole people to constitute a קהל. The call in 2:15 ff. concerns everyone, as it also does in 1:14 where כל ישבי הארץ refers to all the inhabitants of the land. In 2:15 ff. those called are even more delineated. Besides the עם and זקנים also the very young ones and the sucklings (עוללים, ינקי שדים), are called upon as are the bride and the bridegroom (כלה, חתן), who will leave, יצא, their chambers, v. 16. The verb יצא which is used here in reference to the bridegroom's and the bride's "going out" [5] occurs in some other passages as a technical term for a cultic "going out". The same kind of usage is true also of בוא, "to come in",[6] cf. Josh. 14:11, Ex. 28:35, Lev. 16:17 f., Num. 27:21, Ezek. 46:10, Ps. 121:8, 1 Kings 3:7.

In the Ugaritic text Krt. 85 ff.//176 ff., there are some parallels to Joel 2:16 and the multitude of the people mentioned there which may throw further light on the Joel passage. In this text Keret's "army" is described as one which everyone will join. For example, the widow is said to hire [7] a substitute (for her husband?), the bride-

---

[1] *Joel*, p. 60.

[2] *SEÅ* 12/47, p. 231, cf. A. S. Kapelrud, *Joel Studies*, p. 86, H.-J. Kraus, *Psalmen*, p. 182, S. Mowinckel, *Studien zu dem Buche Ezra-Nehemia* I, 1964, pp. 86 ff. J. D. W. Kritzinger's book *Qᵉhal Yahwe* (1957) was not available to me.

[3] Ahlström, *Psalm* 89, p. 59, L. Dequeker, "Le qedôšîm du Ps. LXXXIX à la lumière des croyances sémitiques", *Ephem. Theol. Lovaniensis* 39/63, pp. 487 f., J. Coppens, "Les Saints dans les Psautier", *Ibid*, 39/63, pp. 485 ff.

[4] Cf. Ps. 81:4, Isa. 27:13, Lev. 25:9.

[5] We can notice that the word for bridegroom's chamber, חדר, is the same as that one used for Keret's nuptial chamber, Krt:26.

[6] In my article "Solomon, the Chosen One", *History of Religions* 8/68, pp. 93-110, I have dealt with these terms.

[7] R. de Langhe "Les textes de Ras Shamra-Ugarit", *Ephem. Theol. Lov.*, 16/39, p. 314, n. 5, *Les Textes de Ras Shamra-Ugarit* II, Paris, 1945, p. 516. C. Virrolleaud

groom leaves his bride, the blind one reveals secrets (?) [1] the invalid carries his bed, the man who is alone closes his house and goes out.[2] The "army" consists of three hundred myriads of persons, 1:89, going out to occupy the field as locusts, *'erby*, cf. Judg. 6:5, 7:12, and as grasshoppers, *ḥsn*, and for seven days they go until they reach *'udm rbm* and *'udm ṯrrt*, "the big *'udm* and the little *'udm*",[3] Krt. 108 f. These two latter terms may refer to a city and its center, the sanctuary; *ṯrrt* is then the actual temple area.[4] The description of the "army" makes it somewhat difficult to see it as a direct parallel to Joel 2:16. We can, for example, note in the Krt text the difference that the groom leaves the bride. However, the description of king Keret's army is not exactly that of a regular army going out to war. It seems to be an exceptional army, so that it is possible we are dealing with some kind of cultic "exodus" [5] described, perhaps, in the Ugaritic categories of the "holy war". Therefore what we have here are two Near Eastern texts each with its own description of an army and a קהל, in which some common motifs can be seen. What is of importance here is that both texts prescribe that almost everyone must participate. We are dealing with the totality of the people. In Joel all should come before Yahweh, their god, and all should return (שוב) to him.

Before concluding our discussion of the above ideas, one further observation must be made. Joel 2:15 begins with—as does 2:1—the imperative to sound the שופר horn, and thus to summon the people to an official cultic event, a fast. It is interesting to observe that the שופר is not mentioned in that passage which might be called a holy

---

(*La légende phénicienne de Keret, roi de Sidoniens*, 1936, p. 76) and I. Engnell (*Studies*, pp. 157 f.) among others translate *škr* by "to drink'.

[1] Cf. Num. 24:3 and the man with the closed eye divining.

[2] The passage is not quite clear, see, for example, J. Gray, *The Krt Text in the Literature of Ras Shamra²*, 1964, pp. 38 ff. which should be compared with A. Aistleitner, *Die mythologischen und kultischen Texte aus Ras Shamra*, 1964, p. 91.

[3] C. H. Gordon, *Ugaritic Textbook*, Glossary, p. 352.

[4] Cf. L. R. Fischer, "The Temple Quarter", *JSS* 8/63, pp. 34 ff.

[5] Cf. I. Engnell who calls this text "the Ugarit form of the Canaanite *hillulim* and the Jerusalem *sukkōt*", *Studies in Divine Kingship*, p. 157. J. Gray understands the Krt-text as a social myth that has had some connection with the new year festival, but belonged in a situation where it was "recited on occasion of the wedding of the kings of Ugarit", *The Krt Text²*, pp. 9 f., cf. R. de Langhe, "Myth, Ritual, and Kingship in the Ras Shamra Tablets", *Myth, Ritual, and Kingship*, pp. 147 ff. The locusts mentioned in Krt are only used as a symbol for the multitude of the army. Thus, there is no parallel in the use of the motif in Krt and Joel, since in Joel the locusts are the enemies.

war passage, Joel 4:9 ff.[1] We can, therefore, conclude from these two
passages that the שופר motif is not always used for a summons to
(holy) war. Its setting may as well be seen in a special liturgical
celebration; Ps. 47:6, Ps. 81:4, 98:6, Lev. 25:9, 2 Sam. 6:15. It is
not necessary, however, to make this distinction too sharp since
Yahweh's war against his enemies is a mythical event which is
performed, heard, and/or seen in cultic actions.[2] Furthermore the
blowing of the שופר always served to summon the people, cf.
Num. 10:9, 10. Perhaps by the time of Joel the שופר could have been
one of the typical features of the Jerusalem cult.[3]

There is still another motif which must be mentioned in connection
with the sounding of the שופר, namely that it sometimes symbolizes
the coming of Yahweh, Ex. 19:16 ff., as king, Ps. 47:6, cf. Zeph. 1:16.
In Joel 2:1 it is used to announce the coming of the disastrous day
of Yahweh.[4] Thus the prophet has used the שופר motif with a different
meaning, namely to announce the coming of Yahweh and of one of
his holy days, cf. Ps. 81:4. They should sound the שופר and the people
should shout and rejoice before Yahweh, their king, Ps. 98:6, when
he comes to judge the land and the earth, Ps. 98:9. We have here the
"divine king coming to judgement".[5] It is this old new year's day

---

[1] According to H.-P. Müller the sounding of the שופר in the holy war was not
originally at home there, "Die kultische Darstellung der Theophanie", *VT* 14/64,
p. 188.

[2] S. Mowinckel, *Psalmenstudien* IV, p. 44, cf. *ZAW* 48/30, p. 267.

[3] The תרועה which is often connected with the שופר is in Ps. 27:6 also to be
seen in connection with some kind of sacrifices having been performed after a
victory over enemies, cf. *Roš haššanah* 16a and the sacrifice of Isaac. For some of
the inconsistencies in P. Humert's discussion about תרועה (*La "terouʿa"*, Recueil
de travaux publié par la faculté de lettres 23, Neuchâtel 1946) see my book, *Psalm
89*, p. 84, n. 7.

[4] For J. Morgenstern the שופר announces the advent of the new year's day,
"The Cultic Setting of the Enthronement Psalms", *HUCA* 35/64, p. 15 ff. The
שופר can also be used as a symbol for the voice of Yahweh, cf. Ex. 19:19, see
A. Weiser, "Zur Frage nach den Beziehungen der Psalmen zum Kult: Die Darstellung der Theophanie in den Psalmen und im Festkult", *Festskrift A. Bertholet*,
1950, p. 523. For שופר and תרועה as moments in the enthronisation ritual cf.
H.-J. Kraus, *Psalmen*, p. 351, cf. 1 Kings 1:34, 39, 41, 2 Kings 9:13. For trumpet
blowing in Israel see H. Seidel, "Horn und Trompete im alten Israel unter
Berücksichtigung der 'Kriegsrolle' von Qumran", *Wissenschaftliche Zeitschrift
der Karl-Marx Universität Leipzig*, 1956-57, p. 589, Cf. Also Y. Kaufmann, *The
Religion of Israel*, p. 120. For the שופר in Judaism, cf. E. R. Goodenough, *Jewish
Symbols in the Greco-Roman Period* IV, pp. 167 ff.

[5] H. M. Segal, *The Pentateuch. Its Composition and its Authorship and other Biblical
Studies*, 1967, p. 160. Segal has shown that three main themes of the pre-exilic
psalmody also occur in "the liturgy of the Synagogue for the New Year's festival"

motif which Joel has made full use of in his utterances about the two
aspects of the day of Yahweh which occur in his book. In 1-2:17 we
find it used negatively against Judah and Jerusalem; in chapters 3
and 4 it is used positively for Judah and Jerusalem, but negatively
against the גוים.

At this point we must consider the phrase שוב את־שבות. The *kĕtîb*
has in Joel 4:1 אשוב את־שבות, but the *qĕrē* indicates a hiphil אשיב and
thus interprets the text to mean that Yahweh leads back the prisoners
(taking שבות from שבה) of Judah and Jerusalem.[1] However, there
is no compelling reason to depart from the *kĕtîb* because in the preceeding chapters the text is not talking precisely about the return of
the population, scattered by the Exile or some other disaster.[2] In
4:1 we hear about a radical change which will take place to the
benefit of the inhabitants of Judah and Jersalem, a change which will
begin at the same time Yahweh sits down to judge the foreign nations,
כל־הגוים, in the valley of Jehoshaphat. The picture given in chapters
1-2 as well as in ch. 3 (3:5 may be an expression for the prophetic
futuristic hope) concerns the cult congregation of Jerusalem. The
phrase שוב שבות refers to the "turning of the fate" of Yahweh's own
people, a restoration, not only as experienced of old in the cult, but
also as a promise for the national immediate future, which at the
same time connoted an unfavorable fate for the גוים. We can thus
say that Joel also in this case is dependent upon old theological and
cultic ideas as they were at home in the performances of the temple
cult at Jerusalem. To simply understand the phrase שוב שבות[3] as

---

and that this "cannot be a matter of chance", p. 159. These three themes are: "the
creation of the world on the New Year, the manifestation of God's kingship over
the world on the New Year, and the judgement of the world by God on the
New Year", p. 158. According to Segal "the liturgy of the Synagogue...is the
direct descendant of the older liturgy of the Temple". His conclusion is that the
pre-exilic psalms using these themes "have the festival of the New Year as their
subject", p. 159. The conclusion we can draw here is then that these kinds of
themes also have been at home in the liturgy of the second temple. For the mention
of the cult day "at the turning of the year", Ex. 34:22, cf. 23:16, Dt. 16:13 ff.,
see Ahlström, *Journal of Religion* 46/66, p. 336.

[1] See among others A. Merx, *Die Phrophetie des Joel*, 1879, p. 30.

[2] Cf. M. Bič, *Das Buch Joel*, p. 85.

[3] Cf. Pss. 14:7, 53:7, 85:2, 146:1. For this phrase see, among others, E. L.
Dietrich", שוב שבות. Die endzeitliche Wiederherstellung bei den Propheten",
BZAW 40/25, E. König (the phrase does not occur "in einer unbestritten nach-
exil. Prophetie"), *Einleitung in das Alte Testament*, 1893, p. 347, S. Mowinckel,
Psalmenstudien II, p. 75 f., 287 f., who compares the Hebrew phrase with the Akkadian *sim šimti* "fixation of the fixed" which took "place in the council of gods
every year at the new year festival", *The Psalms in Israel's Worship* I, p. 147, n. 123,

always referring to eschatological happenings,[1] is not in accordance with what Joel actually says. It would be enough to refer to Job 42:10 and Lam. 2:14.[2] Thus, as has been advocated by, for example, P. Volz,[3] and S. Mowinckel, the phrase שוב שבות ought to be seen in connection with the Day of Yahweh, the day upon which Yahweh acts and restores the cosmos and the right conditions for his people according to the covenant with them and, in so doing, *ṣĕdāqāh* and *bĕrākāh* will be established.[4] This day, which phenomenologically can be called a new year's day is the day we encounter in the book of Joel.

It should be emphasized that the restoration was never meant as "only" a cultic phenomenon which had nothing to do with life outside the temple such as, for example, the political sphere. Ideally the acts of Yahweh concerned all aspects of life, and in the cult the foundations for them were laid. Such a concept of cult underlies the book of Joel. After the description of the disaster in chapters 1 and 2 we not only have the idea of a restoration of the right cult which gives the right *bĕrākāh*, but also following this the right order, *ṣĕdāqāh*, for the whole society and the ideal future, Ch. 3-4. Apropros of שוב את־שבות in Joel 4:1, one may note that the idea of a restoration, a turning of the fate, or a coming back to stability, i.e. the harmonious order,

---

cf. also II, p. 294 f. where Mowinckel emphasizes the original idenpendence of this phrase as to eschatology. Cf. H. Ringgren, *Israelite Religion*, p. 199, A. R. Johnson, *The Cultic Prophet in Ancient Israel*[2], p. 66, n. 4. See also W. L. Holladay, *The Root šûbh in the Old Testament*, 1958, pp. 110 ff., R. Borger, "Zu שוב שבו/ית", *ZAW* 66/54, pp. 315 f., H. Gottlieb, "Amos und Jerusalem", *VT* 17/67, pp. 455 f. A. Guillaume sees שבות as belonging to a root שבת II which he compares with

the Arabic ثُبُوت, "stability", "Hebrew and Arabic Lexicography, a Comparative Study", *Abr-Nahrain* III, 1961-62, p.8.

[1] So f. ex. Dietrich, *op. cit.*, p. 36 f., H. Gunkel, *Die Psalmen*, p. 235, Ed. Jacob, *Theology of the Old Testament*, 1958 pp. 310 320 f., H. W. Wolff, *Hosea* pp. 156 ff.

[2] S. Mowinckel, *The Psalms in Israel's Worship* II, p. 250, W. Holladay, *The Root šûbh in the Old Testament*, pp. 112 f. In Job 42:10 the term "has nothing to do with captivity, for Job had never been a prisoner or an exile", A. Guillaume, *op. cit.*, p. 8. Thus a form of שבה is out of the question. In Ps. 85:2 (cf. Am. 9:14) שוב שבות does not necessarily refer to the Exile, cf. Bentzen, *Salmerne*, pp. 468 f., 625, F. F. Hvidberg, *Weeping and Laughter*, pp. 133 f. A. Neher, *Amos*, 1950, p.144. שיבת which occurs in Ps. 126:1 H.-J. Kraus considers as "ein Schreibfehler" for שבות, *BK* XV, p. 853. However, the phrase השבו שיבת is found on an inscription from Sefire, see A. Dupont-Sommer, *Les inscriptions araméens de Sfiré*, 1958 (stele III; line 24), p. 128. This makes it probable that in Ps. 126:1 we have an old variant of the usual Hebrew phrase. M. Noth views שיבת as "die ursprüngliche Form der bekannten alttestamentlichen Redewendung" שוב שבות, "Die historische Hintergrund der Inschrifte von *sefire*", *ZDPV* 77/61, p. 149, n. 85.

[3] *Das Neujahrsfest Jahwes*, 1912, p. 42, n. 80.

[4] *Op. cit.*, I, p. 146 f.

includes a restoration of the people as such. Therefore the phrase שוב שבות may include also the scattered ones returning to Jerusalem and Judah.[1] The idea involved in שוב שבות is an idea of salvation for the whole society in all facets of its life. The religious as well as the political-national situations will be ideal, cf. Isa. 52:7 f. The cultic reality in which Yahweh creates the new time and its contents was thought of as creating a better world for his people. This is exactly what Joel's book is all about. The cult prophet takes the cult seriously; for him a better world starts with a true cult that gives a true *ṣĕdāqāh*, a true order, cf. Ps. 14:7. When Yahweh in the valley of Jehoshaphat has passed judgement on all the גוים, 4:2, 12, because they, among other things, have scattered his people among themselves, then the Day of Yahweh becomes the "inauguration" of a new time for his own people. This is exactly what should happen and what did happen in the cult. This could be called the cultic reality, even if this reality never became the same as the political reality. According to Joel 3:5 the destiny of the people changes and there will be a פליטה at Zion.[2] This "remnant", the ideal cult congregation, will consist of all those who call upon the name of Yahweh who at the same time are all those whom Yahweh has called. In the book of Joel the present historical situation or reality has been so combined with the cultic that they are inseparable. The right cult is the only foundation for the future of the people.[3] With such a viewpoint Joel comes close to Haggai and Zechariah.

---

[1] Even if the book should have been composed a long time after the Exile, there were still Jews outside the homeland.

[2] It should be noted that Judah is not even mentioned.

[3] One could add that the Book of Joel could be understood as a refutation of H. H. Rowley's concept of the Israelite religion. Rowley thinks that the ritual acts are unable to "lift men to present themselves before God in spirit and truth", *Worship in Ancient Israel*, 1967, p. 167.

CHAPTER FOUR

THE DAY OF YAHWEH

The locusts in Joel (1:4, 2:25) represent a real catastrophe which, perhaps, has been the propelling power for the message and composition of the book.[1] From 2:25 it is seen that the locusts are to be understood as a historical phenomenon.[2] This verse tells us that Yahweh will restore to the people that which the locusts have destroyed.[3] Perhaps the prolonged disaster caused by the locusts was the reason Joel examined why it had happened, and his conclusion —after examining the religion—was that the cult had not been of the right kind. He sees the locusts as the "messengers" of the terrible day of Yahweh which will follow them. In 2:11 he calls them the army of Yahweh.[4] Thus, after mentioning the locusts as his starting point, he continues his description of what the day of Yahweh will look like by using common terminology concerning the destruction caused by enemies. The categories best fitted for this purpose are mythological ones, and especially those common in lamentations.[5] However, it should be noted here that in lamentations locusts are not usually a part of the structure.

---

[1] Cf. H. Birkeland, *Zum hebräischen Traditionswesen*, 1938, pp. 64 f.

[2] Cf. Th. Chary, *Les prophètes et le culte à partir de l'exil.* p. 210.

[3] Cf. Mal. 3:11, which also mentions a disaster caused by locusts which Yahweh promises to rebuke.

[4] Compare also Yahweh's use of locusts in Ex. 10:4-20, cf. Quran, Sura 7:134. See also Am. 4:6-9, 7:1-3. Cf. E. Kutsch, "Heuschreckenplage und Tag Jahwes in Joel 1 und 2," *ThZ* 18/62, pp. 86 f.

[5] Compare A. S. Kapelrud who says that already in 1:11 f. "it becomes evident that symbols and trains of thought emerge, other than the domains and phenomena characterized by the locusts", *Joel Studies*, p. 17. The literal interpretation of the locusts has been advocated by, among others, J. A. Thompson, "Joel's Locusts in the Light of Near Eastern Parallels", *JNES* 14/55, pp. 52 ff. It should also be mentioned that the picture of hostile peoples as locust-swarms is not uncommon in the Near East. Thus, in "The Curse of Agade", the Gutians are described as locusts, sent by Enlil, covering the earth and causing famine, A. Falkenstein, "Fluch über Akkade", *ZfA* 57 (N. F. 23), 1965, pp. 58, 70, 1. 160, S. N. Kramer, "Sumerische literarische Texte in der Hilprecht-Sammlung", *Wissenschaftliche Zeitschrift der Friedrich-Schiller-Universität Jena*, V, Gesellschafts- und Sprachwissenschaftliche Reihe 6, 1955/56, p. 760, cf. *The Sumerians*, 1963, p. 64, B. Albrektson, *History and the Gods* (Coniectanea Biblica, OT Series 1), 1967, p. 90. See also *CAD* under *erbu, erebiš*. For Ugarit see I Krt :103 ff., 192 ff., ʿnt II:10. Cf. Kapelrud, *op. cit.*, p. 16.

It has been maintained that the disaster mentioned in Ch. 2 is not of the same kind as that described in the first chapter, and neither can the army of Ch. 2 be the same as the destruction-causing force, the locusts, in Joel 1. The reason for this distinction is said to be the fact that in Ch. 2 it is Yahweh himself that leads the army, v. 11. Therefore the army mentioned in Ch. 2 has been characterized as "ein apokalyptisches Heer".[1] It is right that Yahweh is the one who leads the army, but it should also be recognized that what is described in this chapter is not only a plague of locusts, but also the consequences issuing from a wrong cult. Because of the "wrong" kind of worship the locusts are coming as an announcement of the impending day of Yahweh. In 2:25, Yahweh calls the locusts "my army", חילי, which means that there is a great possibilitiy of seeing the locusts and the people of the North, הצפוני, 2:20, as expressions for one and the same idea, namely, that the army has been sent against Yahweh's own people according to the will of their god, cf. also 1:6. The book of Joel, which uses cultic motifs and liturgical language in so many instances, is in this case in accord with the dramatic actions and ideas of the annual festival, in which Yahweh "created" the right order, blessings and righteousness. The "enemies" may "work" for a time, but the deity himself comes and puts an end to their dominion and work of destrcution. With this in mind one cannot deny the possibility that the גוים of 2:17 belong to the same category as the locusts—that they are enemies too. This does not mean that they have to be identical with the locusts. On the other hand, the עם-motif of 2:2 is an expression for the same thing that the locusts stand for.

Thus in Ch. 2, when the prophet calls upon the people to be prepared for the day of Yahweh and calls for a cultic fast, he does this in expressions and motifs that are proper in this connection— namely, religious phraseology, the aim of which was best to describe the coming day of Yahweh.[2] Taken together these phrases and motifs may be seen therefore as indications for this day as an old cultic day.

Much has been written about the day of Yahweh, יום יהוה, and it would seem unnecessary to discuss it again. However, because of the different viewpoints advocated concerning this theme, it is necessary to deal with it at some length in connection with Joel. It

---

[1] So Wolff, Joel, pp. 48 ff. Every futuristic aspect in a prophetic book cannot be understood as apocalyptic, cf. below.

[2] Cf. A. Weiser, *The Old Testament. Its Formation and Development*[2], 1963, p. 238.

has been maintained that the יום יהיה had its roots in the holy war concept.[1] Among the indications for this connection is the fact that the שופר of Joel 2:1, 15,[2] as well as the תרועה,[3] are phenomena which also occur in connection with holy war.[4] On the other hand, it has been maintained that the יום יהוה originally was a cult day, a special cultic festival marking the coming of Yahweh, which meant destruction for the enemies of Yahweh and blessing for his own people.

Concerning this second interpretation, Amos 5:18 serves as the starting point of the discussion:

> "Woe unto you (who) long for the day of Yahweh.
> What is to you the day of Yahweh?
> > (or: What will the day of Yahweh be unto you?)
> It (הוא) will be darkness and not light.

The same idea is repeated in Amos 5:20.[5] The succeeding verses (21-27) clearly show that Amos is concerned with the cultic festivals of Israel, and how wrong they are. Thus, the only conclusion that can be drawn from Amos 5:18 ff. is that the Day of Yahweh was a well known cultic day, which now will not be the usual festival of light, but instead will turn out to be a day of disaster for Israel. The

---

[1] G. von Rad, "The Origin of the Concept of the Day of Yahweh", *JSS* 4/59, pp. 97 ff., *Old Testament Theology* II, pp. 119 ff., cf. K.-D. Schunk, "Strukturlinien in der Entwicklung der Vorstellung vom 'Tag Jahwehs'", *VT* 14/64, pp. 319 ff., H. Reventlow, *Liturgie und prophetisches Ich bei Jeremia*, pp. 107 f.

[2] Cf., however, above, pp. 58 f.

[3] The admonition to shout for joy on the holy mountain of Yahweh occurs with the verb הריע in Joel 2:1.

[4] Cf. H. W. Wolff, *Joel*, p. 46; see also the same author, *Hosea* (BK XIV:1) pp. 59 ff. where Wolff calls this day a "Heilstag". Concerning these two terms, Wolff has not really investigated their cultic use. He only says that "der Aufruf zum Hornblasen" can also be found in cultic connections "allerdings sonst nicht für die Aufrufe zur Volksklagefeier", *Joel*, p. 47.

For the cultic use of these two terms see my book, *Psalm* 89, pp. 84 f. שופר in 2 Sam. 15:10 is also been by J. Morgenstern as an announcement of the arrival of the New Year's Day. Thus, Absalom began his rebellion in connection with a cultic festival, "The Cultic Setting of the 'Enthronement Psalms'", *HUCA* 35/64, pp. 15 f. Absalom's promise to go to Hebron "refers to a special cultic action", according to C. Lindhagen, *The Servant Motif in the Old Testament*, p. 283, n. 4. The occurrence of שופר in Ps. 81:4 is reason enough for considering it to have been used in cultic festivals from antiquity, cf. M. Dahood, who considers Ps. 81 to be of "North Israelite origin", *Psalms* II, p. 263.

[5] G. von Rad has argued that this passage "is not sufficiently unequivocal to be used as a suitable starting point for an examination" of the concept of the Day of Yahweh, *JSS* 4/59, p. 98, cf. *Old Testament Theology* II, p. 119.

prophet has used a common religious idea about a special cult day [1]
but turned it into its opposite. From this passage it is impossible to
conclude that the people of Israel knew nothing of a day that could
be termed יום יהוה. Instead, the text gives clear evidence—from the
negative—that a special Yahweh day existed, with which some
concepts of light (with all its associations) were connected.[2]

The day of Yahweh has been compared with the Akkadian *ûm ili*,
the day of the god,[3] which is a cult day, and also with ימי בעלים, the
days of the Baals, mentioned in Hos. 2:16. This latter phrase Wolff
characterizes, without any discussion, as Canaanite cult festivals.[4] Of
further interest here is the phrase מה תעשׂו ליום מועד וליום חג־יהוה from
Hos. 9:5; cf. Ex. 3:16, Dt. 16:8. Here the prophet explicitly mentions
that Yahweh has a special cultic day. Remembering Amos 5:18, 20,
one ought ask whether there really is any difference between יום

---

[1] See, among others, H. Gressmann, *Der Ursprung der israelitisch-jüdischen
Eschatologie* (FRLANT 6), 1905, pp. 8 ff., G. Hölscher, *Die Ursprünge der jüdischen
Eschatologie*, 1925. For S. Mowinckel, the day was originally the day of Yahweh's
enthronement, *Psalmenstudien* II, pp. 264 ff., *The Psalms in Israel's Worship* I, p. 116,
n. 35, "Jahves Dag", *NTT* 59/58, pp. 5 ff. See also L. Černy, *The Day of Yahweh
and Some Relevant Problems*, 1948, A. J. Wensinck, "The Semitic New Year and the
Origin of Eschatology", *Acta Orientalia* 1/23, pp. 158 ff., W. A. Heidel, *The Day
of Yahweh*, 1929, p. 356, A. S. Kapelrud, *Joel Studies*, pp. 54 ff., *Central Ideas in
Amos*, 1956, pp. 71 ff., A. Weiser, *ATD* 24, 1949, p. 147, J. Lindblom, "Gibt es
eine Eschatologie bei den alttestamentlichen Propheten", *StTh* 6/52, p. 84, *Prophecy in Ancient Israel*, pp. 317 ff., P. Humbert, *Opuscules d'un hebraïsant* (Memoires
de l'université de Neuchâtel 26), 1958, p. 72, n. 1, R. Largement-H. Lemaitre,
"Le jour de Yahweh dans le contexte oriental", *Sacra Pagina* I, 1959, pp. 260 ff.,
J. Klausner, *The Messianic Idea in Israel*, 1956, pp. 38 f., H. Gese, "The Idea of
History in the Ancient Near East and in the O.T.", *Journal for Theol. and Church*
1/65, p. 64 (or *ZThK* 55/58, p. 144), E. Kutsch, *ThZ* 18/62, pp. 89 f., H. Ringgren,
Israelite Religion, 1966, pp. 199, 265, H. Donner, *Israel unter den Völkern* (SVT XI),
1964, p. 130, E. C. Kingsbury, "The Prophets and the Council of Yahweh",
JBL 83/64, p. 286. J. Jeremias says that the Day of Yahweh is taken for granted
as a well-known phenomenon among the listeners. It is of "vorprophetischen
Ursprunges", *Theophanie*, 1965, pp. 98 f., cf. R. LeDéaut, *La Nuit Pascale* (Analecta Biblica 22) 1963, p. 83. According to J. B. Segal, "Amos may be referring
to the Passover" as the day of Yahweh (referring to Amos: 5:20), *The Hebrew
Passover*, 1963, p. 213, n. 9.

[2] E. Hammershaimb, *Amos*, 1946, p. 85. See also A. Lods, *Les Prophètes d'Israël
et le début du judaïsme*, 1935, p. 78.

[3] "Festtag", B. Landsberger, *Die kultische Kalender der Babylonier und Assyrer*
(Leipziger Semit. Studien VI 1/2) 1915, p. 12, cf. S. Mowinckel, *NTT* 59/58,
pp. 5, 19. E. F. Weidner has shown that the main cult days of the god Aššur
(*ûm il âli^(ki)*) fell on the 6th of Nisan, 22nd of Šebaṭ and 3rd Adar, "Der Tag des
Stadtgottes", *AfO* 14/41-44, pp. 340 f.

[4] *Hosea*, pp. 47 f., cf. E. Sellin, *SKAT* XII:1, p. 37, W. Rudolph, *Hosea*
(SKAT XIII:1), 1966, p. 71, Mowinckel, *op. cit.*, p. 5.

חג־ יהוה and יום יהוה. When the phrases ימי בעלים and יום חג־יהוה have
the character of being cultic days, the most obvious postulation is
that יום יהוה is also a cultic day in its origin. The preceeding discussion
also confirms this. What else could this day possibly be when we are
specially concerned about a deity? This day is the one on which the
deity shows himself as he really is—a "showing" which takes place
in the temple where he lives. This is the day that the deity works in
a special way for his people, according to his covenant. The day
mentioned in Ps. 118:24 as the day Yahweh acts (takes action),
זה היום עשה יהוה,[1] may be this special day.[2]

Perhaps we could surmise that Amos and the other prophets of
Judah have used a common, popular term for the most important
day of the cultic calendar, the day when Yahweh delivered his people
from chaos and disorder, from enemies and disaster, judging the
enemies, and thereafter reestablishing his covenant with his own
chosen people. Yahweh's day, in other words, can be characterized
as his epiphany day,[3] the day on which he comes to show himself
as he is—mighty, powerful, terrifying his enemies, bringing light and
establishing ṣĕdāqāh for his own people. The cultic character of this
day is clearly hinted at in Zeph. 1:7, where the prophet says that the
day of Yahweh is at hand. Yahweh has prepared a sacrifice and made
his guests holy (הקדיש), he has sanctified them. The יום יהוה is here
conceived as a sacrificial day.[4] All those who worship gods other than
Yahweh will be "sacrificed". In portraying the fate of the unfaithful,
the prophet builds upon the cultic character of the day of Yahweh
as a sacrificial day. From what has been said above, Zeph. 1:14 ff.
should not be understood as a contradiction to the description as a day
of sacrifice, for the motifs of war and natural catastrophes, used by

---

[1] This verse does not refer to "the day which the Lord has made" (RSV).
He has made all the days. In this particular verse, עשה must be translated "act",
"work", because the psalm is talking of Yahweh's acts of deliverance. Because of
these acts the people rejoice, v. 24.

[2] Cf. J. Pedersen, *Israel* III-IV, p. 546. It can be mentioned that S. Herrmann
sees the phrase יום יהוה not as an eschatological one but as "eine Umschreibung
des *Machtpotentials Jahwehs*". He does not, however, connect this "Machtpotential"
in any way with the religious manifestations of Yahweh and his acts in the cultus,
which would be the natural place for the revelation of a god and his acts, S. Herrmann, *Die prophetischen Heilserwartungen im Alten Testament* (BWANT fünfte Folge
5), 1965, p. 122.

[3] For Mowinckel, Yahweh's epiphany day is also a day of battle, *NTT* 59/58,
pp. 13 f.

[4] G. Gerleman, *Zephanja, textkritisch und literarkritisch untersucht*, 1942, p. 125.

Zeph. 1:14 ff., belong to the sphere of concepts connected with the theophany of the deity.[1] His coming meant "war" against enemies, chaos, Leviathan, etc., and therefore this day occurs in another context as a day of his wrath, יום אף־יהוה, Lam. 2:22, cf. Ps. 110:5, Zeph. 2:2 f., Isa. 1:5, 13:13.[2] Thus one ought to be very cautious in declaring that Yahweh's holy war cannot be a cultic phenomenon. On the contrary, it would perhaps be more accurate to affirm that almost every act ascribed to Yahweh has at one time had its place in the cult, in liturgy, oracle, hymn, etc., at the sanctuary where he lived.[3] Only at that place could one really learn to know the god and his acts.[4] This concept comes to the fore in the temple; it is its *raison d'être*. It is the place where the god lives. In other words, the temple is the religious reality that is heaven on earth for the people.

From the "antiphonal liturgy" of Psalm 24, F. M. Cross, Jr. has maintained that there is to be found the "reenactment of the victory of Yahweh in the primordial battle and his enthronement in the divine council, or, better, in his newly built (cosmic) temple",[5] which, of course, is the same as the earthly temple. According to Cross, the ritual procession of the Ark had a "long prehistory in the cult and ritual warfare of old Israel".[6] The use of the ark is a "reenactment

---

[1] M. Weiss has rightly connected the origin of the day of Yahweh with the theophany-phenomenon, but he argues that this is not a cultic event. Furthermore, Weiss argues for the holy-war-motif as not originally being a part of the theophany because it does not occur in Amos 5:18, "The Origin of the 'Day of the Lord' Reconsidered", *HUCA* 37/66, pp. 34 ff., 40. In this way, Weiss opposes von Rad's view of the day as being basicly at home in the concept of holy war. At the same time, Weiss makes the mistake of not seeing the theophany as an integral part of the cultus.

[2] Cf. H. Ringgren, "Einige Schilderungen des göttlichen Zorns", *Tradition und Situation* (Festschrift A. Weiser, ed. E. Würthwein), 1963, pp. 107 ff.

[3] Frank M. Cross, Jr., traces it back to the premonarchic cult, "The Divine Warrior", *Biblical Motifs* (ed. A. Altmann), 1966, pp. 11 ff.

[4] This does not exclude the possibility of seeing Yahweh as acting in history. For the ancient Israelites, there was no real difference in the character of Yahweh's cultic acts and his acts in history. Further, Yahweh's cultic acts could be historified; likewise, history could be a matter of cultic remembrance, or, better, history became a part of the cult and as such, it always retained its aspect of contemporaneity, cf. J. Muilenburg, "A Liturgy on the Triumphs of Yahweh", *Studia Biblica et Semitica*, 1966, pp. 235 f.

[5] Behind this Cross sees the Ugaritic myth of Baʿl going to battle and then becoming king. He also compares it with Marduk's battle with Tiāmat and his receiving a temple and celebrating his kingship, *op. cit.*, p. 21, cf. J. P. Ross, "Jahweh Ṣᵉbāʾôt in Samuel and Psalms", *VT* 17/67, p. 88. See also A. R. Johnson, who says that in Ps. 21, Yahweh as king is not only creator but also judge and warrior, *Sacral Kingship*², p. 74.

[6] Cross, *op. cit.*, p. 24.

of the 'history of redemption', of the Exodus-Conquest theme, preparatory to the covenant festival of the spring New Year".[1] Thus, the ideas of war and battle are to be found as a part of the cultic day of Yahweh.[2] These ideas go far back in time, to the early cult of the Israelite people.

The origin of these ideas involved in the day of Yahweh is difficult to demonstrate. Cross maintains that "the normal locus of holy warfare is discovered in the Exodus-Conquest, not in the primordial battle of creation".[3] However, these categories are not so neatly to be divided. The Exodus, to some degree, is built around the old mythological concept of the battle against the sea, here represented by the Sea of Reeds, cf., Ps. 74.[4] Further, as Cross himself points out, the concept of Yahweh as king is not a late phenomenon. It appears in some of "the earliest Israelite poems": Nu. 23:21, Ex. 15:18, Dt. 33:5, Ps. 68:25.[5] Also, the Canaanite El was worshipped as king. "The elements making up Israel derived from Canaanite and Amorite stock". The language was a Canaanite dialect which had preserved not only Canaanite traditions, but traditions from northern Mesopotamia as well, dating from the second millenium B.C.[6] It should be noted that, according to Cross, in "non-Israelite contexts, the mythopoetic motifs of the creator-king and cosmic warrior" were present.[7] Therefore, could not one ask whether the concept of the deity as a warrior-king could have had its original locus in the primordial battle, even if the emphasis in early Israel had somewhat shifted to the conquest theme?[8] In the royal cult of Jerusalem, the conquest theme may have become weakened from the time of

---

[1] P. 27. Cross sees the later prophetic eschatology as being born of the "wedding of the kingship and Conquest themes in the cultus", p. 30.

[2] Cf. Marduk's war in the *akītu*-festival, W. G. Lambert, *Iraq* 25/63, pp. 189 f.

[3] *Biblical Motifs*, p. 25.

[4] Cf. H. Ringgren, *Israelite Religion*, pp. 81 f.

[5] Niek Poulssen repeats the arguments of these texts as being late and therefore the concept of Yahweh as king on Zion is also late, *König und Tempel im Glaubenszeugnis des Alten Testaments*, 1967, pp. 139 f.

[6] Cross, *op. cit.*, p. 24, n. 43. For the symbiosis El-Yahweh, see Ahlström, *Aspects of Syncretism in Israelite Religion*, pp. 12 f., "Some Remarks on Prophets and Cult", *Transitions in Biblical Scholarship*, pp. 128 f.

[7] Cross, *op. cit.*, p. 28.

[8] For the "exaltation of Yahweh" in connection with the Exodus, see W. W, Hallo—J. J. A. van Dijk, *The Exaltation of Inanna* (Yale Near Eastern Researches 3). 1968, pp. 67 f.

Solomon, and the heritage of Canaan may have played a greater role again.[1]

The cultic day of Yahweh is a day of his coming, his theophany, his war against his enemies, and his reestablishment of the covenant, complete with its accompanying ṣĕdāqāh, for his people. That the idea of epiphany has been a basic part through the years may be concluded from Mal. 3:1 f.[2] Here it is said that Yahweh will suddenly come to his temple, and when he comes, "who can stand when he appears", מי העמד בהראותו (v. 2)?

Mowinckel [3] and Cross,[4] among others, have underlined both the royal motifs as well as the cosmic motifs connected with this day. Among the former was mentioned above the shout of joy, תרועה, (cf. Pss. 47:6, 89:16, Num. 23:21, Isa. 52:7 f.), upon the occasion of Yahweh's having become king, and the שופר, cf. 2 Sam. 6:15.[5] As one of the characteristic features of the day as an epiphany day, Mowinckel has mentioned the שוב שבות.[6] He could as well have included the renewal of the covenant in this connection, for Yahweh also comes on this day to reestablish his covenant and, in so doing, to turn destiny in the right direction. His coming meant judgment and darkness [7] for his enemies, but light and vindication for his own

---

[1] On syncretism in Jerusalem, see, among others, H. S. Nyberg, "Studien zum Religionskampf im Alten Testament", *ARW* 35/38, pp. 372 ff., G. Widengren, *The Accadian and Hebrew Psalms of Lamentation as Religious Documents*, 1937, pp. 70 f., A. R. Johnson, *Sacral Kingship*[2], pp. 74 f., H. Schmid, "Jahwe und die Kulttraditionen von Jerusalem", *ZAW* 67/55, p. 197, Ahlström, *VT* 11/61, pp. 113 ff., and *Aspects of Syncretism*, pp. 34 ff., G. Henton Davies, "The Ark in the Psalms", *Promise and Fulfilment*, 1963, p. 57, n. 32, H. H. Rowley, *Worship in Ancient Israel*, pp. 72 ff. Cf. also J. A. Soggin, "Der offiziell geförderte Synkretismus in Israel während des 10. Jahrhunderts", *ZAW* 78/66, pp. 182 ff. On p. 186, Prof. Soggin complains that my book *Aspects*, p. 42, has not answered how the "veranlasstein Neugestaltung des Kultes" by David should be understood in relation to the narratives in 2 Sam. 6-7 and 1 Chr. 21 ff. The answer to this is given tentatively in *VT* 11/61, pp. 113 ff., to which I had referred already.

[2] See Mowinckel, *NTT* 59/58, p. 8.

[3] *Op. cit.*, pp. 8 f.

[4] *Biblical Motifs*, pp. 18 ff., 38 ff.

[5] Cf. R. A. Carlson, *David, the Chosen King*, p. 89.

[6] *Op. cit.*, p. 6, cf. *The Psalms in Israel's Worship* I, pp. 146 f.

[7] It ought to be mentioned that the motif of the god judging mankind at the New Year's Day can be traced back to Sumerian times, S. N. Kramer, *The Sumerians*, pp. 124 f., cf. E. Lipiński, *La royauté de Yahvé*, p. 211. It is quite natural that the judging and the battle against chaos-enemies go together in Israelite religion. Thus, Yahweh as a war hero is a mythic idea with its natural and original "Sitz im Leben" in the cultus.

people.[1] Further, it meant at the same time that צדקה and שלום were guaranteed according to the covenant when it was reestablished.[2] This is exactly the main concern in the book of Joel.

Mention was made above about the Day of Yahweh as a day of his war against his enemies. Because of the opinions of G. von Rad, it is necessary to dwell upon this phenomenon somewhat. In his study of holy war in Israel,[3] von Rad has not dealt with one of the most basic ideas of the war—namely, that Yahweh is the leader, the chief or king of the heavenly assembly [4] which is the same as his army. This omission on the part of von Rad is the more astonishing in the face of such Old Testament phrases as בני אלים,[5] קהל קדשים, or סוד קדשים. These phrases refer to the attendant deities which constitute Yahweh's army, צבא, which meaning also lies as the root idea in the term צבאות of Ps. 89:9. It is to these that Joel 4:11 refers when the text asks Yahweh to let his *gibbōrīm* go down,[6] cf. Ps. 103:20, Isa. 13:3. In the Joel passage, beginning with 4:9, the holy war motif occurs. First there is the phrase, קדשו מלחמה, "make holy the war", 4:9. Then in v. 10 the people are urged to make their tools of peace into swords and spears, and the weak one is to say that he is a *gibbōr*, a hero. In v. 11, Yahweh is asked to let his *gibbōrīm*, who are irresistable, go down,[7] and after the victory, Yahweh will sit in judgment in the valley of Jehoshaphat, cf. Ps. 9:6-9. Verses 12 f. indicate that the "harvest" is ripe. All these expressions about Yahweh indicate that he is pictured as a king, a war lord, cf. Ps. 24:8. He and his heroes, the heavenly hosts, are fighting the war, and after the battle, Yahweh judges the nations, the enemies, as a king, v. 12.[8]

---

[1] For the light characteristics of Yahweh's nature, see my book, *Psalm 89*, pp. 85 ff.

[2] According to A. Weiser, the theophany is "the heart of the Covenant Festival", *The Psalms, A Commentary*, Philadelphia 1962, p. 38.

[3] *Der heilige Krieg im alten Israel*, 1951.

[4] Rightly observed by P. D. Miller, Jr., *Holy War and Cosmic War in Early Israel* (Unpubl. diss. Cambridge, Mass., 1963), p. 17. Cf. F. M. Cross, Jr., "The Divine Warrior in Israel's Early Cult", *Biblical Motifs* (ed. A. Altmann), 1966, p. 17.

[5] W. Hermann, "Die Göttersöhne", *Zeitschrift für Religions- und Geistesgeschichte* 12/60, pp. 242 ff.

[6] For הנחת, see above, pp. 1 f.

[7] Concerning גבור, see, among others, Cross, *op. cit.*, pp. 11 ff., Ahlström, *Psalm* 89, pp. 77, 101.

[8] H. W. Wolff has emphasized that Yahweh in 4:12 can no longer be found as a warrior, but as a judge on his throne, judging the peoples of the world, *Joel*, p. 97. This is quite right. One should, however, remember that the basis for Yahweh as both warrior and judge is that he is the king. As such he is a warrior in 4:11 and a judge in 4:12.

The fact that von Rad does not discuss this reveals his unwillingness to come to terms with Yahweh's ritual and mythological battle against the powers of chaos, against his enemies. However, this aspect cannot be neglected; its occurrance is to be found in too many texts to be ignored,[1] cf. Pss. 74:13 f., 77:17 ff., 68:22, 31, 89:10, 97:3, Ex. 15:8, Hab. 3:8 f., 15, Isa. 51:9 f. It has been advocated by von Rad and others that Yahweh does not fight or engage in battle with such mythological figures as Tiamat, Yamm or Mot, but that his battles are historical ones in which the enemies are Israel's political enemies, the foreign nations.[2] This is correct only to a certain degree, because, as one can see from the passages just mentioned, Yahweh has been thought of from antiquity as fighting the sea, Yamm, or Leviathan (in Uga., Lotan), Rahab or Tannin, cf. further Job 3:8, 9:13, 26:12, 40:25 (7:12), Pss. 74:14, 89:11, Isa. 27:1.[3] It may be argued that the mythological side of the question has been subordinated to the historical events and purposes of the life of Israel, which is the picture one can easily get in reading the historical books of the Old Testament. But even in these it is possible to see the important role mythology played in Israelite historiography. "The quite natural and free way in which to the Israelite mind the ideas and notions pass from a sphere that we call 'historical' to what we think a 'mythical' sphere and vice versa should warn us not to draw any fixed line of demarcation between" what is characterized as history and myth in Israelite thinking.[4] Myth was the category

---

[1] The ritual aspects of Israel's wars cannot be completely differentiated from the theological aspects—to which the cosmological belongs. P. D. Miller (*op. cit.*, p. 250) has not observed that in the world of religion, the rituals are expressions for theological-mythical concepts, cosmological as well as soteriological.

[2] G. von Rad, *Der heilige Krieg*, pp. 32 f. Claus Westermann follows the same line of reasoning, *The Praise of God in the Psalms*, 1965, p. 93, Cf. also P.-E. Langevin, "Sur l'origine du 'Jour de Yahwé'", *Sciences Ecclésiastiques* 18/66, pp. 359 ff.

[3] For lit. see my book, *Psalm* 89, pp. 69 ff. See further R. de Vaux, "Les combats singuliers dans l'AT", *Analecta Biblica* 10/59, pp. 372 f., O. Kaiser, *Die mythische Bedeutung des Meeres in Ägypten, Ugarit und Israel* (BZAW 78/59), pp. 141 ff., G. Fohrer, *Studien zum alttestamentlichen Prophetie* (BZAW 99/67), p. 52, M. Dahood, *Psalms* II, pp. 205 f.

[4] G. Widengren, "Myth and History in Israelite-Jewish Thought", *Culture in History* (Essays in Honor of Paul Radin), 1960, p. 483, cf. also F. M. Cross, Jr., *Biblical Motifs*, pp. 27 ff., H. G. May, "Cosmological Reference in the Qumran Doctrine of the Two Spirits and in Old Testament Imagery", *JBL* 82/63, pp. 7 f., S. B. Frost, "Apocalyptic and History", *The Bible in Modern Scholarship* (ed. J. Ph. Hyatt), 1965, p. 101. For the composition of the epic cycle of the David traditions as resembling the Keret epic, see C. H. Gordon, *Introduction to the Old Testament Times*, pp. 294 ff., R. A. Carlson, *David, the Chosen King*, pp. 190 ff.

through which the Israelites expressed historical origins and events, as well as divine actions.[1]

In this discussion, the concern has not been with the political, historical holy war, with all its ritual preparations, the deity, the ark, marching with the army, etc. Instead, the main concern has been with aspects of holy war as they are found in the cultic-mythic sphere. It is from the cultic-mythic sphere that the prophets have gotten their language, their concepts, even their inspiration. They have, as in the case of Joel, built upon these old, well-known motifs from the theological-mythological sphere, and they have adapted them for their own purposes. However, the terminology of holy war— whether cultic or political—is very much the same, which is to be expected, since both represent a war between gods.[2] In the political war the deities are marching with their armies [3] as well as the deity in the cultic war. Both are thought of as conquering other deities.[4] The phrase יהוה צבאות thus refers to both categories of holy war, either earthly or heavenly armies. For the cultic war, the cult congregation may also be included, because in the temple, Yahweh's hosts includes his people.[5]

The next problem to be considered is the ideological—or, should one say, theological—meaning behind the use of such phrases as are found in Joel. The basic concept is the Israelite temple symbolism.

---

[1] From an Israelite point of view, H.-J. Kraus' statement that "myth destroys history", *Worship in Israel*, p. 21, is a misunderstanding. On the contrary, the use of mythological motifs and patterns is a help in narrating the history. "Der Orientale erlebt in Symbolen", C. A. Keller, "Über einige alttestamentliche Heilig-tumslegenden", *ZAW* 68/56, p. 92. Perhaps one should rather say that history sometimes destroys myth.

[2] Cf. H. S. Nyberg, *Studien zum Hoseabuche*, p. 47, A. Goetze, "Warfare in Asia Minor", *Iraq* 25/63, pp. 128 f. For the political holy war, see, among others, Fr. Schwally, *Semitische Kriegsaltertümer* I. *Der Heilige Krieg im alten Israel*, 1901, G. von Rad, *Der Heilige Krieg im alten Israel*, 1951, N. Lohfink, "Darstellungskunst und Theologie in Dtn 1, 6-3, 29", *Biblica* 41/60, pp. 110 ff., E. Nielsen, "La Guerre considérée comme une religion et la Religion comme une guerre", *StTh* 15/61, pp. 93 ff., P. D. Miller, *Holy War and Cosmic War in Early Israel*, 1963, J. H. Grønbaek, "Juda und Amalek", *StTh* 18/64, pp. 26 ff., H. P. Müller, "Die kultische Darstellung der Theophanie", *VT* 14/64, pp. 183 ff. It could be mentioned that J. R. Porter has criticized von Rad's opinion about the holy war as having died out in the time of the monarchy, *Moses and Monarchy*, 1963, p. 25, n. 91.

[3] Cf. *ARM* II, 50:12 f. Cf. A. E. Glock, *Warfare in Mari and Early Israel*, (Unpublished diss. Univ. of Michigan) 1968, pp. 24, 30.

[4] For holy war in the Mari texts, cf. E. Nielsen, *StTh* 15/61, pp. 103 ff., P. D. Miller, *Holy War and Cosmic War*, pp. 27 ff.

[5] Cf. Ex. 7:4, 12:41, I Sam. 17:26.

The temple was considered to mirror everything that happened in the heavens; it was a replica of the heavenly abode of the deity. The phenomenon can be expressed in the idea that the temple "was" the deity mountain. When a deity acts for his people, either culticly or in a prophet's vision, it is always according to the pattern of life that was believed to exist in heaven, yea, in the temple, cf. Ps. 11:4, Isa. 6:1 ff., Hab. 2:20. "Heaven and earth reflect or image each other", says S. A. Cook.[1] This is particularly true of the relationship between heaven and temple.[2] This concept is one of the foundations for the prophetic utterances about the future ideal time. What has often been called eschatology is really but prophetic use of the old cosmogony as it was expressed in liturgy. Therefore it is difficult to decide whether a text can be characterized as eschatological or not. Especially is this true of prophetic texts, which, in this case, should rather be characterized as futuristic. The occurrance of the term יום יהוה in the book of Joel can thus a priori not be labeled eschatological.

From the description of Joel 4:14 ff., one can see that judgment occurs in connection with the day of Yahweh, יום יהוה, the day when Yahweh's epiphany is experienced, vv. 15 ff. Sun and moon become dark, and the stars "gather in" their brightness, their brilliance, their radiance, נגה, v. 14, cf. 2:10, 3:4, and Am. 5:20.[3] This is the prelude

---

[1] "Notes on the Relevance of the Science of Religion", Festschrift A. Bertholet, 1950, p. 122.

[2] G. B. Gray, Sacrifice in the Old Testament, 1925, pp. 148 ff., W. Brede Kristensen, The Meaning of Religion, 1960, pp. 369 ff., Ahlström, Psalm 89, pp. 60, 74, Ph. Reymond, L'eau, sa vie, et sa signification dans l'Ancien Testament (SVT VI), 1958, pp. 235 ff.,H.-J. Kraus, Psalmen (BK XV:1), p. 351.

[3] F. R. Stephenson understands Joel 3:4 (Eng. 2:31) as referring to a "total lunar and solar" eclipse, and therefore he dates the book around 350 B.C., because Joel and the people must have remembered the eclipse of 357 B.C., "The Date of the Book of Joel", VT 19/69, pp. 224 ff. One has to be grateful to a geophysicist for helping to fix the dates of such phenomena. However, all the other kinds of evidence can not be disregarded. When it is known that the kind of language used in Joel in connection with Yahweh's coming is epiphany and theophany phraseology, then one cannot at all be certain that the prophet in 3:4 would have left this kind of language and suddenly have spoken of a particular eclipse. When one remembers that the day of Yahweh is a day of his coming in judgment upon the nations, that it is the day of his epiphany, then it necessarily has cosmic proportions. It is the lord of the cosmos who comes and acts on this day. Thus, Joel has used mythological motifs here, cf. J. Lindblom, Prophecy in Ancient Israel, p. 421. According to J. S. Holladay, Joel 3:3-4 shows the "most 'orthodox' use of solar and lunar omina", "The Day(s) the Moon Stood Still", JBL 87/68, p. 173.

The prayer of Joshua (Josh 10:12) might also be brought into the discussion. The prayer is addressed to the sun and the moon, indicating that they are to be understood as deities, cf. F. M. Th. Böhl, "Het Ontstaan en de Geschiedkundige

of events which announce the coming of the greatest brightness, namely, the shining forth of Yahweh on his day, cf. Judges 5:4, Pss. 18:8, 68:9, 77:14, Isa. 13:10, 13, Jer. 4:28, Ezek. 32:7, Nah. 1:5. Yahweh roars from Zion, ויהוה מציון ישאג,[1] and from Jerusalem he gives his voice,[2] יתן קולו, cf. Am. 1:2. The effect of this is that heaven and earth tremble, v. 16. The people knows these phonomena and has experienced them several times in the "reality" of liturgy.[3] Such is the coming of Yahweh on his own day, when he conquers and judges his enemies. When one encounters an explanation in 4:17 to verse 16, namely, וידעתם כי אני יהוה אלהיכם, "and you shall know that I, Yahweh, am your god", then this can be seen as an indication that Joel has used a liturgical phrase which also occurs in Am. 1:2.[4] Further, Joel has added the same kind of liturgical explanation as in 2:27. Thus, it is natural to ask whether Joel's book could be called a liturgy,[5] but more about this later on.

Waarde van Oud-Testamentische Verhalen", *Nieuwe Theologische Studiën* 13/30, pp. 54 f. Therefore, the prayer of Joshua can be seen as originally referring to a cultic situation which the tradent has used in a historical context. For the ideas in Josh. 10:12 f., one can compare a hymn to Adad, see H. Zimmern, *Babylonische Hymnen und Gebete in Auswahl* I, 1905, p. 12. E. Nielsen sees Josh. 10:12 f. as a "fragment of an ancient song", *Shechem*, p. 303. Cf. J. Jeremias: a "Siegeslied", *Theophanie*, p. 145, n. 4. J. S. Holladay dogmatically states that the "leader of the Host of Israel" could not have been praying to "Shemesh and Yārīah," *JBL* 87/68, p. 167. This will be hard to prove.

[1] The stem שאג does not occur in the very late texts. It is used in connection with the deity in Am. 1:2 and Jer. 25:30 in addition to its use in Joel 4:16. In Ps. 74:4 the צררים are roaring in Elohim's assembly, מועד. In Job 37:4, it expresses the thunder of El's voice. שאג is used in connection with a lion, Jer. 2:15, 51:38, and Zech. 11:3. The noun, שאגה is found in Ezek. 19:7 in connection with the king of Judah ("lion among lions" in v. 6), and in Ps. 22:2, the crying of the suffering servant is termed שאגה.

[2] Cf. Ps. 18:14, Ps. 68:34, Isa. 30:30, Job 37:4 f., see also Ps. 104:7.

[3] The idea of the voice of deity as thunder which both creates and judges is not uncommon in the Near East, cf. J. A. Knudtzon, *Die El-Amarna-Tafeln* (VAB II), 1915, p. 608, cf. Akkad. *iddin rigmašu* and Ugar. *ytn ql*. See among others, M. Held, "The *yqtl-qtl* (*qtl-yqtl*) Sequence of Identical Verbs in Biblical Hebrew and in Ugaritic", *Studies and Essays in Honor of A. A. Neumann*, 1962, p. 287, n. 4, E. Lipiński, *La royauté de Yahwé*, pp. 140 f., Jörg Jeremias, *Theophanie*, pp. 13, 76, cf. W. G. Lambert, *Babylonian Wisdom Literature*, 1960, p. 192, 1. 18, and p. 334. For the OT, see also Ex. 19:16, 20:18, Ps. 46:7.

[4] Joel 4:16, according to J. Lindblom, is "not a quotation from Amos, but taken from the same liturgy", *Prophecy in Ancient Israel*, p. 116.

[5] According to I. Engnell, Joel's book was originally a liturgy, but it is possible that in its present form, it is worked over and revised, "Joels Bok", *SBU* I², col. 1185. In the view of N. K. Gottwald, Joel 4:16 ff. is a part of "an ancient prophetic scroll which was apparently also employed" by Joel, *All the Kingdoms of the Earth*, 1964, p. 104.

Because of the situation with which Joel deals,[1] he has emphasized again in chapter 4 that Yahweh, and nobody else, is the god of the people. Note, therefore, the parallelism between chapters 2 and 4. In Ch. 2 the oracle ends with the affirmation that the people will know that *Yahweh* is their god, 2:27, and in Ch. 4, the theophany ends with the same phrase, v. 17. Thus both verses, with their emphasis on Yahweh as *the god* of the people (and none else), are to be seen as the climax of these passages.[2] Joel has seen the main reason for the disaster of the people as the abandoning of Yahweh. Instead of worshipping Yahweh in his temple, other gods have been worshipped. Thus, Jörg Jeremias' statement that Yahweh had no competitors [3] is not accurate.

It has been maintained previously that the idea of Yahweh as giving (forth) his voice, or roaring, from Zion may be older than both Amos [4] and Joel.[5] It is possible that both of them could have used an old liturgical and cult-prophetic phrase. The history of this kind of phrase cannot be written simply because our knowledge of the history of cult is inexact, both the Jerusalemite cult and that of any other Canaanite-Israelite cult place. The occurrence of the root, שאג, in mostly late pre-exilic and exilic texts leads one to conclude, however, that Joel is not too far removed from these times, but that he has used an old cultic terminology that has not been quoted by any of the prophets before Amos. H. W. Wolff has argued that Joel has taken over this motif word for word from Amos, but his argument

---

[1] It is this kind of situation that Dt. 11:13 ff. cautions against.

[2] A. S. Kapelrud has maintained that 4:9-17 is the climax of the whole book, *Joel Studies*, p. 8.—It must be said that the name "Joel" is very appropriate for the message of this book, a message which so often emphasizes that Yahweh is *the* god; Joel, i.e., Jo is god or Jo is El. Thus, this name is to be compared with the form of such other names as Yahweh-El, cf. Ahlström, "Some Remarks on Prophets and Cult", *Transitions in Biblical Scholarship* (Essays in Divinity VI), 1968, pp. 128 f. For the Amorite *Jahwi-il, Jawi-ilâ*, see M. A. Finet, "Iawi-ilâ, roi de Talhayûm", *Syria* 41/64, pp. 177 ff., W. F. Albright, *Yahweh and the Gods of Canaan*, 1968, p. 149, and H. B. Huffmon, *Amorite Personal Names in the Mari Texts*, 1965, p. 72.

[3] *Theophanie*, p. 79.

[4] Cf. N. K. Gottwald, *All the Kingdoms of the Earth.*, p. 104.

[5] J. Lindblom calls the phrase in Am. 1:2 "a fragment of a cultic hymn", *Prophecy in Ancient Israel*, 1962, p. 116, cf. Aa. Bentzen, "The Ritual Background of Amos I:2-II:16", *OTS* 8/50, p. 95, A. S. Kapelrud, *Central Ideas in Amos*, 1956, pp. 17 f., J. Steinmann, *Études sur les prophètes d'Israël*, 1954, p. 168, G. Farr, "The Language of Amos, Popular or Cultic?", *VT* 16/66, pp. 312 ff., cf. Ahlström, "Some Remarks on Prophets and Cult", *Essays in Divinity* VI, p. 118, Jörg Jeremias, *Theophanie*. p. 13. See also Ps. 50:2.

depends upon a misinterpretation of the change of locality that occurs in the text—namely, from the valley of Jehoshaphat to the holy mountain of Jerusalem, Zion.[1] These two places should not necessarily be exclusive of each other in the same context, for there may lie some liturgical tradition behind this text in which Yahweh was at one moment in the valley (conquering the chaos-waters, the Reed Sea?) and in the next moment back at Zion again, cf. Ps. 24:6-10.[2] As is known, Joel is rooted in the Jerusalemite cultic tradition, and in this tradition the associations of valley and temple mountain occur.[3] Therefore, it is possible that liturgical events from this tradition are mirrored in the book of Joel.[4]

On the basis of the above, the ideas of Sellin may be dismissed. He believes that the judgment in the valley is the reflection of an older eschatological tradition in which all judgment took place in a valley.[5] It is much older than this. Perhaps it is as old as the tradition of Yahweh as a warrior—at least as far as Israel is concerned. It is quite true that the prophets refer to a valley in connection with judgment, but the prophets, Joel included, have not invented the idea. Far back in the antiquity of Canaan, the mythological concept of a deity slaughtering his enemies in a valley occurs. For example, in the Ugaritic text, 'nt:II:5 ff., there is described the fighting of the goddess 'Anat. In a valley, $b\,'mq$, between the two cities,[6] she slaugh-

---

[1] *Joel*, p. 98, Jörg Jeremias, *op. cit.*, p. 99.

[2] פניך יעקב in Ps. 24:6 can be read, with M. Dahood, "the Presence of Jacob", which is "a divine appellative", *Psalms* I, p. 152. One could perhaps see the phrase as an old reminiscence of the deity name, Jacob-El. Cross considers the "received reading impossible", and puts אביר before יעקב, *Biblical Motifs*, p. 20. However, this is impossible, because no MS has that reading.

[3] Cf. my book, *Psalm* 89, pp. 144 f. For the valley in general as a cult place, see Leo Krinetzki, "'Tal' und 'Ebene' im Alten Testament", *BZ* 5/61, pp. 212 ff.

[4] It is, of course, impossible to determine whether the name "Valley of Jehoshaphat" has been chosen not only because of its meaning—"Yahweh judges"—but also because of the events described in 2 Chr. 20:16. Among those advocating a connection with king Jehoshaphat's victory over Moab and Ammon in the valley of Berakah is K. Jensen, "Indledningsspørgsmaal i Joels Bog", *DTT* 4/41, pp. 98 ff. Jensen combines this valley with Lysia's defeat in 163 B.C., to which Joel, according to Jensen, is referring. The position taken in this investigation is that the name is a symbolic one.

[5] *SKAT* XII:1, p. 173. Sellin refers to Jer. 7:32, Ezek, 39:11, Isa. 22:1, 5, Zech. 14:4, and Apoc. 16:16. On Ezek. 39:11, see W. Zimmerli, *Ezechiel* (BK XIII), p. 966, and for Zech. 14:4, see B. Otzen, *Studien über Deuterosacharja*, pp. 199 ff.

[6] C. H. Gordon, *Ugaritic Textbook*, Glossary No. 1873, 1874. The phrase $b\,'mq$ could also be rendered "with strength", but the phrase following, $bn\ qrytm$, "between the two cities", makes the translation given above more probable.

ters people.[1] It is possible that in the cultic life of Canaan and Israel, there was a symbolic annihilation of enemies in the valley at a certain point in the liturgy, just as mentioned above.[2] Joel has exploited this tradition, 4:2, 12 (cf. v. 14), but he has put the emphasis on judgment—therefore the name "valley of Jehoshaphat". Thus Joel is in tune with an old cultic tradition in which the valley has long meant something special to the people of Yahweh. It is in this valley that destiny, שוב שבות, is restored, along with the harmonious order, צדקה, both in connection with the judgment of the nations, the enemies, 4:1 ff.[3]

---

[1] Cf. also I. Engnell, *Studies in Divine Kingship*, p. 111. J. Aistleitner, *Die mythologischen und kultischen Texte aus Ras Schamra*, 1964, p. 25, A. S. Kapelrud, *The Violent Goddess*, 1969, pp. 49 f.

[2] Cf Ps. 23:4, Mic. 1:6.

[3] A. S. Kapelrud maintains that it "is doubtful whether in our passage there is any dependance or direct antithesis to the places in Jeremiah", *Joel Studies*, p. 145. That Joel does not depend on Jeremiah in this matter can now be seen. On the contrary, there is a difference. Jeremiah may be said to be dependant upon the same tradition as Joel, but the difference is that Jeremiah has inverted it. Joel is faithful to the tradition, which may be explained as being natural for a cult prophet. One ought remember here that the Mount of Olives was a cult place, a holy mountain, which had been connected with some of the rites of Jerusalemite religion. These were abandoned during the reform of Josiah. At the same time the cult place, Tophet, was desecrated, 2 Kings 23:10, 31. For the Mount of Olives as a cult place, see J. B. Curtis, "An Investigation of the Mount of Olives in the Judeo-Christian Tradition", *HUCA* 28/57, pp. 137 ff., 169 f., B. Otzen, *Deuterosacharja*, pp. 202 ff. W. A. Heidel has connected the story of David's leaving of Jerusalem during Absalom's rebellion and going up the Mount of Olives (2 Sam. 15) with maṣṣot-passover rites, *The Day of Yahweh*, 1929, pp. 310 f., cf. J. Morgenstern, "The Cultic Setting of the 'Enthronement Psalms', " *HUCA* 35/64, pp. 15 ff., *Id.* "The King-God among the Western Semites and the Meaning of Epiphanes", *VT* 10/60, pp. 180 ff. J. Wilcoxen, building upon Curtis, has maintained that in connection with the reform of the *pesaḥ*, king Josiah's order to the Levites to put the ark in the Temple, 2 Chr. 35:3, must be understood to mean that the ark should no longer be carried outside the temple, and that all the rites outside the temple were abandoned, *The Israelite Passover in Context and Function in the Later Old Testament Period* (Unpublished Diss., Univ. of Chicago) 1967, p. 295. That Josiah's reform was not a lasting one can be seen from, for example, such passages as Jer. 11:9-13, 32:30 ff., Ezek. 8:1 ff. Cf. J. Pedersen, *Israel* III-IV, p. 252, J. Lindblom, *Prophecy in Ancient Israel*, p. 357, H. W. Robinson, *Two Hebrew Prophets*, 1948, p. 67, A. Alt, *Kleine Schriften* II, p. 300, V. Maag, "Erwägungen zur deuteronomischen Kultzentralisation", *VT* 6/56, p. 18, J. Bright, *A History of Israel*, 1960, p. 311, cf. S. B. Frost, "The Death of Josiah? A Conspiracy of Silence", *JBL* 87/68, pp. 369 ff., 376 f., E. W. Nicholson, *Deuteronomy and Tradition*, 1967, p. 87, W. Zimmerli, *Ezechiel*, p. 151, H. Ringgren, *Israelite Religion*, p. 166. Also the phrase, "he did what was evil in the eyes of Yahweh", which is used in reference to kings who were judged as apostates from Yahweh and his religion, supports this thesis because it is used in connection with Jehoahaz, Jehoiakim, and Zedekiah, 2 Kings 23:32, 37, 24:19, 2 Chr. 36:5,

As mentioned above, the name, "valley of Jehoshaphat", is probably symbolic of judgment, and is used by Joel to emphasize the seriousness of Yahweh's acts of judgment. As a background for understanding this valley motif, the preceeding paragraph has given a tradition belonging to the old Jerusalemite cult—a tradition which must have had some kind of relevance also in the time of Joel. The next question to arise is, can this valley mentioned in Joel be identified with some valley in Jerusalem's vicinity? When dealing with symbolic place names for which no information is given in the textual material, only possibilities can be mentioned. One such possibility may be the brook of Kidron, which is located between Jerusalem and the Mount of Olives.[1] Some Passover rites seem to have established a relationship between the temple mountain and the Mount of Olives.[2] 2 Sam. 15:32 may indicate that a cult place existed on this mountain from before the time of David.[3] In later Hebrew tradition, this holy mountain was named הר־המשחית, "Mountain of the Destroyer", 2 Kings 23:13. The figure of the "Destroyer" is so closely associated with the Passover that one may certainly see a connection of the mount with some rites in the *pesaḥ* festival.[4]

Because of its location, the valley between the temple mountain and the Mount of Olives may have been playing a significant role in the religious traditions and rituals of the Jerusalemite cult. Two well-

---

12. Y. Kaufmann maintains that 2 Kings does not mention the fact that the cult reverted back into its old ways again after the death of Josiah, *The Religion of Israel*, pp. 405 f. However, the above mentioned phrase about the three kings who followed the reign of Josiah speaks against Kaufmann's position and the information given in 2 Chr. 36:14 shows that the position of this author must be the fact. 2 Chr. 36:14 can be seen as evidence that the pre-Josianic cultus was reestablished.

[1] Cf. A. von Gall, "Über die Herkunft der Bezeichnung Jahwe als König", *Studien zur Semitischen Philologie und Religionsgeschichte Julius Wellhausen zum siebzigsten Geburtstag am 17. Mai* 1914 *gewidmet* (BZAW 27) 1914, pp. 158 f., J. Morgenstern, *HUCA* 35/64, p. 21.

[2] W. A. Heidel, *The Day of Yahweh*, pp. 310 f., J. Wilcoxen, *The Israelite Passover*, pp. 290 ff.

[3] Cf. 1 Kings 11:7. The entire area, according to M. R. Lehmann, was dedicated to Mot as a sanctuary, "A New Interpretation of the term שדמות," *VT* 3/53, p. 365, n. 5. J. B. Curtis believes that the Mount of Olives was at one time the "akitu shrine of Šalim", *HUCA* 28/57, p. 168.

[4] J. Wilcoxen, *op. cit.*, p. 295. Morgenstern argues that the deity of the Mount of Olives was the dying and resurrecting Tammuz, and in the later Israelite times, it was Tammuz-Yahweh, *HUCA* 35/64, pp. 25 ff. The latter statement, however, is contrary to textual evidence. Yahweh of Jerusalem was not considered a dying and resurrecting god.

known Jebusite cult places, the Stone of Zohelet at En-Rogel and Gihon spring,[1] were located here, I Kings 1:9, 33. Since royal enthronement rites were performed at these two cult places, one can also surmise that other rites connected with the enthronement of the king, such as the subduing of the enemies (cf. Ps. 110), may have been performed in this valley close to one of these cult places. E. Lipiński suggests that the triumph of Yahweh in his war against his enemies has been celebrated on the same spot where the consecration of the king took place.[2] This may well be correct. From what has been said above, Yahweh conquers his enemies in a valley. It is thus natural that the rejoicing over his victory begins in the valley and from there the jubilant procession starts its way up to Zion, cf. Ps. 24:7 ff., 47:6 ff. Just as Solomon was anointed at Gihon, the holy spring in the Kidron valley, and began his enthronement procession from there, so also can Gihon have been the place from which some other cultic processions started.[3] Perhaps it was here that Yahweh smote and destroyed, מחץ ("to strike, break into pieces"), his enemies. [4]

The religious significance which must be given to the Kidron valley is also shown by its function in the reforms of the Judean Kings Asa, Hezekiah, and Josiah. In these reforms, each of the three Kings had altars and temple idols destroyed in this valley,[5] 1 Kings 15:13, 2 Kings 23:4. 6, 12, 2 Chr. 15:16, 29:16, 30:14, cf. Jer. 31:40. These actions may have taken place in connection with some cult days, for that was the proper time and "place" for ritually destroying

---

[1] Cf., among others, A. von Gall, *BZAW* 27/14, p. 158, J. P. Peters, *The Religion of the Hebrews*, 1932, p. 159, A. Lods, *Israël des origines au milieu du VIIIe siècle*, 1930, p. 418, J. Pedersen, *Israel* III-IV, (Eng. ed.), p. 239, E. Nielsen, *Shechem*, p. 330, Ahlström, *VT* 11/61, p. 115, A. R. Johnson, *Sacral Kingship²*, p. 119, E. Lipiński, *La royauté*, p. 444. R. de Vaux believes that the sanctuary of the Ark was located at Gihon, *Ancient Israel*, 1965, pp. 102, 278.

[2] As support for this, Lipiński refers *inter alia* to Sukkah 4:9-10 and Isa. 12:2-3. He considers the latter passage to be part of a liturgy originally spoken by the king; this part was later inserted into the book of Isaiah, *La royauté*, pp. 444 f.

[3] It is possible that Ps. 110:5, 7 should be connected with rituals performed at Gihon, cf. G. Widengren, *Psalm* 110 (UUÅ 1941:7, 1), pp. 1 ff., H.-J. Kraus, *Psalmen*, p. 762.

[4] The verb מחץ is mostly used in poetic texts referring to Yahweh's and the king's slaughter of enemies, Num. 24:8, 17, Dt. 32:39, 33:11, 2 Sam. 22:39 //Ps. 18:39, Pss. 68:22, 110:5 f., Hab. 3:13, Job 5:18, 26:12. Cf. E. Lipiński, *La royauté*, pp. 128 f. See also M. Held, "*mḫṣ/*mḫš* in Ugaritic and other Semitic Languages," *JAOS* 79/59, pp. 169 ff.

[5] Cf. Ahlström, *Aspects of Syncretism*, pp. 57, 86 f.

other gods—and thus, also, their גוים.[1] Holy war aspects were then
also involved in this action. Therefore, the ritual custom has given
Asa, Hezekiah and Josiah the opportunity to get rid of undesirable
gods and their cult vessels. In these instances, the ritual has been the
servant of not only purely religious phenomena, but also of religio-
political ideas.

2 Chr. 29:16 clarifies the fact that the temple purification mentioned
above was carried out in a ceremonial way. Everything that was
considered unclean was carried out of the house of Yahweh by the
priests, and handed over at the temple court to the Levites, who
carried it down into Kidron where it was destroyed and burned.
(One should note that these objects were still considered to be holy,
for only temple personnel were allowed to touch them.) Thus, the
priests undertook a ceremony of temple purification, לְקַדֵּשׁ, and the
following verse, 17, states that it began on the first day of the first
month. Then, on the eighth day, they had come to the "vestibule",
אולם, of the temple, and on the 16th day of the same month, the
purification of the entire temple area was completed. This all indicates
that the phenomena here under discussion was connected with one
of the festivals of a new-year character; at least this seems to be the
opinion of the Chronicler.

Thus, Kidron is a place where ritual destruction of other deities
has taken place. This means that the judgment that accompanies the
ritual destruction may have taken place in the same cultic situation,
and therefore it is possible to see the valley of Kidron as a valley of
judgment.[2] This is the valley in which Yahweh smites his enemies and
passes judgment upon them. From this viewpoint, it could also be
possible that Joel's choice of the name, עמק יהושפט, has been inspired
by, or is an expression of, what was a religious reality. It is, of course,
impossible to prove whether this was still the case in the days of
Joel, but one does have the right to assume that some rites existed
which at least could be seen as reminiscences of this reality. However,
Joel was quite familiar with the tradition, and he has drawn quite
richly from this source.[3]

---

[1] Cf. E. Nielsen, "The Burial of Foreign God's", *StTh* 8/54, p. 121.
[2] For this identification, see, among others, A. von Gall, *BZAW* 27/14, pp.
158 f., cf. also L. Krinetzki, *BZ* 5/61, pp. 214 f. For the valley motif in prophetic
texts, see A. S. Kapelrud, *Joel Studies*, pp. 145 ff.
[3] This may explain why the text of Joel is sometimes so parallel to other prophets,
such as Jeremiah, Amos (1:2), Isaiah (ch. 13), etc.

What has been said above can also be used as an explanation for the other symbolic name that Joel gives this valley, namely, עמק החרוץ, "the valley of cutting, decision", Joel 4:14. A. Merx has maintained, for example, that this name represents the threshing that occurred at the end of the harvest.[1] This may be correct, for 4:13 contains several phrases for harvest and for practices belonging to typical fertility rites. Thus, מגל, "sickle", occurs, and the "rich, ripe harvest" (בשל קציר), the exhortation to tread the grapes because the vats and the winepresses are full (גת, היקבים). The "cutting" in the valley will be so great that the valley itself is rightly called the "valley of cutting". The root חרץ, which could mean "to cut, engrave, sharpen", has mostly been used in the sense of "to decide", "to sharpen (the tongue)", Ex. 11:7, 1 Kings 20:40. One should also note that the form חרוץ can stand for "ditch, grave". Sometimes חרוץ refers to a threshing cart or sledge, Amos 1:3, Isa. 28:27, Job 41:22, but in these instances, perhaps מורג should be supplied, as is found in Isa. 41:15.[2] Perhaps this is the meaning of חרוץ in Joel 4:14. The term chosen by Joel in 4:14, thus, is very impressive and suitable with its double meaning of decision and threshing instrument.[3]

Thus far it has been seen that the trembling of nature in the theophany texts is connected with the idea of Yahweh's coming to intervene on behalf of his people [4] or on behalf of his chosen one. In Ps. 18:8 ff., Yahweh stretches out his hand to save the one who is surrounded by the cords of Sheol (vv. 5 f., 17 ff.), and in Ps. 50:2 ff., Elohim shines forth, הופיע,[5] and calls upon heavens and earth gathering his people to judgment, and unto deliverance for the just, vv. 14 f., cf. Ps. 76:7 ff. In the archaic psalm 68, the theophany of Elohim is connected with the blessings of life-giving rain, and thus, with "restoration" for his inheritance. Zion is glad, and the "daughters of Judah rejoice" when Yahweh comes and his righteousness is proclaimed, Ps. 97. The same can be seen from Hab. 3. The

---

[1] Merx, *Die Prophetie des Joel*, p. 74.

[2] E. Hammershaimb, *Amos*, p. 23.

[3] Cf. the picture of ʿAnat chopping up her enemy, Mot, UT 49:II:26 ff. From the discussion given above, it is natural that שאול is said to be located in a valley, Prov. 9:18.

[4] Cf. E. Beaucamp, "La théophanie du Psaume 50 (49)," *Nouvelle Revue Théologique* 81/59, p. 912.

[5] For evidence that this verb is a technical term for the shining forth of deities and heavenly bodies, see Ahlström, *Psalm 89*, p. 88.

coming of Eloah means salvation for his people and for his messiah,
v. 13, cf. also Dt. 33:3, 26. Originally the theophany meant fear for
everybody and everything except his people. This idea has sometimes
been inverted by the prophets. It should be noted that in the book
of Joel, both uses—the original, and the inverted form—are to be
found.

It has been advocated that the brightness, the brilliance, that is
attributed to Yahweh in many of the theophany texts did not originally belong to the description of Yahweh's theophany, and that in
this case one is dealing with non-Israelite influence.[1] This is, of course,
possible, because the Israelites did invade the land, settling in it, and
doubtless were very much influenced by Canaanite phenomena which,
perhaps, were not entirely foreign to them. It should also be remembered, however, that Israel had its own traditions from their
pre-Canaanite days, and both Egyptian and Mesopotamian elements
may have been present in these traditions. How the religion of the
Hebrews began is, of course, quite impossible to describe, nor is
this the place to discuss such beginnings at length. It should only
be emphasized that because of the paucity of knowledge in this matter,
it is impossible to prove how "foreign" these light motifs, which are
used to describe Yahweh, may have been—if at all. The character of
Yahweh as an atmospheric high god invites, of course, all sorts of
heavenly features to be attributed to him. This would also explain
how Yahweh was quickly assimilated in some circles, being identified
with Baal (-Hadad),[2] the one who rides upon the clouds, cf. Ps. 68:5.[3]
At several other places, the close identification of Yahweh with El

---

[1] So P. Humbert, who says that this is a later "décor", *Problèmes du livre d'Haba-
cuc*, 1944, p. 210, followed by Jörg Jermias, who sees this as an influence from
neighboring peoples, *Theophanie*, pp. 63, 90. Cf. also F. Schnutenhaus, "Das
Kommen und Erscheinen Gottes im Alten Testament", *ZAW* 76/64, p. 20.

[2] Cf. the polemics in the book of Hosea.

[3] Geo Widengren, *Religionsphänomenologie*, 1969, pp. 81 f. As far as can be understood, it is not quite proper to use the phrase "early pagan vestiges" when dealing
with Hebrew literature and religion, as W. F. Albright does here, *Yahweh and the
Gods of Canaan*, 1968, p. 159. The term "pagan" is a Christian invention and
therefore should not be used in dealing with other religions.

Concerning ביה שמו in Ps. 68:5, R. de Langhe suggested that the "author"
was thinking of the phrase בעל שמו, because Baal of Canaan was the rider of the
clouds; later on, "un scribe pieux en a fait ביה", *Orientalia et Biblica Lovaniensia*
1/57, p. 85. A. Guillaume reads here the verb בָּיָה, "to remember", and translates
the phrase, "to be mindful of his name", cf. Isa. 26:4, "A Note on Psalm LXVIII.5",
JThSt 13/62, pp. 322 f. M. Dahood reads שמו as a qal masc. pl. imperative of
ysm, "to be pleasant, beautiful," which occurs in Ugaritic, *Psalms* II, p. 136.

and his different local forms—such as El Eljon in Jerusalem—has worked against this assimilation with Baal. In the latter case, some other heavenly light phenomena in the character of Yahweh may have been emphasized. As a matter of fact, these other heavenly light phenomena could already have been present, because Yahweh and El are in reality two forms of the same god.[1]

The terms theophany and epiphany are often used in the above discussion. Before proceeding further, one ought to note the distinction between these two terms made by C. Westermann. According to Westermann, an epiphany has three main features: first, the deity comes or goes forth from a place; second, the presence of "cosmic disturbances which accompany this coming"; third, "God's (wrathful) intervention for or against...". In a theophany, on the other hand, the main features would be the deity's appearance in order to reveal himself at a specific place and at a specific time through a special person who serves "as the mediator of God's activity toward the people".[2] Is it now possible to apply this pattern to the book of Joel? One could answer both "yes" and "no". Using categories of the "epiphany", Ch. 2 describes the coming of Yahweh's army, yea, the coming of Yahweh himself, cf. 2:3, 10. First, in 2:11 it is said that Yahweh himself is coming, i.e. an epiphany. He raises his voice in front of his army. This does not exactly harmonize with Westermann's two "Gattungen". In 3:3-4 are found theophany motifs, but no mention is made of Yahweh's coming. Instead, he himself is promising what he is going to do. After all the portents have been mentioned, 4:16 announces that Yahweh is roaring from Zion and lifting up his voice from Jerusalem, with the usual effect—that heaven and earth tremble. This could, of course, be seen as part of an epiphany if Yahweh is appearing at the same time. Thus it is evident that the prophet did use several motifs belonging to the theophany-epiphany category in describing the coming day of Yahweh. What this day meant for both him and his listeners has been more than clear; it meant exactly as Yahweh himself coming.

Joel contains no particular "Gattung" of a theophany or an

---

[1] Cf. my remarks in *Aspects of Syncretism*, pp. 12 ff., and in *Essays in Divinity* VI, 128 f. For the identification with 'Al(u), see also H. S. Nyberg, *Studien zum Hosea-buche* (UUÅ 1935:6) passim, and "Studien zum Religionskampf im Alten Testament", *ARW* 35/38, pp. 329 ff., G. Widengren, *The Accadian and Hebrew Psalms of Lamentation as Religious Documents*, 1936, pp. 71 f., cf. p. 323, M. Dahood, "The Divine Name 'Ēlî in the Psalms", *ThSt* 14/53, pp. 452 ff.

[2] *The Praise of God in the Psalms*, 1965, pp. 98 ff.

epiphany but rather a prophecy built out of features from these so-called categories. Therefore, what can be separated out in this case by means of literary critical observations is of a lesser importance for the understanding of Joel's message about the day of Yahweh.

However, one could ask here whether Westermann's literary types are accurate. When he says that in an epiphany, the god "comes from" or is "going out from",[1] this could as well mean that the god is coming from a place in order to reveal himself. This latter, according to Westermann, should be a characteristic of a theophany. Further-more, in an epiphany Yahweh is said to intervene for somebody against somebody else. But is this not just another way of saying that Yahweh, who is revealing himself, is making himself manifest in concrete action? One could object to Westermann by saying that when a deity manifests himself as going forth from a place, he could as well come forth at a special place. Even if the epiphany should only mention cosmic happenings (Hab. 3:6, cf. Ps. 18:16, 29:6, 46:7, 77:19) in connection with the deity's intervention, these might as easily have had a context in the sanctuary, which is the natural place for the appearance and manifestation of a deity. The psalms and prophets may very well have decked out the motifs connected with these manifestations. What Westermann has seen as the difference between theophany and epiphany seems rather to be a difference of acting than of literal forms.[2] The weakness in Westermann's thesis is his failure to take into consideration the cultic nature of the revelation or appearance of the deity.[3]

---

[1] *Op. cit.*, p. 98.

[2] For a structural analysis, it would have been more appropriate to take into consideration the Hebrew terms announcing the coming of the deity, cf. F. Schnutenhaus, "Das Kommen und Erscheinen Gottes im Alten Testament", *ZAW* 76/64, pp. 1 ff. Thus, an epiphany should, for example, contain words telling about the deity coming and going out, בוא, יצא, shining forth, הופיע (Dt. 33:2, Ps. 50:2, cf. Pss. 80:2, 94:1), or the going up of Yahweh's *kābōd*, זרח כבוד, Isa. 60:1 ff., or, the forms of the root נגה (Hab. 3:4, Isa. 60:3, cf. Ps. 18:13, 2 Sam. 22:13, Ezek. 10:4), this latter stem showing Yahweh as a being who shines forth as the heavenly bodies shine forth.

Another question to be raised is whether the form and content of an epiphany (or theophany) must always be the same. If so, it would mean that all epiphany texts have come from one and the same place. But surely, the Israelite religion was more complex than that!

[3] Jörg Jeremias separates the theophany from the cult because he supposes the cult to be something static ("das Statische, Stetige, Regelmässige") and the theophany is to be seen as something that comes suddenly, *Theophanie*, p. 122. This is simply a misconception of cultic and religious reality on his part, a misconception of the dynamic character of cultic drama. The liturgical phenomena of

Philologically speaking, both terms under discussion are expressions for a deity's appearance. Theophany means the coming or the shining forth (φαίνω, "bring into the light", "make visible") of a deity (θεός), and epiphany (ἐπι-φαίνω, -φαίνομαι, "make oneself shown", "become visible") is roughly equivalent. From the point of view of the history of religions, an epiphany is the appearance of a deity who usually is hidden (or invisible). The day when he reveals himself is a "day on which he appeared in our world" as he is, according to W. Brede Kristensen.[1] One should add that "our world" refers to the "world" of the temple area outside his usual, holy "hiding place", which is also in the temple (celestial or not). Thus there is no real difference in character between the ideas involved in a theophany compared with those of an epiphany. The manifestations of a god and the circumstances under which he appears may be the same in both cases;[2] thus, it can be concluded that all the acts which he performs when he "shines forth", as well as the reactions of the surroundings in which he appears are also the same in both cases as well. If any difference is to be maintained between these two terms, it would be that a theophany accompanies or includes an epiphany.[3]

Proceeding now with a discussion of the motifs of the day of Yahweh, i.e., the day of his theophany, one should note that after the judgment of the nations in Joel 4:12, 14, the prophetic oracle presents

---

the cult have the character of that which is new, coming just now, even though the liturgy may occur regularly. Again it is to be remembered that when one is in the temple, one is with the deity in his heaven. As a memento against too rigid a concept of the cult as being static, or against theophany as being too novel an experience to be contained in cult liturgy, indeed, as a memento that cult and theophany do belong together, one should note that in Judg. 6:18 ff., the sacrificial term מנחה is connected with theophany phenomena, cf. H.-J. Kraus, *Worship*, p. 115, H. H. Rowley, *Worship in Ancient Israel*, p. 60. The narrative about Gideon's sacrifice and his building of an altar *after* he had sacrificed must be understood as a text which describes the adoption of a cult into the community of Yahweh worshippers. The text could thus be called a cult adoption text.

[1] *The meaning of Religion*, 1960, p. 382. For a discussion of theophanies in the Old Testament, see, for instance, H.-P. Müller, "Die kultische Darstellung der Theophanie", *VT* 14/64, pp. 183 ff., F. Schnutenhaus, *ZAW* 76/64, pp. 1 ff. Jörg Jeremias, *Theophanie*, 1965, J. J. Stamm, "Elia am Horeb", *Studia Biblica et Semitica* (Festschrift Th. C. Vriezen), 1966, pp. 330 ff., E. Lipiński, *La royauté*, pp. 205 ff., cf. also J. Koenig, "Aux origines des théophanies iahvistes", *RHR* 169/66, pp. 30 ff.

[2] Therefore, it is somewhat artificial to deny the existence of theophanies in the cult, cf. H.-P. Müller, *VT* 14/64, p. 191.

[3] For theophanies experienced in visions, see, for example, J. Lindblom, "Theophanies in Holy Places in Hebrew Religion", *HUCA* 32/61, pp. 91 ff.

a picture of the ideal time that will follow the judgment. First, there is a natural emphasis on Yahweh as the only refuge and stronghold of the people, 4:16, cf. 2 Sam. 22:3, Ps. 18:3. Then, there again occurs the statement that only Yahweh is the god of the people. It is he who lives, שֹׁכֵן,[1] on the holy mount Zion, 4:17, cf. Isa. 8:18, Ezek. 20:40. Herein lies a reference to Yahweh as the god of the covenant—the only one who can save the people. Thus they will know that he is *their* god. Jerusalem will become a holy city,[2] cf. Isa. 52:10, and no longer will strangers pass through it, 4:17b. This is to say that Jerusalem will never again be profaned, it will be an inviolable city. This motif also occurs among other prophets as a part of the coming ideal future, cf. Isa. 52:1, Ob. 17, Zech. 9:8, 14:21.[3] It should be underlined that as far as Joel is concerned, this does not mean that the cult will cease to function. On the contrary, the right cult is only possible where Yahweh lives. On the temple mountain, the people will always meet with their god. But the holiness of the city will be established only when the right cult is practiced.[4]

The ideal time pictured in Joel 4:18 is depicted in terms of life-giving waters, of abundance of wine, of fatness. This means that the sources of life and the goodness of life will be guaranteed. The use of "wine" in this context serves as an expression for the joy of life; it is also found in this sense, for example, in Ps. 104:15, Jg. 9:13, Ecclus. 39:25 f. The book of Joel contains no polemics against wine as are found among pre-exilic prophets, who were agitating against Canaanite customs. Pre-exilic prophets viewed wine and its use in the cult not only as demoralizing, but as part of the rites of the Canaanite fertility cult. In the case of Joel, the time for such polemics

---

[1] For the root שׁכן, see, among others, A. Kuschke, "Die Lagervorstellung der priesterschriftlichen Erzählung", *ZAW* 63/51, pp. 84 ff., cf. W. Schmidt, "מִשְׁכָּן als Ausdruck Jerusalemer Kultsprache", *ZAW* 75/63, pp. 91 f. M. Görg considers the שׁכן motif and the tent motif in the OT originally to have been Canaanite, *Das Zelt der Begegnung* (Bonner Bibl. Beiträge 27), 1967, pp. 110 ff. For אהל as referring not only to a tent in Canaan, but also to a temple, see Ahlström, *Aspects of Syncretism*, pp. 28 f. V. W. Rabe has not seen this double use of אהל, "Israelite Opposition to the Temple", *CBQ* 29/67, pp. 228 ff.

[2] W. Staerk, "Zum alttestamentlichen Erwählungsglauben", *ZAW* 55/37, p. 19, J. Lindblom, *Prophecy in Ancient Israel*, p. 412.

[3] Concerning the *topoi* of the holiness of Jerusalem as belonging to traditional language, see H. W. Wolff, *Joel*, pp. 98 f.

[4] Wolff sees the idea of Jerusalem as holy not so much as referring to "kultische Reinheit" as to "seine unverbrüchliche Zuordnung zum Bundesgott", *op. cit.*, p. 99. This "Zuordnung" must, of course, be established in the cult. For Joel, religion is cult.

against this phenomenon is passed. From antiquity, wine had been not only a pleasure that cheered both gods and kings, Judg. 9:13, but also a necessary item in the cult. By means of wine, one came into contact with the divine.[1] In the paradise that is to come, wine will be understood as the gift of Yahweh only—not Baal—and it will be available in abundance.

In considering the use of wine and fatness in Joel, one ought notice that "on that day the mountains shall drip fresh wine, and the hills shall flow with fatness" is similar to Am. 9:13.[2] Reference to a Ugaritic text indicates the great age of these motifs. The text (UT 49:III:6 f., 12 f.)[3] is referring to the time of the resurrection of Baal when it says:

> *šmm šmn tmṭrn* The heavens will rain fatness,
> *nḫlm tlk nbtm* the wadies flow with honey.

In Canaan, this was the imagery for expressing the life-giving powers of a deity.

Connected with this in the same verse is the motif of the temple well, 4:18. This motif is also ancient. The idea that deities lived on a mountain located upon or at the primeval waters is not an uncommon idea in the Near East. Thus, the Akkadian mountain of the gods was located *ina pî nārāti*, "in the mouth of the rivers" or, as it could also be expressed, *ina bērit pî nārāti killān*, "between the mouth of the two rivers" (CT XVI:47:198).[4] This is also the location of the garden of paradise.[5] In Ugarit, El's abode was "at the spring of the rivers in the midst of the stream of the (two) deeps (thmtm)", UT 51:IV:21 f.[6] Ezek. 28:2 is to be compared with this, as well as the

---

[1] H. S. Nyberg, *ARW* 35/38, p. 355. Cf. also J. P. Brown, "The Mediterranean Vocabulary of the Vine", *VT* 19/69, pp. 146 ff. According to R. J. Forbes wine was "an expensive commodity...highly appreciated by the rich" in Mesopotamia, *Studies in Ancient Technology* III, 1955, p. 71.

[2] For the parallelism גבע//הר, see S. Gevirtz, *Patterns in the Early Poetry of Israel*, 1963, pp. 56 f.

[3] Cf. C. H. Gordon, *Ugaritic Literature*, p. 46, F. F. Hvidberg, *Weeping and Laughter*, p. 35, J. Aistleitner, *Die mythologischen und kultischen Texte aus Ras Schamra*, pp. 20 f., I. Engnell, *Studies*, p. 122, H. W. Wolff, *Joel*, p. 100. Fatness and honey are also the foods of the promised royal child in Isa. 7:14 f.

[4] Cf. W. F. Albright, *AJSL* 35/1918-19, pp. 161-195, and S. N. Kramer, *BASOR* 96/44, pp. 18 ff.

[5] G. Widengren, *The King and the Tree of Life*, pp. 6 f., 19.

[6] A. S. Kapelrud, *Joel Studies*, pp. 167 ff., J. Gray, *The Legacy of Canaan*[2], pp. 156 ff., M. Pope, *Job* (The Anchor Bible 15), p. 181. Of course this idea does not mean that El is to be seen as a seagod. If so, what about all the Babylonian gods who live *ina pî nārāti*?

מוֹשַׁב אֱלֹהִים, which is in the midst of the sea, i.e., the cosmic sea. Thus, this motif serves as the prototype for the meaning involved in connecting god-mountain/temple and water/well in Canaanite and Israelite religions. The picture of the abode of the deity, namely, paradise, is the source of the waters (of life), Ps. 36:8 ff.,[1] Ps. 46:5,[2] cf. Ezek. 47:1ff., Zech. 14:8, Gen. 2:10,[3] Ps. 65:10.

Because of the above, Joel 4:18 cannot *per se* be used as an argument for the late date of the book of Joel. Neither can the passage be argued to be eschatological in nature.[4] Both Amos 9:13 and Joel 4:18 present traditional concepts that, from antiquity, have expressed the ideal time which, according to Canaanite and Israelite thinking, would come into existence when the deities fulfilled their functions,[5] cf. Ps. 65:6-14. In these ancient motifs lies the inspiration for the prophetic preaching and promises of the ideal future.

Thus, when Yahweh comes, he will restore everything, and no enemies will ever again trouble his people. The future will be an ideal one. To describe this, the prophet uses the categories and motifs of mythology—which is his theology—making his point fully clear. Therefore references to historical events are not to be found for the most part, and arriving at a date of the composition of this part of the book is more complex than merely discussing such references to historical data. The usual explanation of these motifs in Joel is that they are eschatological and apocalyptic in nature and, thus, late

---

[1] Cf. H. Gressmann, *Der Messias*, pp. 179 ff. The phrase עֲדָנֶיךָ in Ps. 36:9, which is commonly rendered "thy delights", is rendered by K. Yaron as "thy Eden(s)" instead, "The Dirge of the King of Tyre", *Annual of the Swedish Theol. Institute* III, 1964, p. 41.

[2] E. Lipiński believes this to be a reference to Gihon, *La royauté*, p. 445, a correct evaluation on his part, because the stream of paradise is parallel to or a symbol for the temple stream.

[3] For Gen. 2:10, which can be seen as an Israelite expression of the ancient near eastern myth of the streams of paradise, see, among others, O. Kaiser, *Die mythische Bedeutung des Meeres in Ägypten, Ugarit und Israel* (BZAW 78), 1959, pp. 107 ff. Kaiser has, however, not discussed this phenomenon in relation to the temple ideology.

[4] Contra A. Weiser, *ATD* 24, p. 109.

[5] Cf. A. S. Kapelrud, *Joel Studies*, p. 167. Even if Am. 9:11-15 is a later addition to the book, as has been maintained several times (cf. Kapelrud, *Central Ideas in Amos*, pp. 54 ff., J. Lindblom, *Prophecy in Ancient Israel*, p. 281, W. S. McCullough, "Some Suggestions about Amos", *JBL* 72/53, p. 248, cf. also the commentaries by Sellin, *SKAT* XII:1, and Weiser, *ATD* 24), this does not mean that vss. 13-15 must be of late origin. Cf. J. Gray, who understands Am. 9:13 and Joel 4:18 as coming from a liturgy which was probably "associated with seasonal festivals", *The Legacy of Canaan*², p. 70, n. 5.

rather than early. However, if one understands "eschatology" correctly as a doctrine concerning the end of the worldly era, then one must understand that there is almost no eschatology at all in the prophetic books.[1] Prophetic writings refer to the future, to be sure, an ideal future for Yahweh's own people in the land that he has given them, but it is a future in this world, and not at or after the end of this world. If this kind of future is what one means by eschatology, then it would be possible to say that the book of Joel is eschatological.[2]

Years ago, when H. Gunkel maintained that Israelite eschatology was a phenomenon older than the prophets,[3] he was thinking along correct lines, because the texts in which he found this phenomenon must be seen as the sources of inspiration for the prophets. The objection to be raised, however, is Gunkel's choice of the word, "eschatology". Futuristic aspects are certainly to be found in these texts, but this is not the same as eschatology—a term which should be restricted to its true meaning—the end of this world and the beginning of a new one.[4] What Gunkel rightly had seen was that the traditions with which he was dealing were mythological in nature.[5] These traditions, complete with their motifs of Yahweh's coming, his acts, complete with the stylistic pattern of change from disaster/chaos on the one hand to good fortune/order (cosmological and national) on the other, have become an integral part of the prophetic message. This was the language of religion. It is only natural that the prophets used it; it is hardly conceivable that they would have used anything else.

---

[1] Cf. J. Lindblom, "Gibt es eine Eschatologie bei den alttestamentlichen Propheten?", *StTh* 6/52, pp. 80 f. See also the remarks by J. L. McKenzie, "Royal Messianism", *CBQ* 19/57, pp. 49 ff., H. Wildberger, "Jesajas Verständnis der Geschichte", *SVT* 9/62, pp. 114 ff., M. Treves, "The Date of Joel", *VT* 7/57, p. 150. For a summary of the discussion about eschatology in the OT, see O. Plöger, *Theokratie und Eschatologie* (WMANT 2), 1959, W. Köhler, "Prophetie und Eschatology in der neueren alttestamentlichen Forschung", *Bibel und Leben*, 9/68, pp. 57 ff.

[2] Even so, this eschatology, according to Th. H. Robinson, is not developed in Joel to any great extent. For instance, he considers the oracles against foreign nations to be simple in form and unconnected with an eschatological concept, *HAT³* 14, pp. 55 f. In this connection, one should also remember the fact that the scenes of trial in the prophetic utterances are modelled after cultic patterns, according to E. Würthwein, "Der Ursprung der prophetischen Gerichtsrede", *ZThK* 49/52, pp. 1 ff., cf. I. Engnell, "Profeter", *SBU* II², cols. 587 f., E. Jacob, *Theology of the Old Testament*, p. 321.

[3] "Zum religionsgeschichtlichen Verständnis des Neuen Testaments", *FRLANT* 1, 1903, pp. 21 ff.

[4] S. Mowinckel, *He that Cometh*, pp. 125 f.

[5] Gunkel, *op. cit.*, p. 22.

One ought also ask whether or not apocalyptic features are to be found in Joel. If one should follow H. H. Rowley's definition of an apocalyptist-prophet, then Joel cannot be termed an apocalyptist. Rowley maintains that "the prophets foretold the future that should arise out of the present, while the apocalyptist foretold the future that should break into the present.... The apocalyptists had little faith in the present to beget the future". According to the prophets, the world powers were used by Yahweh as a means of destruction and punishment, but in apocalyptic literature, the world powers "were the adversaries of God".[1] As has been seen, the book of Joel predicts an ideal future which will indeed arise out of the presently bad situation. With respect to the world powers, Joel does not mention them by name—perhaps it was dangerous to do so at that time—but he does use the liturgical terms עם and גוים, and also the "Northerner". These terms *may* allude to world powers. The locusts may also have alluded to worldly powers, but in this text, they are more clearly a natural disaster. The fact, however, that world powers are not called by name here is not the important point. More important is the fact that the גוים, being enemies, are both instruments of Yahweh's punishment against Israel, and objects of Yahweh's wrath—which is a liturgical pattern. Thus, their punishment will be the salvation of Yahweh's people. In this case, Joel is in the same tradition as the other prophets and in telling of the annihilation of enemies and of the coming future of his own people, he has used liturgical motifs, both cosmological and mythological.[2] It may be that a "paradisiacal" time will come after the judgment of all the nations, but this need not be called apocalyptic, even though the same motifs used in Joel have been used by later apocalyptists. Joel does speak, as do all the other prophets, from a point of view that is in the present, and he does portray a future that is paradisiacal, which will be established after the imminent day of Yahweh. One should note that there is no indication in this book that the prophet has tried to revert back into Israel's history and speak under the name of one of Israel's famous men of the past.[3] Neither are there any of the general characteristics

---

[1] *The Relevance of Apocalyptic*. A Study of Jewish and Christian Apocalypses from Daniel to the Revelation[3], 1963, pp. 38 f.

[2] Rowley, *op. cit.*, pp. 42 f., F. M. Cross, Jr., in *Biblical Motifs*, pp. 18, 30.

[3] Rowley, *op. cit.*, p. 39, cf. J. Klausner, *The Messianic Idea in Israel*, 1956, pp. 227 f. One should also note that the utterances of the prophets are usually in poetic form, but the apocalyptic writings are in prose, F. Dingermann, "Die

of apocalyptic, such as riddles, speculations, secret knowledge, allegorical theories about the end of this world. Instead, there is mentioned only the beginning of a better time for Judah and Jerusalem all in the continuum of this world. Thus, Joel is not an apocalyptic book. However, the strong emphasis upon the ideal, paradisiacal future, complete with its unrealistic exaggerations, could be seen as a definite intensifying of the old, cult-mythological motifs about Yahweh's establishing of the right órder (צדקה) in heaven and on earth, with the right, ideal life for his people. Thus, Joel may have contributed to the beginning of apocalyptic—or, he may even have inspired that beginning—a trend which became so important in later, post-exilic times.

It is possible that some of the motifs usually connected with the day of Yahweh have been associated with similar phenomena belonging to another חג, such as, for instance, the Passover. Because of the creation and re-creation ideas and motifs, and the *rite de passage* character of this festival, it has been understood as another form of the Near Eastern new year's festival.[1] Therefore, even though the day of Yahweh in Joel is mostly dependent upon the autumnal festival for its setting, the prophet may very well have also used motifs from the Passover which were appropriate for his theme. Joel 4:18 f. may lend support to this thesis. Here, the phrase נחל השטים occurs, along with the names of Israel's traditional enemies, Egypt and Edom.[2] These names, which were intimately connected with the Exodus and the wilderness wanderings, are a part of the Passover traditions. The name שטים, an important place name in the Jordan valley opposite Jericho, occurs also in Num. 25:1, 33:49, Josh. 2:1, 3:1, and Mic. 6:5. Besides these passages, Judg. 7:22 mentions a place בית השטה, which is also located in the Jordan valley. The problem is whether שטים in Joel 4:18 is a place name (geographical) or a symbolic name.

Botschaft vom Vergehen dieser Welt und von den Geheimnissen der Endzeit. Beginnende Apokalyptik im Alten Testament", *Wort und Botschaft* (ed. J. Schreiner), 1967, p. 333. For the characteristics of apocalyptic writings, see also H. Ringgren, "Apokalyptik", *RGG* I³, pp. 464 f., P. Grelot, "Apokalyptik", *Sacramentum Mundi* I, 1967, cols. 224 ff., L. Hartman, *Prophecy Interpreted* (Coniectanea Biblica N.T. Series 1), 1966, pp. 23 ff.

[1] Cf. W. A. Heidel, *The Day of Yahweh*, pp. 78 ff., also J. B. Segal, *The Hebrew Passover from the Earliest Times to A.D.* 70 (London Oriental Series 12), 1963, p. 238.

[2] According to H. W. Wolff, Edom became an arch-enemy of Israel after the fall of Jerusalem in 587 B.C., *Joel*, p. 101. However, the hatred between the "twin-peoples" seems to go further back in time, cf. 2 Sam. 8:14, 2 Kings 8:20 ff., 14:7, 1 Chr. 18:12 ff., 2 Chr. 28:17, 1 Kings 11:14 ff., Am. 1:11 f.

The best solution would be to see it as a parallel to the valley of Jehoshaphat.[1] Prior to the occurrence of this name, the prophet has been using the motif of the valley of judgment and cutting (= valley of death) as a means of telling the fate of the גוים. Now, in 4:18, he mentions the valley of שטים as being blessed with the water which flows out of the temple of Yahweh. The idea here is that this water will irrigate the desert (= place of death) and make it fertile, cf. Isa. 41:18 f., Zech. 14:8 ff. Shittim will benefit from this water. From this kind of argument, a strong case for understanding Joel's use of Shittim as symbolic can be made.

In spite of the case for a symbolic understanding of the name, Shittim, one must realize that the name carries such strong associations with it that one wonders whether the symbolic interpretation is the *only* one.[2] In the first place, the name has a meaning, namely "acacias" or "acacia tree", and, in the second place, the geographical place name, Shittim, could have played some role also in the oracle of Joel. In Josh. 3:1, Shittim is the starting point for the holy war and passover activities; thus, it is part of a tradition which signifies a new era for the people.[3] In Joel, this era will witness the end of Egypt and Edom, both of whom are accused of having poured out the innocent blood of the sons of Judah, 4:19.[4] Thus, the curses of the covenant will have gone into effect.[5] W. A. Heidel, among others, considers Josh. 3 to belong to what he calls the "New Year's Passover".[6] He strengthens his theory by pointing to the עבר-motif [7]

---

[1] Cf. E. Sellin, *SKAT* XII:1, p. 177.

[2] E. Sellin prefers to change Shittim to שדים, "demons", *SKAT* XII:1, pp. 177f.

[3] Cf. J. A. Wilcoxen, "Narrative Structure and Cult Legend", *Essays in Divinity* VI. Transitions in Biblical Scholarship, 1968, pp. 69 f.

[4] Cf. Jer. 49:7 ff., Ezek. 25:12 ff., Ps. 137:4, Lam. 4:21, Ob. 10 f.

[5] For curses of foreign nations at the new year festival, cf. Aa. Bentzen, "The Ritual Background of Amos I 2-II 16", *Oudtestamentische Studiën* VIII, 1950, pp. 91 ff.

[6] *The Day of Yahweh*, p. 164, cf. N. Füglister, *Die Heilsbedeutung des Pascha*, 1963, p. 216, J. B. Segal, *The Hebrew Passover*, pp. 237 f., see also H.-J. Kraus, *Worship in Israel*, 1966, pp. 156 ff., F. M. Cross, Jr., in *Biblical Motifs*, p. 26, n. 56.

[7] *The Day of Yahweh*, pp. 79 ff., 95, 161 ff. R. A. Carlson considers "the *ʿābar* pericope in Josh. 3... a Deuteronomic composition in a cultic-literary style", *David, the Chosen King*, p. 102, n. 3, cf. p. 175. Concerning Josh. 3-4, A. R. Hulst advocates that "der Bericht des Durchzugs durch den Jordan ursprünglich in einer selbständigen und unabhängigen Form (der Wortlaut weist darauf hin) bekannt gewesen ist. Es ist sogar möglich, dass diese ursprüngliche Darstellung weder die Lade noch Josua erwähnte." In later time, this tradition should have been influenced by the Exodus legend, "Der Jordan in den alttestamentlichen Überlieferungen," *Oudtestamentische Studiën* XIV, 1965, p. 181.

which is present both here and in the Passover, cf. Josh. 4:10 f., 5:1. After the crossing of the Jordan on the tenth day of the first month, Josh. 4:19, the *pesaḥ* began four days later, 5:10.[1]

In Josh. 3 ff., the themes of holy war and Passover occur in sequence. In the light of this, it would be possible to see Shittim in Joel 4:18 as a reference to the holy war that preceeded the Passover. This is supported by the fact that holy war terminology is found in Joel 4:9 ff. One cannot disregard consideration that the prophet may have used the name Shittim with such an intention in mind. In the historical traditions Shittim is the place from whence the people started into the promised land,[2] and this has been commemorated in the cult. Thus, נחל השטים in Joel 4:18 could be considered as a reference to the place where the people in the cultic tradition of Passover prepared themselves for the holy war, which once ended at Gilgal.[3] Therefore, it is in this connection that Egypt and Edom are mentioned as countries that will be desolated and of no more trouble for Yahweh's people, 4:19.

Is it possible then to assume that the memory of Shittim has been kept alive in some Jerusalemite rites performed outside the temple area? If so, then the valley of Shittim could have been associated with the people's passing over some river [4] in one of the valleys around the city.

This is a tentative explanation of the significance of the valley of Shittim; whether or not it can solve the problem is, of course, impossible to say with exactness. Namely, one could ask why the temple well should specifically water the valley of Shittim in the ideal future if Shittim were only a symbolic place in connection with preparations for the Passover. Out of several other important places, why is this particular one mentioned? One is led to suspect that there have been other ideas or phenomena connected with this name—something which required Shittim to play a role not only at a special moment in history, but also through the years for the people or for the temple.

---

[1] The connection between holy war and passover in Josh. 3 ff. supports the thesis that holy war was an old aspect of the religious forms of Israel.

[2] Cf. Mic. 6:5, and see F. M. Cross, Jr., in *Biblical Motifs*, p. 27.

[3] Ps. 114:3 could be taken as an indication that the Jordan River was associated with the Passover, cf. H.-J. Kraus, *Psalmen* II (BK XV:2), pp. 780 f., J. B. Segal, *The Hebrew Passover*, p. 237. See also A. C. Welch, *Prophet and Priest in Old Israel*, 1936, p. 132, J. A. Soggin, "Gilgal, Passah und Landnahme", *SVT* 15/66, p. 271.

[4] Cf. E. Vogt, "Die Erzählung vom Jordanübergang. Josue 3-4", *Biblica*, 46/65, pp. 141, 148.

It goes without saying that the prophet has not chosen this name by chance. When Joel promises that a well will flow forth from the temple of Yahweh, he strikes the tones of paradisiacal chords. Here he is speaking of the ideal time to come. Just as a stream goes out from Eden to water the garden in Gen. 2:10, so also will a spring well up from the temple and water the valley of acacias. This kind of parallel can be drawn because the temple can be compared with the garden of paradise. Accordingly, one ought to find some kind of symbolic or ideological "identity between the *streams* of Eden and the water-sources which will spring forth from the Temple in the days to come".[1] This identity can already be found in psalms such as 36:9 and 63:6. Thus, one could maintain that the trees of the valley of Shittim, the valley of acacias, belong to the same category as the trees of the garden of paradise.[2]

The water flowing forth from the temple well is then given the character of the water of life, which, among other things, will water the valley of acacias, Shittim ; thus, the growth of these trees will be guaranteed. Ideologically, this could mean that the water from this temple well can make "the whole world" into Yahweh's garden.[3] With this in mind, the geographical location of the valley of Shittim is of less importance; what is more important is rather the product of the valley, the acacia trees. There may have been some special significance to them which justified their being mentioned in this prophecy. As is known, acacia wood was often used in the construction of cultic objects such as, for example, the ark, the bars of the tabernacle, altars, poles, the table of shewbread, Ex. 25 ff., 30:1, 5, 35:4 ff., Dt. 10:3. According to Joel, Yahweh is going to provide for these trees.[4] Considering the LXX translation of שטה, ξύλον ἄσηπτον, "the wood that will not rot," one gets some understanding of the lasting value of this kind of wood and, therefore, that it could be desirable as material for cultic objects. Because of this, Kapelrud may be

---

[1] Kalman Yaron, "The Dirge over the King of Tyre", *Annual of the Swedish Theological Institute* III, 1964, p. 41.

[2] H. Gressmann compared the valley of acacias with a valley mentioned in some Egyptian texts—a valley which was located where the Nile came down from heaven, *Der Messias*, p. 139. "The Nile of Egypt was only a continuation of the Nile of heaven", *The Book of the Dead*⁶, tr. E. A. Wallis Budge, New York 1966, p. 190.

[3] In a Sumerian text it is said that "the four corners of the world" grew as a garden for Enlil, see G. Widengren, *The King and the Tree of Life in Ancient Near Eastern Religion* (UUÅ 1951:4), 18.

[4] A. S. Kapelrud, *Joel Studies*, pp. 170 f.

correct in assuming that Joel has mentioned something here which once had importance for the cult, and still had the same importance.[1] The ideal time Joel is predicting is not a time free from cult; on the contrary, Yahweh's temple will be the foundation, the center point of that time.[2] For Joel, cult and religion are inseparable.[3]

What is of importance in this part of the prophecy is the picture of the ideal future—a future without any shortcomings. Joel 4:18 mentions the fresh, sweet wine, עסיס,[4] that will "drip" from the mountains, and the hills will flow with sweet milk, and the Judean water beds will again flow with water.[5] These are to be seen in connection with the temple well,[6] cf. Ps. 65:10. According to Joel 4:18 f., these blessings will be the consequences of the day of Yahweh. As mentioned above, the annihilation of Edom and Egypt are also part of the consequences, for they are here accused of having shed innocent blood, 4:19. The theme of pouring out innocent blood, דם נקיא,[7] is resumed in 4:21, but this time it is Yahweh who will pour out the blood, namely, the blood of Edom and Egypt. Thus, in keeping with his covenant love, he will be an enemy to his people's enemies, cf. Ex. 23:22.[8] The stem נקה in 4:21, as G. R. Driver has maintained, may be an equivalent to Akkadian nequ, "pour out". If so, then the verse contains "a solitary instance in the O.T. of the original sense of נקה".[9] The resultant idea in this passage is that Yahweh will certainly pour out the blood of the enemies who previously had shed

---

[1] Op. cit., p. 171. These trees belonged to the holy sphere.

[2] Cf. Ph. Reymond, L'eau, sa vie, et sa signification dans l'Ancien Testament, p. 236. H. W. Wolff's opinion that Joel had "geringen Eigenintresse am Kult" (Joel, p.101) is thus not valid.

[3] It should be added that there might be another explanation for the phrase נחל השטים, namely, to read השקה as hōf'al (and, as such, a hapax), "drown", "flood", which would then give the meaning of destroying the valley of Shittim— perhaps because of the sin of the people, the sin which was committed with the daughters of Moab, Nu. 25:1. But if so, then the rest of Joel 4:18 would be in contradiction with this, for the temple well is always thought of as bringing forth blessings in the ideal time of the future.

[4] Besides Joel 4:18 and 1:5, this word occurs only in Song of Songs 8:2, Isa. 49:26, and Am. 9:13.

[5] Contrast the picture given in Joel 1:5, 20!

[6] Cf. Ezek. 47:1 ff.

[7] Note the writing of נקיא, which is a late form for נקי.

[8] Cf. F. C. Fensham, "Clauses of Protection in Hittite Vassal-Treaties and the Old Testament", VT 13/63, pp. 141 ff.

[9] "Linguistic and Textual Problems: Minor Prophets III", JThSt 39/38, pp. 401 f., cf. A. S. Kapelrud, Joel Studies, p. 175.

the innocent blood of the Judeans, cf. Ps. 79:10.[1] The particle לא
in verse 21 is then the emphatic or affirmative לא.[2] This means that
verse 21 cannot be explained as a gloss. The structure of the passage
4:18-21 also confirms such a conclusion. As Th. H. Robinson has
argued, these verses appear in a chiastic pattern:[3] A (v. 18)—
B (v. 19)—A (v. 20)—B (v. 21a)—A (v. 21b). It is an artful composition that ends the book of Joel. In some way, one could say that
verse 21 sums up what has been dealt with before: the annihilation
of the enemies, and Yahweh's perpetual inhabitation of Zion. This
is the guarantee of the future, of the well-being of his people. With
Yahweh inhabiting the temple on Zion, and with enemies unable to
profane the city, 4:17, Jerusalem will indeed become a holy city.

Such is the future that this prophet promises the people. This
future will be established by Yahweh as the consequence of his
restoring acts on the יום יהוה. This is the content of the שוב שבות, 4:1,
a term, therefore, that cannot be understood as a purely eschatological
one.[4] One finds in this book aspects of disaster and happiness, both
of which are in relation to Yahweh's own people. In the first part of
the book, the day of Yahweh comes with disaster for Judah and
Jerusalem, but in the second part, it comes as a day of joy and happiness, resulting in an ideal future.[5] Through their god, Judah will
triumph, cf. Zeph. 3. What one can observe here is that the prophet
emphasizes old mythological and cosmological motifs and concepts [6]
which are combined with the present day liturgical and historical
situation. Again it ought to be maintained that the message of Joel's
book is not apocalyptic.[7] Joel's prophecy is prior to the period of
apocalyptic literature, but Joel may be characterized as one of the
prophets who served as a source of inspiration for the apocalyptists.[8]

---

[1] For the fact that the shedding of innocent blood calls for retaliation, see A. R.
Johnson, *The Vitality of the Inidividual in the Thought of Ancient Israel*[2], 1964, pp. 71 f.

[2] See the discussion above, Ch. I, p. 12, and cf. Kapelrud, *op. cit.*, p. 175.

[3] *HAT* 14, p. 69.

[4] Cf. above, pp. 59 ff. and Job. 42:10. S. Mowinckel calls it a *restitutio in integrum*,
NTT 59/68, p. 30, cf. J. Lindblom, *Prophecy in Ancient Israel*, p. 220.

[5] Cf. J. Bourke, "Le jour de Yahvé dans Joël", *RB* 66/59, pp. 5 ff.

[6] Mowinckel, *op. cit.*, p. 20. Cf. Cross, who says: "As late prophecy and rem-
nants of the royal ideology flow together to create the apocalyptic movement,
we may say that the old mythological themes rise to a new crescendo", in *Biblical
Motifs*, p. 18, cf. p. 30.

[7] Cf. above, pp. 90 f.

[8] Cf. M. Delcor, *La Sainte Bible* VIII, p. 137. According to Lindblom, "ideas
of what will occur before the coming of the great day are rare in the prophetic
literature, but appear frequently in apocalyptic", *Prophecy in Ancient Israel*, p. 421.

This understanding of Joel is not incompatible with the view that Joel was a prophet who was seriously concerned about the right cult, which was the only guarantee for a right religion and a socio-political life according to the צדקה. The source of Joel's material and inspiration is the cult with all its cosmological-mythological concepts and soteriological ideas, all of which he uses as a prism through which to view the past, the present, and the future. The cult is the center of life, even the center of nature as well, and the cult is necessarily tied to the temple where Yahweh alone should live. There he meets with his people. There they learn his ways and his will. When the covenant has been broken, as in the book of Joel, צדקה is impossible, and the people need a מורה who is in accord with the צדקה to show them the right way, 2:23, and thus reestablish the צדקה. The צדקה in Joel cannot therefore be understood as a purely ethical[1] or forensic[2] idea, as it could in later times. Here it is a cultic religious concept, the basic foundation of the right cult. To this should be added only that the right cult yielded the right ethic as its fruit.

To conclude, the צדקה can only be established through a right covenant relationship with Yahweh.[3] That means that all of Yahweh's commands and statutes given in the covenant must be kept. Thanks to the re-established צדקה, there will be a right sequence for the seasons which are so necessary for human life.[4] Only through a rightly established and rightly kept covenant can life in all its aspects be guaranteed; for Joel, as for all the other prophets, this can be accomplished only by a correct Yahweh cult. Thus, one can say that the norm expressing these aspects is the צדקה.[5]

---

[1] Cf. E. Kautsch, *Die Derivative des Stammes ṣdq im alttestamentlichen Sprachgebrauch*, 1881, pp. 9 f. For צדקה as "charity" in Judaism, see F. Rosenthal, "Sedakah, Charity", *HUCA* 23:1/50-51, pp. 411 ff.

[2] Cf. W. Eichrodt, *Theologie des Alten Testaments* I[5], 1957, p. 161.

[3] Cf. G. von Rad, "'Gerechtigkeit' und 'Leben' in der Kultsprache der Psalmen", *Festschrift A. Bertholet*, 1950, p. 423.

[4] H. Ringgren, *Israelite Religion*, p. 134.

[5] Cf. K.-Hj. Fahlgren, *ṣᵉdāḳā*, p. 82.

CHAPTER FIVE

HAMMŌREH LIṢDĀQĀH*

The passage 2:21-27 in the book of Joel is concerned with the blessings and the צדקה that Yahweh will give to his people according to the covenant. The blessings mentioned in the text all belong to the agricultural-pastoral sphere: green pastures, good fruit, and rains which will give good harvests, filling the threshing floors with grain and the winepresses with wine. What the locusts had destroyed will be fully restored again. The people will eat and drink and be satisfied. Never again will they be put to shame. Because of this they will praise Yahweh, v. 26. Thus, the blessing and well-being of the people is intimately connected with the needs of an agricultural society. All this will be dependent upon, or made possible through, המורה לצדקה, v. 23, that Yahweh will give the people. What this phrase means has long been a matter of dispute. However, this is not the place for describing that history, but it should be mentioned that the versions differ in translating this phrase. The Vulgate renders it *doctorem* (or *pastorem*) *justitiae*; the Targum מלפיכון בזכו; Symmachus has τὸν ὑποδεικνύοντα. Thus, these versions have based their interpretations of מורה upon the hiph. of what has been considered as ירה III, "to teach, point one's finger at, instruct". The LXX on the other hand has τὰ βρώματα, "food", which means that one has read בְּרְיָה here instead of מורה,[1] which also seems to be the reading behind Vetus Latina's *escas justitiae*,[2] as well as the Peshiṭta's ܡܐܟܠܬܐ. מורה can also be seen as a hiph. ptc. of ירה I, "to throw, shoot, cast",[3] cf. Ugar. *yry/w*, or of ירה II, for which Köhler-Baumgartner's dictionary gives no translation. It has been doubted whether one really should have

---

* This chapter is a reprint of my article in *Supplements to Vetus Testamentum* XVII, 1969, pp. 25-36, and is used by permission of E. J. Brill, Leiden. Only a few changes and corrections have been made.

[1] The LXX is followed by, among others, J. A. Bewer, *Obadiah and Joel*, (ICC 26) 1911, pp. 115 f., H. W. Wolff, *Joel* (BK XIV: 5), 1963, pp. 64 f.

[2] It would not be difficult to read a poorly written מורה as בריה, cf. E. Sellin, *Das Zwölfprophetenbuch übersetzt und erklärt* (SKAT XII:1)²⁻³, 1929, pp. 167 f. For a survey of the different translations, see E. Sellin, *op. cit.*, pp. 167., A. S. Kapelrud, *Joel Studies*, 1948, pp. 114 f., H. W. Wolff, *Joel*, pp. 75 f.

[3] Thus J. Weingreen, "The Title Môrēh Ṣedek", *JSS* 6/61, pp. 169 f.

these three stems ירה; thus, for instance, Brown-Driver-Briggs'
dictionary, which only lists one stem ירה.[1]

In connection with this problem, one should note 2 Chr. 15:3,
where מורה is found referring to a priest. The phrase כהן מורה in this
verse can be translated "oracular priest".[2] J. Morgenstern has
maintained that the occurrence of *tōrāh* in this verse gives a sense
of "oracular decision" or "revelation" to the phrase.[3] In this passage,
מורה and תורה are so intimately connected that they are to be considered
as belonging to the same stem, cf. Mic. 4:2. Thus, one may be somewhat skeptical towards the idea of *tōrāh* as being a pure loan word,
the Akkadian *tertu* (from (*w*)*āru*). Rather, the Akkadian (*w*)*āru* and
the Hebrew ירה should be seen as etymologically the same, both
having as a derivate a t-preformative. Be this as it may, the question
here is whether there is any possibility of finding out what המורה in
Joel 2:23 means.

From the discussion concerning the stems, three meanings of מורה
have been deduced. First, it has been understood as an "archer" in
1 Sam. 31:3 and 1 Chr. 10:3. In both places, the form is plural,
מורים. In the latter passage occurs also the form היורים. The word is
connected with קשת, "bow"; thus, מורה and יורה mean the one who
shoots the bow.[4] Second, מורה is rendered with "rain" in the sense
of early rain. This is to be found in Joel 2:23, מורה ומלקוש, and also
in Ps. 84:7.[5] (It is doubtful that מורה would occur in Joel 2:23

---

[1] This is the same problem as with תורה, which has been derived from ירה
I, "to cast, throw"; in the hiph., "to shoot". That this verb in the hiph. may have
developed the meaning "to instruct" is not impossible to believe. An oracle is
thought of as giving the will of the deity. Therefore, all oracles show "the way of
the god"; they are his law. It should also be mentioned that some have seen the
term *tōrāh* as a loan-word, namely the Akkadian *tērtu*, "oracle(-message)", from
*tawirtum > *ta'irtum*, √ *wa'aru*, *āru*, "to send (a message)", cf. *Codex Ham.* III:51.
For a discussion about *tōrāh*, see G. Östborn, *Tōrāh in the Old Testament*, 1945,
pp. 5 ff. Östborn denies a connection between ירה, "to shoot, cast", and ירה,
"to instruct". I. Engnell (*Israel and the Law*, Symbolae Biblicae Upsaliensis 7/54,
2nd ed., p. 1 ff.) and A. Deissler (*Psalm* 119 (118), 1955, pp. 75 f.) both affirm
(correcting Östborn) that *tōrāh* is to be connected with the Akkad. *tērtu*.

[2] R. Meyer renders it "weisenden Priester" and says that in this particular
passage it means the high priest. According to Meyer, מורה can be a teacher, a
priest or a prophet, "Melkisedek von Jerusalem und Moresedek von Qumran",
SVT XV 1966, pp. 234 f.

[3] J. Morgenstern, "The Oldest Document of the Hexateuch", *HUCA* 4/27,
p. 108. Cf. Isa. 2:3 (and Mic. 6:2), "for from Zion goes forth תורה and from Jerusalem דבר יהוה". *Tōrāh* and Yahweh's word are here identical phenomena; the
word of Yahweh comes as an oracle.

[4] I. Rabinowitz, "The Guides of Righteousness", *VT* 8/58, p. 393, cf. Ps. 11:2.

[5] Cf. J. Barr, *Comparative Philology and the Text of the Old Testament*, 1968, p. 249.

designating the early rain twice. See below.) Third, מורה has been translated "teacher" or "oracle-giver", Prov. 5:13, cf. 6:13 and the above mentioned 2 Chr. 15:3. In 2 Kings 17:28 the priest who was sent back to Bethel after the fall of the northern kingdom, Israel, is said to have become a מורה for the people, a "teacher" of the religion of Yahweh, cf. also Isa. 30:20. In Isa. 9:14, the ordinary prophet is called מורה שקר, "teacher" or "oracle-giver of lies",[1] cf. Hab. 2:18. In Job 36:22, El is called a מורה. These passages all express the hiph. meaning, "to give oracles or priestly teachings"; cf. also Isa. 2:3, Hab. 2:19, Mic. 3:11, 2 Kings 12:3, Ex. 35:34, Lev. 14:57, 2 Chr. 6:27, 15:3.[2]

It has been maintained that אלון מורה at Shechem, mentioned in Gen. 12:6 and Dt. 11:30,[3] refers to the same tree as Judg. 9:37,[4] אלון מעוננים, "the oak, terebinth of the soothsayers". In Judg. 7:1, there occurs the phrase "the hill of המורה".[5] Note here the determinative. C. F. Burney sees this מורה as "the giver of tōrāh", explaining it as "decision or counsel purporting to be dictated by divine or supernatural agency."[6] A similar opinion is advocated by H. Gunkel.

---

[1] Cf. Morgenstern, "the prophet who makes false oracular utterances", "Amos Studies", *HUCA* 11/36, p. 50, n. 52., cf. R. Meyer, "ein Prophet, der Falsches weissagt", *SVT* XV 1966, p. 233. The title מורה הצדק in the Qumran texts could be translated "right teacher, leader". The term הצדק may be in "adjectical position", as, for instance, is הראש in כהן הראש, which A. Sperber renders with "headpriest", *A Historical Grammar of Biblical Hebrew*, 1966, p. 602, cf. also F. M. Cross, Jr., *The Ancient Library of Qumran*, 1961, p. 113, n. 3. However, צדק cannot always be said to be in an "adjectical position". For a discussion of this title in Qumran, see, for instance, M. R. Lehman, *Revue d'Qumran* 1/58-59, pp. 391 ff., T. H. Gaster, *The Dead Sea Scriptures in English Translation*, 1956, p. 5, M. Martin, *The Scribal Character of the Dead Sea Scrolls*, I, 1958, pp. 135 f., J. Weingreen, *JSS* 6/61, pp. 162 ff., G. Jeremias, *Der Lehrer der Gerechtigkeit*, 1963, pp. 308 ff. (with lit.), Per Wallendorf, מורה הצדק, *Rättfärdighetens lärare*, Helsingfors 1964. Cf. also R. Meyer, "'Elia' und 'Ahab'", in *Abraham unser Vater* (Feschrift O. Michel), 1963, pp. 362 ff., C. Roth, "The Teacher of Righteousness and the Prophecy of Joel", *VT* 13/63, pp. 91 ff.

[2] Another text which mentions the priest as teacher of Yahweh's tōrāh and as the keeper of the דעת יהוה is Mal. 2:7. Here also the prophet calls the priest a מלאך יהוה, a messenger of Yahweh. Can one surmise from this that the non-cultic prophetic activity of later monarchic times no longer had a function to fulfill?

[3] E. A. Speiser renders it "the guiding 'oracular' therebinth", *Genesis* (The Anchor Bible 1) 1964, p. 87.

[4] R. de Vaux, *Ancient Israel*, (McGraw-Hill Paperbacks) 1965, p. 279, cf. H. Gunkel, *Genesis* (GHK 1), 1902, p. 147.

[5] C. F. Burney, "the hill of the Oracle-giver", "The Topography of Gideon's Rout of the Midianites", *BZAW* 27/14 (Festschrift J. Wellhausen), p. 90, cf. *The Book of Judges*, 1918, pp. 205 ff., G. Östborn, *Tōrā*, pp. 25 f.

[6] *The Book of Judges*, p. 206, n.

Translating אלון מורה in Gen. 12:6 with "Orakelterebinthe", he explained מורה as a man of God, איש אלהים,[1] who understands how to give oracles. He also mentioned that the deity himself could be called a מורה,[2] as is shown by Job 36:22. In these places, מורה is referring to a person.

Now, the place called אלון מורה, Gen. 12:6, can be nothing other than a reference to a sanctuary, a holy place,[3] which was probably well known to both Canaanites and Israelites since ancient times as a famous site of oracular acitvity. It is also possible to see אלון מורה as a parallel expression to מקום שכם in the same verse, because מקום often signifies a cult place,[4] and the phrase עד מקום שכם is immediately followed by עד אלון מורה as an explanative apposition to Shechem's מקום.[5] In Gen. 12:6 ff. it is said that Abram built an altar at this cult place, and in this way, the sanctuary got its Israelite legitimation.[6]

---

[1] Cf. Johs. Lindblom, *Prophecy in Ancient Israel*, 1965, p. 94.

[2] *Genesis*, pp. 146 ff., cf. A. von Gall, *Altisraelitische Kultstätten* (BZAW 3, 1898), p. 111. Von Gall changed הַמֹּרִיָּה, Gen. 22:2, to המורה, *op. cit.*, pp. 112 ff. However, this is doubtful, cf. E. Nielsen, *Shechem*, 1955, pp. 333 f.

[3] Cf. J. Lindblom, "Die Vorstellung vom Sprechen Jahwes zu den Menschen im Alten Testament", *ZAW* 75/63, p. 277. Y. Aharoni, "Arad; Its Inscriptions and Temple", *BA* 31/68, p. 27.

G. Greiff considers אלון as originally having had the meaning "Hügel", "Was war ein elon?", *ZDPV* 76/60, pp. 164 ff. E. A. Speiser says that the "best technical evidence favors" the translation "terebinth", *Genesis*, p. 86. This may be the place to mention that H. Holzinger, among others, thought of אלה as a feminine form of אֵל, *Genesis*, 1898, p. 137, cf. E. Hammershaimb, *Amos*, 1946, p. 48, n. 1, F. Zimmermann, "ᵓEl and Adonai", *VT* 12/62, p. 193, W. F. Albright, *Yahweh and the Gods of Canaan*, 1968, p. 165. Thus the Old Testament may contain a word for goddess after all. Because of its close connection with the oak or terebinth, the אלה became the usual word for this kind of tree or for some other mighty tree, cf. Zimmermann, *op. cit.*, p. 193. For trees as deity symbols, see, for instance, A. Ermann, *Die Religion der Ägypter*, 1934, p. 153, W. Brede Kristensen, *The Meaning of Religion*, 1960, pp. 110 ff., G. Östborn, *Tōrā*, pp. 24 f., cf. H. Ringgren, *Israelite Religion*, 1966, p. 25, G. Widengren, *The King and the Tree of Life* (UUÅ 1951:4), pp. 8 f., I. Engnell, *The Call of Isaiah* (UUÅ 1949:4), pp. 49 f., K. Yaron, "The Dirge over the King of Tyre", *Annual of the Swedish Theological Institute* III, 1964, pp. 41 f. From Dt. 16:21 f. it is clear that the Israelites have had the wooden post, the ᵓashērāh, as a divine symbol; for this, cf. Ahlström, *Aspects of Syncretism in Israelite Religion*, 1963, pp. 50 ff., 57 ff.

[4] H. Gunkel, *Die Urgeschichte und die Patriarchen* (Die Schriften des AT I:1), 1921, p. 136., cf. B. W. Anderson, "The Place of Shechem in the Bible", *BA* 20/57, p. 11, F. F. Hvidberg, "The Canaanite Background of Gen. I-III", *VT* 10/60, p. 286, E. A. Speiser, *Genesis*, p. 86.

[5] אלון מצב in Judg. 9:6 may be another term for the same place. E. Nielsen maintains that since "the Amarna Age Shechem may have been the residental city of a king", *Shechem*, p. 238.

[6] That the Israelites took over an originally Canaanite royal ritual at Shechem,

It has been mentioned above that an oracle gives the answer and
the will of the deity; thus, it is quite right to render מורה as "teacher,
oracle-giver", and the hiph. הורה as "to teach, instruct." According
to J. Weingreen, it can also be used in a "purely forensic sense".[1] He
understands the phrase מורה שקר in Isa. 9:14 and Hab. 2:18 as a
person who "misdirects or distorts the law".[2] Thus, his conclusion
is that "the significance of this word [מורה] is not instructive, but
legal".[3] However, going back to the phrase מורה שקר, Isa. 9:14,
Hab. 2:18, the aspect of giving oracles is perhaps much more at hand
in both passages than is the legal activity. Isaiah condemns other
prophets as being false prophets, giving false oracles as if they were
the words of Yahweh. The prophet, who, together with the elder
and the honored one, was supposed to lead the people the right way,
is leading them astray, according to Isaiah. In Hab. 2:18, the phrase
is found in association with מַסֵּכָה, אֱלִיל, and פסל; i.e., statues of
deities, idols.[4] Therefore, the מורה שקר here must refer to these idols.
They are deities of lies, false deities; therefore their words cannot be
true, divine words.[5] Thus, one must conclude that Hab. 2:18 and
Isa. 9:14 portray an "oracle-giving" or "teaching" (= religion),
which, according to these prophets, is false.[6]

Thus far, it has been shown that מורה means "teacher, oracle-
giver", and it can be added that because it refers to the one who
gives the law, the divine will, it ought sometimes to be rendered
"leader". To impart the divine will to the people was a function of
the leader of the society, cf. Moses and Joshua.[7] This leader, as

---

see, among others, G. Östborn, *Tōrā*, pp. 67 f., E. Nielsen, "The Burial of Foreign
Gods", *StTh* 8/54, 1955, pp. 107 f., 121 f., *Shechem*, pp. 237 ff., B. W. Anderson,
BA 20/57, p. 11.

[1] He denies, however, that הורה makes any reference to "teaching, showing or
guiding", *JSS* 6/61, p. 171.

[2] *Op. cit.*, pp. 171 f.

[3] P. 173.

[4] Cf. Ahlström, *Aspects of Syncretism*, pp. 46 ff.

[5] J. Morgenstern, "a false revealer", *Some Significant Antecedents of Christianity*,
1966, pp. 3, 5, n. 7. H. Wildberger says the phrase concerns "das heidnische
Lügenorakel", *Jesaja* (BK X), p. 219.

[6] That Hab. 2:18 should deal only with the "deliberate distortion of justice
by the judges" (Weingreen, *op. cit.*, p. 171) is in my opinion an overinter-
pretation. Because Weingreen does not pay enough attention to the oracular
function which is inherent in the stem ירה, he has been lead to overemphasize the
judicial aspect.

[7] For Moses and Joshua as covenant mediators, see. E. W. Nicholson, *Deuteronomy and Tradition*, 1967, pp. 76 f., cf. G. Widengren, *Sakrales Königtum*, p. 29.

G. Widengren expresses it, was the possessor of the *tōrāh*. The king, "as the possessor and reader of the *tōrāh*, acts in the Temple ... service as a *mōreh*, a teacher of the law".[1] This is in accord with the king's covenantal function and thus also with the king as judge, cf. 1 Kings 7:7. The עדות he gets at the enthronement day may be a symbol of the *bĕrīt* [2] and of the divine *tōrāh*. The wisdom the king has as the wise ruler is received from Yahweh, "his father", when he is anointed. At that moment his heart becomes "changed", which means that he is believed to have received the divine spirit, the רוח of Yahweh. In other words, he is ritually "born anew".[3] This is the ideological—or one could as well say the theological—basis for the king's position as the head of the society. Everything ultimately depended upon him and his right relationship to Yahweh. The king had to maintain balance and harmony in the society, just as El or Yahweh had to maintain balance in the cosmos.[4] It can also be expressed thus: the king had to act "as the embodiment of 'righteousness' (צדק, צדקה)".[5] This was mainly done through the cult. As the "son of the deity", or as the "god's representative", the king was the "mediator of the god's will or 'law' ".[6] All this means that the king, properly speaking, is the one who brings the divine mysteries and blessings of life, *tōrāh*, *ṣĕdāqāh* and *mišpāṭ*, to the people, cf. Ps. 72, Isa. 16:5. He is the wise one on the throne, 2 Sam. 14:20, 1 Kings 5:10, cf. Prov. 8:15, 25:2, Isa. 11:2 f., 19:11, Ezek. 28:2 ff.[7]

The king was, as we know, also thought of as the רוח of his people, and it is also said that his people should live among the nations in the

---

[1] "King and Covenant", *JSS* 2/57, pp. 1 ff., p. 21, cf. *Sakrales Königtum*, 1955, pp. 29 f. See also G. Östborn, *Tōrā*, pp. 56 ff., 76 ff., E. R. Goodenough, "Kingship in Early Israel", *JBL* 48/29, pp. 169 ff., J. R. Porter, *Moses and Monarchy*, 1963, pp. 11 ff., 24 f.

[2] Cf. R. de Vaux, "Le roi d'Israël, vassal de Yahwé", *Mélanges E. Tisserant*, 1964, pp. 127 f.

[3] Ahlström, *ThZ* 18/62, p. 207.

[4] Cf. J. Pedersen, *Israel* III-IV, 1959, p. 792.

[5] A. R. Johnson, *Sacral Kingship*[2], 1967, p. 4.

[6] Östborn, *Tōrā*, p. 78. Östborn maintains that "the pre-Israelite Canaanite monarchs also possessed a 'law', which was likewise a kind of 'law of the covenant'", p. 83, cf. p. 84.

[7] Cf., among others, H. Ringgren, *Word and Wisdom*, 1947, pp. 89 ff., N. W. Porteous, "Royal Wisdom", *SVT* 3/55, pp. 247 ff., Ahlström, "Oral and Written Transmission", *HTR* 59/66, p. 76, n. 25.

In Prov. 25:3, it is said that just as nobody can investigate the heights of the heavens and the depths of the earth, so also can nobody investigate the king's heart or mind. For the above mentioned passage, Isa. 11:2 ff., the Targum renders verse 3 as מורה ית דינא.

king's shadow, Lam. 4:20.[1] As the *rūaḥ* of his people, the king's *ṣĕdāqāh* was dependent upon his keeping the covenant, Ps. 89:29 ff.[2] The covenant was established in the cultus, and there all its stipulations were made known.[3] There was no life without a rightly established and rightly kept covenant. The king's cultic function was to guarantee this. In fulfilling his cultic duties in accord with the *ṣĕdāqāh*, the king fulfilled the function of giving life. This role is expressed in the idea of the king as rain, or as the one who causes the rain to come down.[4] For instance, in Ps. 72, which mentions the blessings that the king gives to his people and to his country, one finds the concept of the king being like the rain: he is "like the rain, falling on the mown grass, like showers that drip on (water) [5] the earth", v. 6, cf. Prov. 16:15. This is a picture of the king as life-giver. In verses 1-2 and 7 are found the motifs of the king as giver and upholder of right and righteousness; in vv. 4 and 12 f., he is the defender of the poor and needy. Furthermore, he is described as the one who causes abundance of grain and fruit, vv. 3, 16. The "center" of the psalm is vv. 5-7 where the king's life is compared with the duration of sun and moon, v. 5, and in v. 6, he is, as said, compared with rain, which in v. 7 is said

---

[1] Cf. W. Rudolph, *Die Klagelieder* (SKAT 17:3), pp. 65. f., G. Widengren, *The King and the Tree of Life*, pp. 57 f., A. R. Johnson, *Sacral Kingship*[2], p. 2. For Akkadian parallels to the king as giver of life and abundance, see the collection in I. Engnell, *Studies*, p. 191 ff., cf. also H.-J. Kraus, *Psalmen*, p. 497.

[2] Cf. K.-Hj. Fahlgren, *ṣĕdāḳā*, nahestehende und entgegengesetzte Begriffe im Alten Testament, 1932, pp. 78 ff., Ahlström, *Psalm 89*, p. 81.

[3] It has become very common to compare the Israelite covenant idea with the Near Eastern political treaties, a treatment which has almost given as a result a new kind of "patternistic" approach. Of course, political and religious phenomena often go together, both in acts and words. However, it should also be noted that there exists a more direct parallel to the Hebrew phenomenon of a covenant between a deity and a king. Such a covenant is known, e.g., from Sumer. King Urukagina of Lagash says that Ningirsu has given him kingship, and that he, Urukagina, made a covenant with the deity, F. Thureau-Dangin, *Die Sumerischen und Akkadischen Königsinschriften*, (VAB I:1), 1907, p. 51, cf. P. van Imschoot, "L'alliance dans l'AT", *Nouvelle Rev. Théol.* 74/52, pp. 791 f., Ahlström, *Psalm 89*, pp. 51 f., S. N. Kramer, *Studia Biblica et Orientalia* III, 1959, p. 194, n. 3, M. J. Buss, "The Covenant Theme in Historical Perspective", *VT* 16/66, pp. 502 f. P. van Imschoot also mentions an example with the Sabean king Karibaʾilu Watar, *op. cit.*, p. 792. The importance of the names Baal-Berith and El-Berith should be stressed here once more, Judg. 8:33, 9:4, 46, which show that the concept of the deity as a partner in a treaty or covenant was familiar to the Canaanites, cf. R. Kittel, *Geschichte Israels*[5] II, p. 308 [384], n. 2, cf. also pp. 42 [95] ff.

[4] Cf. A. E. Cowley, *The Samaritan Liturgies* II, 1909, p. 786; 9 ff.

[5] For זרזיף in v. 6, cf. the Judaeo-Aram. זרזיפא, cf. Aage Bentzen, *Salmerne*, 1939, p. 414.

to make righteousness flourish. Here we have rain quite clearly connected to righteousness. This is not merely a matter of "courtstyle",
as so often has been maintained since the days of H. Gressmann.[1]
These motifs are expressions for a religious belief. These royal functions had their foundation and were actualized in the cult, probably
in the annual autumnal festival.[2] In this festival, there was an intimate
relationship between rain and righteousness, something which is quite
natural considering that this feast was held at the time when the early
rain, יורה, was expected.

Here one should note that the rain can be said to "teach the way".[3]
From Solomon's prayer at the consecration of the temple at the
autumn festival, one learns that Yahweh's "teaching of the way"
and the phenomenon of rain are closely connected, 1 Kings 8:35 f.,
2 Chr. 6:27. Solomon asks Yahweh to listen to his prayer and to
forgive the sins of the people and to teach them, תורם, his way and give
them rain.[4] In Job 36:27 it is said that El, who in v. 22 is called a
מורה, "draws up (גרע) the drops of water", and then the skies pour

---

[1] *Der Ursprung der isr.-jüd. Eschatologie* (FRLANT 6), 1905, pp. 258 ff., cf.
H. Gunkel, *Die Psalmen*, 1925, p. 7. According to R. E. Murphy, verse 5 is more
a matter of hyperbole than court-style, *A Study of Psalm* 72 (71), 1948, p. 72.
Perhaps, but then this could aslo be said about several other theological statements.

[2] For non-Israelite parallels to the motif of the king associated with water and
rain, cf. Engnell, *Studies*, pp. 39, 44. Also, the prophets associate the messiah with
rain, B. Vawter, *A Path through Genesis*, 1965, p. 56. One should also note that in
I QH VIII 16, the מורה says that God has put something that is like early rain in
his mouth, A. Dupont-Sommer, "Le Livre de hymns découvert près de la mer
Morte", *Semitica* 7/57, p. 65, J. Maier, *Die Texte vom Toten Meer* I, 1960, p. 94,
II p. 99 f., G. Jeremias, *Der Lehrer der Gerechtigkeit*, 1963, p. 313.
In his treatment of 2 Sam. 21, A. S. Kapelrud has shown the connection between
the king on the one side and welfare and fertility on the other. The text tells about
a famine that has long plagued the country and one learns that this famine could
be considered as an omen showing "that David was not the right man on the
throne of Saul", David, therefore, had to find a way to stop the famine "through
some device which might serve to promote fertility". Therefore he sacrificed the
descendants of Saul and in so doing he also "got rid of the only family which
could seriously threaten his position", "King and Fertility: A Discussion of II
Sam. 21:1-14", *Interpretationes ad vetus testamentum pertinentes Sigmundo Mowinckel
septuagenario missae*, 1955, pp. 117, 121. For the king as being responsible for the
rites of atonement and mourning, cf. 2 Sam. 24.

[3] *Tōrāh* compared with water and rain is a common motif in Judaism, H. L.
Strack and P. Billerbeck, *Kommentar zum NT aus Talmud und Midrash* II, 1924,
p. 434, cf. R. Patai, "The 'Control of Rain' in Ancient Palestine", *HUCA* 14/39,
pp. 251 ff.

[4] Cf. Zech. 14:17 ff. This text may be taken as an indication that rain and
fertility aspects are connected with the succoth festival, P. Volz, *Das Neujahrsfest Jahwes*, 1912, pp. 30 ff., B. Otzen, *Studien über Deuterosacharja*, 1964, p. 211.

it down upon man in abundance, and by flashes of lightening, El
judges the peoples, v. 29 ff. Here one sees how rain and judgment are
closely bound together. It is, therefore, no surprise that the LXX has
rendered the Hebrew מורה with δυνάστης in Job 36:22.[1] The one who
judges the people is the ruler.

A few other texts should be noted. Ps. 68:8 ff. combines rain and
justice in a theophany which can be said to give salvation to the
people. These motifs also occur in Isa. 45:8:

> Let drop, O heavens, from above,
> and let rain down (יזלו) justice (צדק);
> let the earth open,
> that salvation may sprout forth,
> and it may cause righteouness (צדקה) to spring up also.

Or, compare Hos. 10:12:

> Sow for yourselves according to righteounsness (לצדקה),[2]
> gather in according to חסד;
> break up new ground,
> yes, it is time to seek Yahweh,
> that he may come and rain (יורה) justice (צדק) upon you.

It is understandable that the Vulgate has translated יורה here with
"teach", *docebit vos iustitiam*. However, the picture given in this verse
makes it more probable that the original meaning of יורה here is "to
cause it to rain, to let it rain justice", which, of course, may very well
be understood as "teaching the right way". The symbolism of the
verse is that there will not be a good harvest unless Yahweh's צדק
can "rain down" from heaven.[3] In this text there is a polemic against
the Canaanized cult in Israel, the northern kingdom. The prophet is
underlining what for him is the only way to obtain blessing and a
good future, namely, through the right worship of Yahweh, through
the correct Yahwistic cultic performances, which, for the prophet,
is the "right cultic way". Then Yahweh will give the rain with right

---

[1] R. Meyer says, "Schwerlich liegt in δυνάστης eine Fehlübertragung von
MWRH vor", "Melkisedek von Jerusalem und Moresedek von Qumran", *SVT*
15/66, p. 236. Meyer translates *mōreh ṣedeq* with "wahrer Herrscher", p. 237.

[2] Cf. H. S. Nyberg, *Studien zum Hoseabuche*, 1935, p. 83, H. W. Wolff, *Hosea*
(BK XIV:1), p. 232, W. Rudolph, *Hosea*, (SKAT XIII:1), 1966, p. 200.

[3] For *ṣedeq* as a hypostasis, see, for example, H. Ringgren, *Word and Wisdom*,
pp. 150 f. Originally, Ṣedeq was a god; for lit., see Ahlström, *Psalm 89*, p. 79,
n. 5, R. A. Rosenberg, "The God Ṣedeq", *HUCA* 36/65, pp. 161 ff.

and righteousness.[1] With this passage should be compared Hos. 6:3, which says that Yahweh, not Baal,[2] comes as the rain, גשם, "as the late rain (מלקוש) he will rain (יורה) upon the earth".[3]

The relationship between the "teaching of the way" (i.e., the right cult, religion, cf. Ps. 27:11) and the rain occurs also in Isa. 30:20 ff.[4] It is said that Yahweh, the מורה, will give rain and seed for the ground and there will be plenty of good produce. Here again, Yahweh—not Baal—is the one who gives or teaches "the right way" which gives rain and blessings. This was obviously one of the most difficult concepts the prophets tried to get through to the people. In this passage, one finds a strong emphasis upon the right words, oracles, tōrāh, from the right deity who gives the right order, צדקה, fertility and blessings.[5] This can, for instance, be illustrated by Zech. 10:1 f., where the prophet says that the people will ask Yahweh for rain at the time of the latter rain, בעת מלקוש, v. 1. As a contrast to this, v. 2 says that the těrāphīm are nothing other than vanity, speakers of wickedness, and the diviners (oracle-givers)[6] see visions of lie. These passages show us not only the connection between rain and fertility as being given by the deity (here Yahweh), but also the connection between rain and oracles. Thus, the deity may be called מורה לצדקה, cf. Mic. 4:2, Ps. 32:8.

It is now possible to return to Joel 2:23. As mentioned before,

---

[1] Cf. Am. 5:24, Lev. 26:3 ff.

[2] "When Israelite desert tribes penetrated into the land of Canaan...they entered a world where all food for animal and man was due to the rain sent by Ba'al", F. F. Hvidberg, Weeping and Laughter in the Old Testament, 1962, p. 79, cf. A. Soggin, "Der offiziell geförderte Synkretismus in Israel während des 10. Jahrhunderts", ZAW 78/66, p. 180.

[3] According to F. Perles, יורה should be read יָרֶוה, Analekten zur Textkritik des Alten Testaments, 1895, p. 90. So also several commentators; for instance, J. Johansson, Profeten Hosea, 1899, p. 160, E. Sellin, SKAT XII:1, p. 66, J. Lippl and J. Theis, Die Zwölf kleinen Propheten (HSAT), 1937, p. 50, H. W. Wolff, Hosea, p. 134, T. H. Robinson, HAT 14, 1964, p. 24, A. Deissler and M. Delcor, Les Petits Prophètes (La Sainte Bible), 1961, p. 74. This suggested reading is also in accord with the Syriac ܪܡܟܘܐܘ. H. S. Nyberg maintains that the Masoretic text "ist ganz im Ordnung: יורה, 'benetzen', ein der späteren Zeit nicht mehr geläufiges Verbum, wurde durch ירוה ersetzt bzw. in מורה 'Frühregen' korrigiert", Studien zum Hoseabuche, p. 40. However, יורה may be a noun here. Thus, one has in this verse first the mentioning of rain, גשם, and then in the parallel half-verse, the explanation of what kind of rain; namely, the two important seasonal rains, מלקוש and יורה. Then there occurs an asyndetic construction in the last half-verse.

[4] Cf. Prov. 5:13 ff.

[5] Cf. Dt. 11:13 f.

[6] Note the choice of terminology here. When the prophet is rejecting the prophets of the těrāphīm, he uses the word הקוסמים.

מורה probably does not mean rain in both places in this verse. It is said that Yahweh gives the people המורה, and then he will let the rain, גשם, come down. The next line explains, then, what kind of rain it will be: early rain, מורה, and the latter rain, מלקוש.[1] Furthermore, when one takes into consideration that in 23b the determinative form, המורה, occurs (which is not the case in the next line), then, considering what has been said above, המורה in v. 23b may refer to a person, the one Yahweh will give to the people, in order that this person might show them the "right" cultic way causing rain to come and all its blessings with it.[2]

After what has been said, it is possible to see המורה as a title: "the teacher, leader, oracle-giver", who, as the leader of the cult congregation, "teaches the right cultic way", according to which צדקה is established and rain and fertility are given to the land and the people. Thus, I cannot agree with A. S. Kapelrud in his opinion that the translation, "teacher of justice", could be "by no means adequate to the context". This translation, he says, "would be rather out of place in this enumeration of Yahweh's great deeds".[3] On the contrary, it is much more adequate than perhaps it seems to be,[4] because this is one of the great deeds of Yahweh through which the other great deeds are done, cf. להפליא, 2:26. In a way, the word "justice" is a translation for the Hebrew צדקה, but "justice" does not encompass the same breadth of meaning as ṣĕdāqāh did for the Hebrews.[5] The preposition ל in the construction לצדקה המורה announces that המורה will be the one who gives, or is in agreement with, or acts according to the צדקה. He can be seen as the "personification" of the צדקה, the one who establishes the צדקה. Because of him there will be rain, both early

---

[1] Cf. Hosea 6:3.

[2] C. von Oreilli, among others, understood המורה as the prophet himself, *The Twelve Minor Prophets*, 1893, p. 90. He also maintained that the translation must be "teacher" because of 1 Kings 8:36 and 2 Chr. 6:27, *op. cit.*, p. 90. Cf. also A. Merx, *Die Prophetie des Joel*, 1879, pp. 72 f., M. Schumpp, *Das Buch der Zwölf Propheten* (Herders Bibelkomentar X/2), 1950, p. 86.

[3] *Joel Studies*, p. 115.

[4] "Rain at the proper time" is a common translation; cf. Deissler-Delcor, *Les petits prophetes*, pp. 162 f., Kapelrud, *op. cit.*, p. 115, H. Ringgren, *Israelite Religion*, p. 83, cf. M. Dahood, "rain in abundance", *Psalms* I (The Anchor Bible 16), 1966, p. 146.

[5] E. Sellin, "Lehrer zur Gerechtigkeit", *SKAT* XII:1, p. 167. T. H. Robinson gives the alternatives; "Entweder 'in rechten Masse' oder 'als ein Zeichen der (wiederhergestellten) Gerechtigkeit'," *HAT* 14, p. 64. Sellin, however, prefers to follow Ehrlich and change the text so that אות "sign", should be read instead of מורה, *op. cit.*, p. 168.

rain and late rain through his perfect cultic performance and "teaching", and this will give fertility and life. Thus, it will be an ideal time. Without him there would be no rain or fertility, no life; in other words, no *ṣĕdāqāh*. This shows that the prophet is quite bound to cultic categories in his thinking.

The conclusion to be drawn here is that המורה in Joel 2:23 designates the leader and the covenant mediator of the Jerusalem temple cultus.[1] Upon the "teaching" of this man and upon his cultic actions everything, religiously speaking, depended.[2] The leader of the Jerusalem cult, as well as the shepherd of the people,[3] was the king in the pre-exilic era and the high-priest in post-exilic times. Therefore, when the oracle says that Yahweh will give the people המורה לצדקה, one could ask the question: will this one come and replace someone else who has been taken away? Does this text, therefore, refer not only to the cult, but also to the political situation?[4] It is not possible to give a definitive answer to this question. However, a probable time would be the first decades of the existence of the second temple.[5] The cultic apparatus in this temple cannot be assumed to have differed very much from that of the pre-exilic temple in the last decades of its existence[6]—even though the influence of Ezekiel may have already played some role. One has to remember that no cultic (i.e., temple) tradition other than the pre-exilic one was known or acknowledged.[7]

---

[1] For a comparison of the position of the *hammōreh liṣdāqāh* as the cult leader, one should note with R. Meyer that "der gleichsetzung von *môrâ* und *mārê* im sinne von 'Herr' oder 'Herrscher' in unmittelbare Nähe von *mælæk* und *ʾādôn* kommt, die sich beide ebenfalls in Zusammensetzungen mit *sædæq* belegen lassen". Meyer goes on to say that for those who stood in the zadoqite and priestly tradition of Jerusalem, *môreh ṣedeq* meant more than just a "teacher of righteousness". It was synonymous with Melkizedeq who in one person united both "Priester- und Fürstentum", the one who ruled on Zion, *Festschrift O. Michel*, p. 363.

[2] Cf. C. Plöger who writes: "In jedem Falle erfolgt die Wiedergutmachung durch Jahwe in Verbindung mit den kultisch-rituellen Massnahmen der Zionsgemeinde", *Theokratie und Eschatologie* (WMANT 2), 1959, p. 120.

[3] Cf. Mic. 5:3, where it says that the future king shall רעה, "feed", his flock.

[4] Having such a cultic-political background in mind, it is understandable that המורה in this text has been given a messianic interpretation, cf. the discussion by Merx, *Die Prophetie des Joel*, pp. 72 ff., 242.

[5] See the arguments given in the next chapter.

[6] The foundation ritual and the dedication of Zerubbabel's temple, Ezra 3:10 f., 4:16 ff., are, according to J. M. Myers, mainly in agreement with the dedication of the temple of Solomon, I Kings 8:22 ff., 2 Chr. 7:4 ff., Myers, *Ezra, Nehemiah* (The Anchor Bible 14), 1965, p. 53.

[7] Cf. J. Morgenstern, "The Cultic Setting of the 'Enthronement Psalms'", *HUCA* 35/64, p. 38.

Thus, chapters 1-2 in the book of Joel can be seen to suit the period of the first decades of the temple of Zerubbabel as well as the pre-exilic period. The liturgical performances had to be—if possible— the same in the second temple. With the new temple should come a new, ideal time. Zerubbabel was to reestablish the Davidic dynasty. The expectations of the ideal time were to be fulfilled. As is known, nothing of this happened.

Could one assume, then, that Joel's book reflects the time after Zerubbabel had disappeared from the political scene? If so the prophet, in using the phrase המורה לצדקה, promised the people a new leader and teacher. There was still hope. But now, when the prophet gave forth the oracle, he had to choose a phrase which was quite intelligible for his own people, but politically unintelligible for the Persian officials.

CHAPTER SIX

THE TIME OF THE BOOK

One will recall that Joel 2:23 presents some aspects of fertility. The word צדקה, which can be called the central concern of the book of Joel, also expresses some of the aspects of fertility. As a continuation of these aspects, the following verse, Joel 2:24, gives the promise that Yahweh is the one that will fill the threshing floors and the wine presses of the country. In so doing, he will effect a restoration to the people (2:25) for the disaster caused by the locusts he had sent. This will be the result of the re-established צדקה by the מורה. Specifically mentioning גרן and יקב (threshing floor and wine press), Yahweh tells the people through the oracle that he, not Baal, is the only one who gives the harvest! As mentioned before, the two terms גרן and יקב sometimes designate cult places where agricultural rites of fertility have taken place; cf. Hos. 9:1 f.[1] When Hosea 9:2 says that גרן and יקב "shall not feed them" (לא ירעם), it means that these places and their deities cannot perform the task of being the shepherds of the people. Only Yahweh is their true shepherd; only he can feed them. Here in Joel 2:24 Yahweh underlines that he is their god that gives the people a good harvest. Thus, he is their shepherd, and nobody else. This means that at the time of Joel, Yahweh was not yet acknowledged as the only god, not even as the real giver of fertility.

Again can be stated the fact that in the time of Joel, the Judean people did not worship Yahweh alone, and, as far as can be concluded from Joel, this was the case even in the temple cultus. One can then ask as to what time such a cult could possibly have existed in the

---

[1] Cf. above, pp. 46 f. and see my discussion in *VT* 11/61, pp. 115 ff. As an illustration from Mesopotamia, one can mention that "the marriage of Nabu at Calah was celebrated on a threshing floor", S. Smith, "The Practice of Kingship in Early Semitic Kingdoms", *MRK*, p. 43. In arguing against H. Gottlieb (*DTT* 26/63, pp. 167-171). B. Albrektson asks: "Is it altogether improbable that a prophet in an agricultural people could have come to use the metaphor of threshing without the intermediation of the cult?", *History and Gods*, 1967, p. 72, n. 14. It is certainly not improbable, but in the light of the fact that harvest always was connected with some rites, the word גרן always carried such associations. Cf. also A. S. Kapelrud, *Joel Studies*, pp. 117 f. H. W. Wolff does not discuss גרן and יקב at all. He only reaffirms that "alles ist aus der nachexilischen Situation einer Erntenot verständlich", *Joel*, p. 33.

Jerusalem temple—what time is reflected in Joel's utterances?
Perhaps a better question would be whether there could have been
any time other than the pre-exilic time. Is it conceivable that such a
cult could have existed in the second temple? If so, then one must
determine exactly when in the post-exilic Jerusalem temple such a
cult tradition occurred—a cult tradition which was patterned after
the pre-exilic, agricultural traditions.[1] Prior to Ezra and Nehemiah
would be the logical time. From what has been said above, the book
of Malachi may give some indications for the existence of non-
Yahwistic cult practices in the post-exilic temple.[2] Thus, the time
from 515 B.C. down to the time of Malachi should come under
consideration. However, before pursuing this line of reasoning, other
arguments and indications for the possible date of Joel have to be
dealt with.

The results of chapter 1 of this study indicated that some of the
terms and phrases in Joel point to a late rather than an early period
of the Hebrew language. At the end of the third chapter, it was
mentioned that Joel's understanding of the importance of the temple
cult was rather close to that found in Haggai and Zechariah.[3] In
Hag. 1:5-11 the crop-failure and the bad harvests as well as the poor
living conditions are due to the fact that the temple has not been
built. This means that the צדקה cannot be established. In the discussion
concerning Joel's mentioning of the valley of Shittim, it was assumed
that the acacia trees were of a lasting value, and that, because of their
usefulness in the making of cult objects, they would still have the
same importance in the future.[4] Here one should note that, as far as

---

[1] See above, p. 109.

[2] Cf. above, pp. 27 f., 49 f. An indication for the existence of cult practices of this
kind in Judah may be found in Isa. 57:13; cf. J. L. McKenzie, *Second Isaiah* (The
Anchor Bible 20), 1968, p. 158. For קבוציך as meaning "gods", cf. S. Gevirtz, "A
New Look at an Old Crux: Amos 5, 26", *JBL* 87/68, p. 268. For Isa. 57:3-13, cf.
also D. R. Jones, "The Cessation of Sacrifice after the Destruction of the Temple
in 586 B.C.", *JThSt* 14/63, pp. 18 f. P. R. Ackroyd calls these cult phenomena a
"revival of Canaanite practice, or allusions of wrong thinking described in the
conventional terms of idolatry", *Exile and Restoration*, 1968, p. 229, n. 43. This
seems to be less accurate. This is rather a continuation of the old cult practices,
of the religion that was natural in this country. This also shows how difficult the
task of the prophets had been.

[3] Cf. J. M. Myers, "Some Considerations Bearing on the Date of Joel", *ZAW*
74/62, pp. 193 ff. Thus, Kapelrud is accurate when he says that "Joel is influenced
by Jeremiah", *Joel Studies*, p. 190. This does not necessarily mean that he must be a
contemporary of Jeremiah.

[4] See above, pp. 94 f.

can be judged, the use of cedar was impossible—at least in the amounts used in the Solomonic temple—in the construction of the second temple. Ezra 3:7 mentions plans of shipping cedars from Lebanon to Joppa, but from Ch. 4 it is learned that other Palestinean groups prevented the temple from being built. When the temple finally could be built, one hears nothing according to Hag. 1:7 about cedar trees. The prophet only tells the people to go up into the hills and get wood for the building. Thus it is not out of place to assume that greater quantities of acacia wood were used than formerly; thus they could have been of current interest in the days of Joel.

This investigation has also maintained that Joel did not prophesy during the time when apocalyptic was popular, but that he may be seen as a source of inspiration for the later apocalyptics.[1] This would lead one to think of Joel as belonging to a late prophetic time.

To this could be added the results of S. Mowinckel's investigation of the day of Yahweh mentioned above.[2] Mowinckel has maintained that the cosmic aspect of the day of Yahweh has been pushed into the background in the latest stage of the prophetic form of this motif. This may be so. Mowinckel's work results in the judgment that the יום יהוה in Joel—as well as in Zech. 14—belongs to this latest stage of the prophetic form of this motif, namely the Judahite hope of national restitution.[3] What should be noticed here is that in Joel 4:9 ff., the nations come to Jerusalem not of their own free will, but because Yahweh has called them; cf. Ez. 38:4, 39:2, Zech. 14:2. In *summoning* them to Jerusalem, Yahweh intends to judge them and to destroy them. This is not the usual way the גוים are pictured in the Old Testament psalms and prophecies. As a rule, they are in the prophets the means by which Yahweh punishes his own people.[4] Therefore, with Mowinckel, one could conceive of the change in the motif as pointing to a late period.[5]

Th. Chary has understood the book of Malachi as having been preoccupied with the renewal of the traditional cult. In effecting this renewal, Malachi wanted to reform the cult and in some way to cut off the ties which connected the post-exilic cult with the pre-exilic

---

[1] Cf. above, p. 96.

[2] "Jahves dag", *NTT* 59/58, pp. 1-56, 209-229.

[3] *Op. cit.*, pp. 50 f.

[4] Cf. Joel 1-2. Being a cult prophet Joel has used the liturgical pattern of the cultic holy war, but in chapter 4 he has somewhat changed the structure of the motif.

[5] *NTT* 59/58, p. 50; cf. G. von Rad, *Old Testament Theology* II, pp. 293 f.

one. Moreover, in his zeal for a pure religion, Malachi should have
been somewhat influenced by Zoroastrian doctrines.[1] These aspects
are not found in Joel. At the time of Malachi, Persian concepts may
very well have been known outside Persia, and may have exerted
influence in some circles within the Persian empire. Joel, on the
other hand, is concerned about the preservation of the old Jerusalemite
cult—a preservation which was free from its "Baalistic ballast"; the
only true way for him. Thus, Joel could belong to a time prior to
the impact of Persian influences in Judah.

Furthermore, it should be underlined that Malachi gives a very
detailed criticism of the cultic apparatus and of the priests. As far as
can be known from the book of Malachi, there seems to have been
more negligence of most of the cultic rules and statutes than is the
case in the time of Joel. Also, the ethical demands are more stressed
in Malachi than in Joel.[2] From all this, one may conclude that Joel
belongs to a time when the cult had not yet "decayed" in such a way
as it had in the time of the prophet Malachi.

Some decades ago, W. F. Albright advocated that the book of Joel
belonged to "the period of Haggai". The mentioning of the wall in
2:7, 9 "proves nothing" concerning the date, he maintained, because
it could very well be that "some sort of rampart around the city was
constructed before the liquidation of Zerubbabel by the Persians".[3]
This may have been so. In this connection it is of some importance to
note how the enemy will conquer the city. The description in Joel
2:7, 9 uses phenomena that are to be associated with an army overrunning a city, but he also refers to the enemies in such a way that
one is reminded of the Akkadian female demon, Lamaštu, who often
enters houses via the windows.[4] From the description of the enemies
as an army overrunning the city, it would be difficult to argue that
one special word, as חומה, must be singled out as pointing to a particular historic event. Would it be possible that here one has to deal
with the same kind of phenomenon as in Jer. 41:5? This verse
mentions that, after the destruction of the Solomonic temple, eighty

---

[1] *Les prophètes et le culte à partir de l'exil*, pp. 182 f. Cf. also S. Mowinckel, *op. cit.*,
pp. 35 f.

[2] According to E. Hammershaimb, the ethical admonitions in Malachi "sound
like clichés merely, pale reminiscences of the older prophets of doom", *Some
Aspects of Old Testament Prophecy from Isaiah to Malachi*, 1966, p. 109.

[3] Albright (in a review of R. H. Pfeiffer, Introduction to the OT) *JBL* 61/42,
p. 120.

[4] Cf. S. M. Paul, "Cuneiform Light on Jer. 9:20", *Biblica* 49/68, pp. 373 ff.

men from the province of the former northern kingdom came to Jerusalem with offerings for the temple of Yahweh, בית יהוה.[1] The temple, as well as the walls, had been destroyed; yet, they existed in some remnant fashion. Their remains were there, and perhaps parts of the wall were still standing.

When discussing the city wall of Jerusalem, one should note that Neh. 3:8 contains a hint to the effect that some parts of the wall were not completely torn down. Nehemiah relates the rebuilding of the wall by Nehemiah's men, and in so doing they did not extend it to the old "Broad Wall". The text reads: ויעזבו ירשלם עד החומה הרחבה, "and they left out (abandoned) Jerusalem unto the Broad Wall".[2] This means that the whole area of the late, pre-exilic Jerusalem was not encircled by Nehemiah's wall.[3] This passage may also be understood as indicating that this part of the old wall system was not completely damaged.[4] C. G. Tuland has drawn attention here to the choice of words in Neh 3. Sometimes the verb בנה, "to build", is used, but several times the text has החזיק, "to strengthen", "to repair".[5] This choice of verbs may also point to the fact that there were several parts of the wall that were only repaired and not completely rebuilt again, cf. Neh. 2:13,[6] if the passage really refers to the wall destroyed by the Babylonians.[7] It may be natural to assume that the walls had been partly repaired immediately after the return from Babylon, but that they later were destroyed or weakened by attacks from neighboring peoples.

So far in this discussion, serious doubts have been expressed to the thesis that חומה necessarily refers to the wall that Nehemiah had repaired. From this point, one can go one further step in discussing the time of the book. Albright has pointed to the fact that Joel 4:8

---

[1] K. Galling maintains that the foundations of the temple were not completely destroyed, *Zur Geschichte Israels im persischen Zeitalter*, 1964, p. 129, cf. pp. 130 f.

[2] Thus, for example, the Swedish Bible Transl. For a discussion of this chapter, see C. G. Tuland, "*ZB* in Nehemiah 3:8", *Andrews University Seminary Studies* V, 1967, pp. 169 ff.

[3] Cf. K. Kenyon, "Excavations in Jerusalem", *BA* 27/64, p. 45, and "Israelite Jerusalem", *Near Eastern Archaeology in the Twentieth Century*, p. 247.

[4] Tuland, *op. cit.*, p. 176, cf. M. Avi-Yonah, "The Walls of Nehemiah—a Minimalist View", *IEJ* 4/54, p. 241.

[5] *Op. cit.*, p. 178.

[6] Cf. A. Šanda, *Die Bücher der Könige übersetzt und erklärt* (EHAT IX:2), 1912, p. 387. For a resumé concerning the discussion about the walls see J. M. Myers, *Ezra, Nehemiah* (The Anchor Bible 14), 1965, pp. 112 ff.

[7] Cf. below, p. 120.

and the mention of the Sabeans as slave traders establishes a time "not later than the sixth century, since the Mineans controlled Arab trade in the following centuries".[1] This is a very important piece of information, not only because it gives the latest possible date for the book, but also because it gives very little room for seeing 4:4-8 as a secondary insertion, as has often been maintained.[2] If the Sabeans were loosing their control of the trade-routes around 500 B.C.,[3] then the book of Joel must have been composed shortly before or around 500 B.C.[4]

How does all this harmonize with the mentioning of the Philistines in 4:4 and with the sons of the Ionians in 4:6? At the beginning of the post-exilic era, the Philistines were no longer a union of city states. Nebuchadressar had given them the same treatment as Judah,[5] which means that it would be difficult to see them as selling the Judeans as slaves in the period immediately following 604 or 586 B.C. After the destruction of the city states, the term פלשת גלילות, 4:4, can be seen as denoting a part of the Phoenician-Palestine area close to Judah. Even if the independence of the Philistines had completely disappeared, their usual trade business may have been resumed in the later, exilic period and thereafter. Since it is known that the slave trade still flourished in the sixth century B.C., at least to 538 B.C., a post-exilic date for this passage is probable.[6]

What then about the Ionians? According to R. H. Pfeiffer, the passage Gen. 10:2 ff. (which he dates in the fifth century), and the list of the nations mentioned in it, is a text that clearly "reflects the history of Asia Minor and of the Mediterranean during the century

---

[1] *JBL* 61/42, p. 120. Cf. F. W. Winnett, "The Place of the Mineans in the history of Pre-islamic Arabia", *BASOR* 73/39, pp. 3 ff. Cf. also Isa. 45:14, Ezek, 27:22 ff., Job 1:15, 6:19.

[2] See for instance H. W. Wolff, *Joel*, p. 3, J. Lindblom, *Prophecy in Ancient Israel*, p. 277, E. Sellin—G. Fohrer, *Einleitung in das Alte Testament*[10], 1965, p. 470. A. S. Kapelrud maintains that there are no "grounds for detaching it from other sections" of the book, *Joel Studies*, p. 159.

[3] Cf. M. Rostovtzeff, *Caravan Cities*, 1932, p. 23.

[4] Albright dates the book in "the critical years between 522 and 517 B.C.", *JBL* 61/42, p. 120, cf. Myers, *ZAW* 74/62, pp. 186 ff.

[5] Cf. H. Tadmor, "Philistia under Assyrian Rule", *BA* 29/66, p. 102, T. C. Mitchell, "Philistia" in D. Winton Thomas (ed.), *Archaeology and Old Testament Study*, 1967, p. 416.

[6] See J. M. Myers, *ZAW* 74/62, pp. 186 ff., 190, also S. Dubnov, *History of the Jews from the Beginning to Early Christianity* I, p. 367. For pre-exilic events, cf. Am. 1:6, 9, where Israelites are said to have been delivered to Edom by the Philistines and the Tyrians.

710-610 B.C.".[1] In this list, יון is mentioned as a son of Japhet, v. 2, and the sons of Jawan are listed as Elishah (Alašia), Tarshish, Kittim, and Dodanim, v. 4. Furthermore, it is clear that there were many mercenary troops in the Egyptian army from the time of Pharaoh Psammetichos I (663 B.C.),[2] and the Iudeans knew this.[3] At the time of the 8th and 7th centuries, the Ionians were known in the Near East. This is testified, for instance, by inscriptions of Sargon II and Sennacherib.[4] In this time, the Ionians controlled the trading routes that lead through Asia Minor. In their trading, they later became the main competitors of the Phoenicians. Thus, it would be hazardous to assume that the people of pre-exilic Judah had no knowledge of the Ionians.[5] Ezechiel mentions the Ionians as traders, רכליך,[6] in Ezek. 27:13, but this does not mean that they were first known as such by this prophet. Rather, he expresses what was probably common knowledge among the Judeans about the Ionians; this common knowledge may have included the fact that the Ionians were slave traders.[7]

It has been argued that the mention of the Ionians in a plural form,

---

[1] "Hebrews and Greeks before Alexander", *JBL* 56/37, p. 92. "The seventh century saw the first great flowering of Ionian civilization and was the most active period in the Greek colonial expansion", p. 92.

[2] A. Moret, *Histoire de l'orient* (Histoire Ancienne I), 1936, pp. 724 ff. Cf. E. Otto, *Ägypten. Der Weg des Pharaonenreiches*, 1953, pp. 233, 238 ff., W. F. Albright, *From the Stone Age to Christianity*, 1951, p. 259, D. Auscher, "Les relations entre la Grèce et la Palestine avant la conquête d'Alexandre", *VT* 17/67, p. 14. O. Procksch has already given attention to this, "König Josia", *Festgabe für Theodor Zahn*, 1928, p. 28, cf. also J. Myers, *ZAW* 74/62, pp. 178 ff., B. Otzen, *Studien über Deuterosacharja*, pp. 52 ff.

[3] Cf. Zech. 9:13. See also H. Tadmor, *BA* 29/66, p. 102, n. 59.

[4] *ANET*, pp. 284 ff.

[5] See A. S. Kapelrud, *Joel Studies*, pp. 154 ff., Y. Kaufmann, *The Religion of Israel*, p. 350, n. 2, D. Auscher, *VT* 17/67, pp. 8 ff. For the cultural contacts between Greece and Judah one should notice that pottery characterized "an East Greek import of the type brought to Palestine in the 7th century" has turned up at Tell Goren at En-Gedi among other south Palestinian places, see B. Mazar, Trude Dothan, I. Dunayevsky, *En-Gedi, The First and Second Seasons of Excavations*, 1961-1962 ('Atiqot V), 1966. pp. 30 f.

[6] For רוכל, see B. Landsberger, "Akkadisch-hebräische Wortgleichungen", *Hebräische Wortforschung* (Festschrift W. Baumgartner, SVT 16), 1967, p. 187. This passage in Ezekiel 27 may, according to W. Zimmerli, be pre-exilic, *Ezechiel* (BK XIII), p. 661.

[7] One should pay attention to Homer, who mentions that slave trade existed between the Greeks and the Phoenicians, Odyss XV, 415 ff.,cf. D. Harden, *The Phoenicians²*, 1963, p. 161, A. Neher, *Amos; contribution à l'étude du prophétisme*, 1950, p. 209. Concerning slavery see I. Mendelsohn, *Slavery in the Ancient Near East*, 1949, and *BA* 9/46, pp. 74 ff.

בני היונים, Joel 4:6, should indicate that Joel is to be dated in the same time when the Chronicles were written, for such constructions also occur in the Chronicles; see, for instance, בני הקהתים instead of בני (ה)קהת(י), and בני הקרחים for בני קרח.[1] However, the books of Chronicles are inconsistent in this matter. 1 Chr. 1:7 has בני יון,[2] and בני הקהתי is to be found in 1 Chr. 6:18, 9:32, 2 Chr. 29:12. In 1 Chr. 6:7, there occurs בני קחת. The plural בני הקהתים is found in 2 Chr. 20:19, and 34:12. The use of the plural in this kind of construction, thus, is not consistent. Concerning קרח, the phrase בני הקרחים does not occur at all in the Chronicles, but the plural is to be found, as should be expected, in the phrase לבית אביו הקרחים, 2 Chr. 9:19. This inconsistency can, of course, be explained if one remembers that, in some cases, the Chronicler has been using older sources and therefore has retained their style; cf. the parallels Gen. 10:2, 4//1 Chr. 1:5, 7; Num. 3:17 ff.//1 Chr. 6:16 ff.; 2 Kings 22:3-7//2 Chr. 34:8-13. Therefore one could agree that the form היונים (בני) in Joel 4:6 might point to a relatively late stage in the Hebrew language. However, this is not the same as to say that Joel must be dated as late as the time of the Chronicler. Such a decision cannot be made on the occurrence of one particular form.[3]

Joel 4:6 accuses Tyre, Sidon, and the Philistines of having sold Judeans as slaves to the Ionians. J. M. Myers, who has taken up Albright's points of argumentation, affirms that this passage fits best into the historical situation "after the middle of the sixth century B.C., when the devastated Judean territory was more or less at the mercy of the neighboring states". Furthermore, Myers advocates that this could only have happened around the time of "the decline of the Neo-Babylonian empire", but before the Persians conquered the West. Thus, he maintains that a date between 550-525 would be probable.[4]

However, one must also consider Joel's mentioning of the temple and his many references to liturgical events and phenomena in the temple of Yahweh, 1:9, 14 f., 16, 2:17, 4:18. These lead to the conclusion—if the book is not pre-exilic—that the book must be from a

---

[1] So, for instance, Julius A. Bewer, *Obadiah and Joel* (ICC 26), 1911, p. 61. Cf. Holzinger, *ZAW* 9/89, p. 94.

[2] Cf. verse 5.

[3] Kapelrud makes the objection that in "1 Kings 20:35, 2 Kings 2:3, 5, 7, 15, etc." one can find בני הנביאים, *Joel Studies*, p. 154. However, this is not exactly the same kind of word. נביא is not a *nomen proprium*!

[4] "Some Considerations Bearing on the Date of Joel", *ZAW* 74/62, p. 190, cf. D. N. Freedman, "The Law and the Prophets", *SVT* 9/62, p. 262.

time after 515 B.C. A date immediately after the beginning of the exile in 586 [1] is thus excluded.

If the utterances of Joel 4:4-8 are to be understood as an integral part of the prophetic message, and still assuming that the book is post-exilic, then this passage may refer to both the early post-exilic period immediately following the rebuilding of the temple as well as the time before. When one approaches the time of Ezra and Nehemiah, the relations between Tyre and Sidon on the one hand and the Judeans on the other seem to have been more friendly.[2] One should remember that Tyre was subdued by Nebuchadressar; cf. Ezek. 29:18.[3] It is possible that the city escaped destruction via tribute payment to the Babylonians. Be that as it may, it became a vassal to Babylonia. Tyre, as a Babylonian vassal or province,[4] may still have been able to carry on its usual trade businesses. Ezr. 3:7 and Neh. 13:16 indicate that the Tyrians were again an important factor in trade and shipping.

But what forces one to assume that Joel 4:4 ff. refers only to exilic and post-exilic events? The passage in question may as well be understood as telling past historical events; in particular, the history of Tyre, Sidon, and the Philistines participating in selling Judeans to the Ionians, which events could have taken place also before the exile.[5] Because of this, Yahweh says in 4:7 f. that he will cause these peoples to be given to the Judeans and through them sold to the Sabeans. Thus, it is of less importance exactly when the Phoenicians and the Philistines were selling Judeans as slaves. What is of importance for establishing the date of Joel 4:4-8 is that Yahweh's punishment of these peoples must have been promised before 500 B.C.[6] when the Sabeans were still the undisputed masters of the trade routes.

---

[1] W. Harrelson, *Interpreting the Old Testament*, 1964, p. 335.

[2] Cf. A. S. Kapelrud, *Joel Studies*, p. 149.

[3] For the date of the Babylonian siege of Tyre, see W. B. Fleming, *The History of Tyre* (Columbia Univ. Or. Studies X), 1925, p. 44, O. Eissfeldt, *Kleine Schriften* I, 1963, pp. 1 ff., A. Moret, *Histoire de l'Orient* (Histoire Ancienne I), 1936, p. 739, cf. M. Noth, *Geschichte Israels*[3], p. 265, J. Bright, *A History of Israel*, p. 333, W. Zimmerli, *Ezechiel*, p. 718, W. Eichrodt, *Der Prophet Hesekiel* (ADT 22:2), 1966, p. 278, Y. Aharoni, *The Land of the Bible*, 1967, p. 354.

[4] Cf. E. Unger, "Nebukadnezar II. und sein Šandabakku (Oberkommissar) in Tyrus", *ZAW* 44/26, pp. 314 ff.

[5] Cf. A. Neher, *Amos*, pp. 209 f.

[6] S. R. Driver also places Joel after Haggai and suggests a date around 500 B.C. However, he says that "the possibility must be admitted that it *may* be later, and that it dates in reality from the century after Malachi", *The Books of Joel and Amos* (The Cambridge Bible), 1915, p. 25.

One may assume that the mention of Edom in Joel 4:19 referred
to a historical event,[1] as is the case in Ezek. 36:5. The neighboring
nations mentioned in Joel are Edom, Tyre, Sidon, Philistia, and
Egypt. There are historical reasons for mentioning the Phoenicians
and the Philistines because of their slave trade. Since these nations
are mentioned in the context of judgment and doom, it is not sur-
prising to find Egypt in this company, not so much because of its
political aspirations, but because Egypt, from the Old Testament
viewpoint, can stand theologically for the powers of chaos and death.
In this respect Egypt is closely associated with the Israelite traditions
about Exodus and the Passover. In a similar connection, perhaps it
would be possible to see the name of Edom as being related to the
traditions of the wanderings in the wilderness. However, knowing that
hatred existed between the Israelites and the Edomites, one could
raise the question whether the mentioning of Edom in a book that
also mentions the Phoenicians and the Philistines does not mainly
refer to a historical event. From Ezek. 36:5 is learned that the neighboring peoples, and especially Edom, have attacked the Judeans and
have taken some part of their country; cf. Jer. 49:7 ff., Ezek. 25:12 ff.,
Lam. 4:21 f., and Ob. 1 ff. The Edomites have moved into Judah and
have settled in the southern part with Hebron as their center.[2]

In one way, the book of Obadiah is a parallel to Joel; namely, in
that both of them mention Edom and that this name in both books
occurs in connection with the יום יהוה-motif, Ob. 15. Could one
conclude from this that these books are not far apart from each
other with respect to their dates? It is possible to see Obadiah as
belonging to the sixth or early fifth century.[3] The threats from Joel
and Obadiah against Edom (reflecting Ezek. 25:12 ff. and Jer. 49:7 ff.)
may therefore refer not only to the devastating raids by the Edomites
immediately after 586 B.C., but perhaps to later attacks as well.[4]

---

[1] Properly speaking, of course, there are several possibilities in connection
with the occurrence of a name of one of the neighboring peoples.

[2] Cf. Josephus, *De Bello Judaico* IV, 529.

[3] Cf. S. Dubnov, *History of the Jews* I, 1967, p. 392, A. Deissler, *La Sainte Bible*
VIII, p. 240.

[4] From this point of view, the hypothesis of J. Morgenstern about a destruction
of Jerusalem in 485 B.C. could be considered, cf. Ezr. 4:7 ff., "Jerusalem—485
B.C.", *HUCA* 27/56, pp. 101 ff., 156 and 171, cf. "The Dates of Ezra and Nehemiah", *JSS* 7/62, pp. 1 ff. That the temple should have been destroyed at this
time could be discussed, even if it would be strange that the Chronicler has not
reported such an event which is so relatively close to his time. However, 2 Macc.

One should also compare the utterances against Edom in Joel 4:19 with those of Malachi (1:3 f.). The difference between these two passages is that in Joel there is mention of a threat of a coming destruction of Edom, but Malachi gives the information that Edom (Esau) has been ruined and devastated already. There is no information given about the source of the devastation. It has been suggested that it was caused by the Babylonians,[1] because Edom, according to Nelson Glueck, did not have any sedentary population in the period of the Persians.[2] Perhaps a more probable theory is that Edom was crushed by Arab migrations.[3] If this is the case, perhaps one is dealing with the tribes of Qedar and Dedan,[4] or the Nabatéans.[5] The latter in the sixth and fifth centuries settled in some parts of Edom, and thus have been the cause of the Edomite move to the north.[6] Around 400 B.C. the Nabatéans occupied most of Edom and Moab and they also took over the copper mines and the smelting business of the Edomites.[7]

This comparison between Joel 4:19 and Mal. 1:3 f. may indicate that Malachi must be younger than Joel[8] and that therefore the destruction of Edom took place before the time of Nehemiah,[9] if

---

1:18 reports that Nehemiah rebuilt the temple. This shows that another tradition different from the official one could have lived on and been reported here. H. C. M. Vogt sees this tradition as being an oral one, *Studie zur nachexilischen Gemeinde in Esra-Nehemia*, 1966, p. 8 f. Furthermore, it should be mentioned that E. Sellin reckoned with a Jewish rebellion during Artaxerxes and a consequent diaster for Jerusalem, *Serubbabel*, 1898, pp. 56 ff. Cf. also R. H. Kennett, *The Church of Israel*, 1933, pp. 60 f., L. W. Batten, *The Books of Ezra and Nehemiah* (ICC), 1913, pp. 184 f., U. Kellermann, *Nehemia. Quellen, Überlieferung und Geschichte* (BZAW 102), 1967, pp. 184 f.

[1] Thus M. Vogelstein, "Nebuchadnezar's Reconquest of Phoenicia and Palestine and the Oracles of Ezekiel", *HUCA* XXIII:2, 1950-51, pp. 209 ff.

[2] "Explorations in Eastern Palestine", *AASOR* XV/35, pp. 138 ff.

[3] Cf. J. M. Myers, *ZAW* 74/62, pp. 187 f., J. A. Thompson, *The Bible and Archaeology*, 1962, pp. 231 f.

[4] Cf. J. Starcky, "The Nabataeans: A Historical Sketch", *BA* 18/55, p. 86.

[5] Cf. A. von Bulmerincq, *Kommentar zum Buche des Malachi* I (ACUT), 1926, pp. 132 f., A. Kammerer, *Pétra est la nabatène*, 1929, pp. 29, 395, J. Gray, *Archaeology and the Old Testament World*, 1962, pp. 16, 102, M. Delcor, *La Sainte Bible* VIII, 1961, p. 139, M. Rostovtzeff, *Caravan Cities*, 1932, p. 22.

[6] Cf. T. C. Mitchell, "Philistia", in D. W. Thomas (ed.), *Archaeology and Old Testament Study*, p. 417, and R. Dussaud, *La pénétration des Arabes en Syrie avant l'Islam*, (Bibliothèque Archeologique et Historique LIX), 1955, p. 23.

[7] Cf. J. N. Schofield, *The Historical Background of the Bible*, 1948, p. 24, S. Cohen, *IDB* III, pp. 491 f.

[8] Cf. S. Dubnov, *History of the Jews* I, p. 391.

[9] Cf. H. Cazelles, "La mission d'Esdras", *VT* 4/54, p. 122, n. 1.

indeed Malachi, as mentioned before, is to be placed in the time
before Nehemiah's arrival in Jerusalem.[1]

Now it is possible to return to the problem of the temple cult in
the early post-exilic time. As was briefly mentioned in the previous
chapter, the cultic apparatus of the second temple is to be seen as a
continuation of the cult of the last decades of the Solomonic temple,
of course, without the Assyro-Babylonian features. 2 Chr. 36:14
portrays what this cult of the last decades of the Judean kingdom
looked like. One learns that the leaders of the temple cultus, the
higher hierarchy, committed many liturgical offences which were of
such a kind as to be called "abominations", תועבות, characteristic of
the גוים.[2] They are said to have made the temple of Yahweh culticly
unclean. This can only mean that the reform of king Josiah was now
a past event, cf. Jer. 32:20 ff.[3] The terms תועבות in 2 Chr. 36:14 and
שקוציהם in Jer. 32:34 reveal that idols and "foreign" cult objects are
to be found again in the temple; cf. Ezek. 8:3-17, 7:20, 37:23,
43:7 f., 44:6 ff.

When the second temple was built, one can assume that the cultic
apparatus which was instituted was mainly the same as that which
could be understood as the main tradition of the Solomonic temple.
And what else could be expected? There is no evidence that the
rituals of the temple of Zerubbabel during the first years of its
existence differed in any *significant* way from those of the temple of
Solomon,[4] even though the influence of Ezekiel could have played
some role.[5] From the point of view of the history of tradition, the

---

[1] This excludes the possibility of dating Joel between 445-343, as H. W. Wolff
does, *Joel*, p. 3, cf. p. 12.

[2] What one is dealing with here, thus, is not popular belief or "individual instances", but the established, official religion of Judah, a phenomenon which
P. J. Calderone has not grasped in its full extent, *Biblica* 45/64, pp. 452 f.

[3] Cf. above, p. 77, n. 3.

[4] Cf. J. M. Myers, *Ezra, Nehemiah* (The Anchor Bible 14), p. 53. For Ezek. 43:
18-27 as reflecting an old cultic tradition, see W. Zimmerli, *Ezechiel*, pp. 1099 f.

[5] For ignoring Ezekiel in the reorganization of the priesthood of the second
temple, see Y. Kaufmann, *The Religion of Israel*, pp. 195 f. A comparison of the
temple rituals of the first temple with Ezekiel's restoration program seems to be
impossible to make because neither the rituals of the first temple nor the rituals of
the second temple are fully known. Ezekiel mostly gives directions for the building
of the temple and for the duties of the prince in connection with the reorganization of the priesthood and its duties. Some of the information does indicate a
difference, however. From Ezek. 43:7 f., for instance, one can draw the conclusion
that the pre-exilic cult had been too "Canaanite" or too influenced by elements
which, according to the prophet, were foreign to the character of Yahweh. Thus,
the concern of the prophet is the usual prophetic one; namely, a pure Yahweh

most natural way of reestablishing the cultus was to follow the old pattern, perhaps with minor necessary adjustments. An examination of the foundation ritual and the dedication of the temple of Zerubbabel in Ezr. 3:10 f. and 4:16 ff., shows that they seem to be mainly in accord with the dedication of Solomon's temple, 1 Kings 8:22, 2 Chr. 7:4 ff.[1] The new generation of priests responsible for the cult would hardly have invented any new rituals. The time of the rebuilding of the temple and the reestablishment of the cultus was not a time fit for cultic reforms and novelties. At least there are no hints to that effect in the texts. Indeed, the temple liturgies can only have been restored and reenacted as the priests had learned them from the older generations. In other words, the priests of the restored cult did not know of any cultic tradition other than the pre-exilic temple tradition.[2] The new "Davidic" era that the prophets Haggai and Zechariah said would come after the temple was built meant that this new time should be an ideal one in accordance with the promises of the liturgies; that what was said and "done" through the cultic performances should now be a reality. The liturgical truth should be fulfilled into a historical truth.[3] All this shows the importance of the temple ideology with its cultic pattern for the inbreak of the ideal time. Without a temple, there could be no possibility for an ideal future. The temple was ideologically heaven on earth; thus, the only religion that could exist was a temple religion.[4] It is in the temple that Yahweh lives and works (עשׂה). Therefore, only in the temple could the norm for the religious life, which was the norm for the ideal time as well, be guaranteed; namely, the צדקה.

As far as is possible to judge, Haggai and Zechariah have thought of the temple cult as being reestablished mainly in the same form or pattern as formerly.[5] They did not give too much attention to the

---

cultus. However, it "seems unlikely that the strict regulations adumbrated by Ezekiel were inforced", A. Parrot, *The Temple of Jerusalem*, 1957, p. 73.

[1] Myers, *op. cit.*, p. 53.

[2] Cf. J. Morgenstern, "The Cultic Setting of the 'Enthronement Psalms", *HUCA* 35/64, p. 38.

[3] It is this liturgical truth that the prophetical expectations have built upon.

[4] The impact of the Babylonian *golah*'s religious problems and traditions, or new orientation, could not yet have had time to be too deeply felt. That came with Ezra. When the people first returned to Jerusalem, the most important desire was that everything should be restored according to the regular traditions. That meant that first of all, the temple and its cult had to be restored first—and in the pattern already known.

[5] Cf. K. Koch, "Haggais unreines Volk", *ZAW* 79/67, pp. 63 ff.

fact that in the restored liturgical system there were features that did not exactly harmonize with the concepts of Deuteronomistic ideas of a right Yahweh cult, or the prophetic concepts of an ideal future. What was of greater importance for them was, for the time being, the temple itself. It had to be built because it was the center, and the only guarantee of life.[1]

Because of the emphasis in the preceeding which has been laid upon the temple ideology and, in the main, upon the temple as "heaven on earth," the objection could be raised that there is a tendency in Deuteronomy to separate Yahweh and the name of Yahweh. It is Yahweh who lives in heaven, and he has caused his name to dwell in the temple.[2] Therefore, it would be probable to assume that Joel, being of a possibly early date in the post-exilic period, could hardly have been ignorant of this tendency. However, even if this were true, there is no proof in the book of Joel that this cult prophet is an exponent of Deuteronomy's so-called שם-theology. Two things ought to be pointed out. First, Deuteronomy is not the only standard according to which everything in the earliest decades of the second temple has to be measured. Second, according to the thinking of the Semitic mind, name and person are the same. Thus, in saying that the name of Yahweh lives in the temple, the Semitic thinker is not thinking of the name as separate from the person of Yahweh, and this is no proof for the separation of name and person. Properly speaking, it can mean the same thing as saying that Yahweh himself lives in the temple. It will not be denied here that there is some kind of a שם-theology and that this can be seen as the basis for a

---

[1] It is a fact that the building of temples in the Near East is the task and duty of kings, cf. Ahlström, *VT* 11/61, p. 126, A. S. Kapelrud, "Temple Building. A Task for Gods and Kings", *Orientalia* 32/63, pp. 56 ff., R. de Vaux, "Jérusalem et les prophètes", *RB* 73/66, pp. 485, 489. Thus, Zerubbabel's initiative to build the temple only one year after his arrival in Jerusalem, Ezr. 3:8 ff., is quite understandable. He also had permission from Cyrus, 2 Chr. 36:23, Ezr. 1:2 ff. From Haggai's oracle in 2:23, where Zerubbabel is called עבדי, "my servant", by Yahweh, it is evident that Yahweh has chosen Zerubbabel for kingship. Thus, one of his first, main duties was to rebuild the temple. Perhaps he was never enthroned as king; therefore, the title מלך is missing.

[2] Dt. 12:11, 14:23, 16:2, 6, 11, 26:2, cf. 1 Kings 8:27, Jer. 7:12. For the שם-theology, see G. von Rad, *Deuteronomiumstudien*, 1948, pp. 25 ff. (English ed. 1953, pp. 37 ff.), cf. J. Bourke, *RB* 66/59, pp. 197 ff., D. Jones, "The Cessation of Sacrifice after the Destruction of the Temple in 586 B.C.", *JThSt* 14/63, p. 23, J. Schreiner, *Sion-Jerusalem, Jahwes Königssitz*, 1963, pp. 158 ff., E. W. Nicholson, *Deuteronomy and Tradition*, 1967, pp. 31, 55 f. For a discussion of לשבתי in 2 Sam. 7:5 and לשמי in 2 Sam. 7:13, see R. A. Carlson, *David, the Chosen King*, pp. 110 f.

certain thinking about the presence of Yahweh in the temple. In later post-exilic time, this kind of thinking has developed into a theory of Yahweh's name as an independent entity, a hypostasis.[1]

Even though a tendency of this kind can be seen in Deuteronomy, it should be pointed out that there is no consistency in this matter in the book. This is clear, for instance, from Dt. 12:5, where it is said that the place where Yahweh lives is the temple and there he places his name.[2] As Pedersen expresses it, the name can be understood as the soul of the person; soul and name are identical.[3] This can also be seen in Joel 2:26. In Joel 3:5 occurs the phrase כל אשר יקרא בשם יהוה. This cannot be understood, as has been maintained,[4] as an expression for the above-mentioned Deuteronomistic tendency.[5]

As can be expected from a cult prophet, Joel is not able to make a distinction between Yahweh in heaven and Yahweh in the temple —or his name in the temple. From a religious point of view, this would be a contradiction, because of the ideological concept of the temple as heaven on earth. It will therefore be maintained here that what begins as a programmatic tendency in Deuteronomy has not been adopted into the theological thinking of Joel.[6] He is not that logical or rational. Instead, he clearly expresses in 4:17 that Yahweh will live on Zion, his holy mountain. This is such a classical, old idea that it could almost be called orthodox, if one could use such a term here; cf. Ex. 15:17.[7]

From what has been maintained above, Judah of the post-exilic era could be reproached for taking part in cult practices not considered to belong to a "pure" Yahweh cult. Here again one could refer to the book of Malachi and the תועבה he mentions, as well as

---

[1] E. Jacob, *Théologie de l'Ancien Testament*, 1955, p. 67.

[2] "For the Israelites there is upon the whole no difference whatsoever between the idea, the name and the matter itself", J. Pedersen, *Israel* I-II, p. 168. Cf. G. van der Leeuw, who says that the name is "ursprünglich nichts anderes als eine Erscheinung dessen, was man erlebt... Er ist das Wesen des Gottes", *Einfürung in die Phänomenologie der Religion*², 1961, p. 81.

[3] *Op. cit.*, pp. 245 ff.

[4] Thus J. Bourke, *RB* 66/59, p. 201.

[5] For this phrase compare above, p. 54.

[6] Cf. Ezek. 43:7. For a different view, see Isa. 66:1 where the heavens are the throne of Yahweh and the earth his footstool.

[7] For this classical concept still being alive in the communities of Qumran and the New Testament, see B. Gärtner, *The Temple and the Community in Qumran and the New Testament* (Society for New Testament Studies, Monograph Series 1), 1965, pp. 32, 94 ff.

the covering of the altar of Yahweh with tears, 2:10 ff.[1] These abuses
and wrong rituals, some of which may well refer to idolatry, are
probably to be dated in the time before the reform of Ezra.[2] After
this time, the thorough reform of the temple cult and the religious
as well as the social practices having been reformed, the book of
Malachi would then be out of date,[3] even though some "apostate"
practices were still in existence in the later centuries.[4] Besides, there
were also other cult places, as, for instance, the Jewish temple at
Lachish.[5]

One should also notice that it would be much more difficult to see
the book of Joel as originating in the time after Ezra's rigid reform.
The "law religion" that was the ideal for Ezra,[6] and according to
which he made his attacks upon the temple cult and the social structure
as well—which, of course, should be seen as the fruit of the religion—
does not harmonize very well with the ideals of Joel. A few phrases
in the book of Ezra give an impression of what the cultic situation
looked like at the time of Ezra's arrival in Jerusalem. Also Ezra uses
the term תועבות in characterizing the cult as it was before his arrival,
and still is at the time of his arrival. As a parallel to this term,
he uses in the same verse, 9:11, the term נִדָּה, "excretion,
that which is unclean, that which is ejected". Both of these
words are thus used for the purpose of describing the idolatrous
cult of the people of Yahweh. The use of נדה means that the
scribe of "the law of the God of Heaven" has understood the cult
of Judah to be non-Yahwistic and idolatrous. To show his disgust,
Ezra makes use of the usual term תועבה together with the special word
for a woman's menstrual discharge;[7] Ezekiel 7:19 f. also uses this

---

[1] Cf. above, pp. 27 f., 112.

[2] See, for instance, J. M. P. Smith, *Malachi* (ICC), p. 49, A. van Hoonacker, *Les Douze petits prophètes*, p. 697, cf. P. R. Ackroyd, *Exile and Restoration*, 1968, p. 231, U. Kellermann, *Nehemia. Quellen, Überlieferung und Geschichte* (BZAW 102), 1967, p. 189.

[3] Van Hoonacker dates the book of Malachi around 450-445 B.C., *op. cit.*, p. 699, cf. A. Lods, *Les Prophètes d'Israël*, 1935, p. 9, O. Eissfeldt, *The Old Testament*, p. 443.

[4] According to P. R. Ackroyd, there is "ample evidence of idolatrous practices after the exile", *Exile and Restoration*, p. 205, n. 116, cf. S. Segert, "Surviving of Canaanite Elements in Israelite Religion", *Studi sull'Oriente e la Bibbia* (Festschrift P. G. Rinaldi), 1967, p. 159.

[5] See Y. Aharoni, "Trial Excavation in the 'Solar Shrine' at Lachish", *Israel Exploration Journal* 18/68, p. 163.

[6] Cf. H. Cazelles, "La mission d'Esdras", *VT* 4/54, p. 113 ff., 125 f.

[7] Lev. 20:21, Ezek, 22:10.

description.[1] Just as one should refrain from contact with a menstruating, and therefore unclean, woman, so also should one abstain from being polluted by this cult carried out in Jerusalem.[2] This is an extremely harsh denunciation of the religious situation in Judah and Jerusalem.

Having maintained that the phrase יהוה אלהיכם in Joel stresses the fact that Yahweh is the god of the people, and none other, it would also be possible to see the often repeated phrase אלהינו in Ezra 9 [3] as giving emphasis to the same idea; namely, that Yahweh is the god of the people and only him should one worship.[4] This stress upon Yahweh as *the* god ought to be seen in connection with Ezra's reaction against the "foreign" wives of the Jews. According to Ezra, these women had led their husbands into apostasy; i.e., they have not only participated in a wrongly performed Yahweh cult, but they have been idolatrous, Ezr. 9:1 f., 14, 10:2.[5] The mixed marriages had contributed to this. Even if Ezra was one-sided in picking these women as being the cause of the so-called apostasy—perhaps many of these were Yahweh worshippers—he nevertheless gives a picture of the whole population as being idolatrous.[6] Thus one may conclude

---

[1] Cf. Zech. 13:1, 2 Chr. 29:5.

[2] Perhaps it would not be out of place to assume that the law-oriented religion that was introduced and forced upon the Judean community by Ezra had been somewhat inspired by the Zoroastrian surroundings of the Jews in the Persian empire. The term דָּתָא, used for law in Ezr. 7:12, is, as a matter of fact, an Iranian term that can be found as a loan word in the Aramaic of this time. One should notice that the "Persians themselves looked upon religion as a law, *dāta*", G. Widengren, "Iran and Israel in Parthian Times with Special Regards to the Ethiopic Book of Enoch", *Temenos* 2/66, p. 142. One can imagine that Ezra had grown up in a world where two religious traditions, hostile to idols and very law-oriented, had lived side by side. From this point of view, one can understand Ezra's actions of purifying the cult when he really discovered what the Jerusalemite and Judean religious scene was all about.

[3] Ezr. 9:8-10, cf. 10:2 f., 14.

[4] An investigation of the frequency of the phrases יהוה אלהיך and יהוה אלהיכם shows that they occur mostly in Dt.: about 170 times in Dt. to 58 times in the D history work. The former phrase is to be found 126 times in Dt., which is over 75% of its frequency in the O.T. See also J. Bourke, *RB* 66/59, p. 193, n. 1, cf. R. P. Merendino, *Das deuteronomische Gesetz*, pp. 105, 120, 403.

[5] Cf. Neh. 13:25 ff., Ex. 34:11 ff., Deut. 7:1 ff. Foreign women and fornication lead to foreign gods, see G. Boström, *Proverbiastudien* (LUÅ N.F. Avd. 1, 30:3), 1935, pp. 150 f.

[6] According to H. C. M. Vogt, Ezra was more concerned about a pure Yahweh cult than about the pure blood of the people, *Studie zur nachexilischen Gemeinde in Esra-Nehemia*, pp. 155 f.

that thoroughgoing syncretism had taken place. [1] What indications
are there to the contrary? What indications are there that the temple
was untouched by this? Perhaps it would be enough to refer again
to the words of Malachi about Judah's profanation of the temple and
the tears upon the altar of Yawheh, Mal. 2:10 ff.

It seems to be unrealistic to interpret the phrases תועבות, נדה, and
טמאה ("uncleanness, menstruation") in Ezr. 9:11, cf. v. 14, as
referring, in Ezra's opinion, to a cult which was in some way wrong,
but not to a cult which was directed toward the worship of other
gods. [2] As is seen from Ezra 9, Ezra's understanding of the religious
situation is that the whole population is still practicing idolatry, [3] and
that this has come to pass mainly because of the influence of the
mixed marriages. By dissolving these marriages, as well as by cutting
the ties with the motivations behind the originally Canaanite festivals,
it would be possible for the cult and the congregation to be free from
contacts with, and influences from, the neighboring peoples. Thus,
religious life and cultic performance could be carried on in a controll-
able environment, according to the "law reform" of the cult under-
taken by Ezra. [4]

---

[1] Cf. R. J. Coggins, "The Old Testament and the Samaritan Origins", *Annual
of the Swedish Theological Institute* VI, 1968, p. 41.

[2] The weeping by the people at the time of Ezra's recital of the law at the
autumnal festival is to be seen as an old rite, either originally connected with
some Canaanite phenomenon and therefore rejected by Ezra, Neh. 8:9, (so Egon
Johannesen, *Studier over Esras og Nehemjas Historie*, 1946, p. 295), or as part of
the ritual of the renewal of the covenant. After penance came the covenant
renewal, cf. 2 Kings 22:12 ff. (so N. Lohfink, "Die Bundesurkunde des Königs
Josias", *Biblica* 44/63, pp. 284, n. 1, 477, n. 3). These two lines of thought do not
exclude each other. It is probable that an old rite of weeping at the autumnal
festival was connected with the penance, because the covenant had been broken
and was in need of renewal. As a matter of fact, Joel's book is dealing with this
very phenomenon—the broken covenant.

[3] Cf. W. Rudolph, *Esra und Nehemia* (HAT 20), 1949, p. 89.

[4] For a better understanding of the situation with which Ezra was confronted,
one should also consider the sociological side of the problem. S. Mowinckel has
maintained that down through the years of the existence of Israel, there existed
the fiction of blood-relationship, "Blutgemeinschaft".Theoretically this could get
its expression "in quasiwissenschaftlichen Stammbäumen, in denen alte Klan-
namen, Städte, Stände usw. als Zweige an einem weiterverzweigten Stammbaum
des einzelnen Stammes und des ganzen Volkes Israel zusammengebunden waren".
In the monarchic time and especially in the late, pre-exilic time, there is no real
proof for "klanbewusste Geschlechter", *Studien zu dem Buche Ezra-Nehemia* I,
1964, pp. 73 ff. Already by the time of the Judges, the elders of the clans or the
families have mostly been substituted in the text for the elders or men of the city,
cf. Judg. 8:14. Mowinckel's conclusion is that what constituted the society was
not the sense of belonging to a special clan or family, but rather the living to-

Having seen that the cult of the second temple cannot have been free from the "accusation" of being syncretistic and idolatrous, it is therefore possible to maintain that the period between 515 and 445 B.C. is the period which can suit the requirements of the evidence for the date of Joel—evidence which requires a post-exilic date and a syncretistic cultus. Thus, the time between 515 and 500 B.C. for the book of Joel, as maintained before, can be defended.

---

gether in the same geographical area or place ("die Grundlage des Geschlechts-gefühls war das Zusammenwohnen, und das betreffende 'Geschlecht' war eine rein lokale Grösse"), *op. cit.*, p. 76. Anybody could be adopted into the clan and thus become a part of the community and its traditions, having the same part in the traditions of the patriarch of the community and its ancestors. All this is the rationale of the life and community in post-exilic Judah prior to Ezra and Nehe-miah. The old organization has come into existence again, if indeed it ever really did cease. Even though many of the exiles returned to their homes and found their property and fields taken over by others, there was no break with the fundamental theory of living together within the same village or district. Also in this time a משפחה "bestand aus den Bewohnern eines grösseren oder kleineren Ortes", Mowinckel, *op. cit.*, p. 77. According to Mowinckel, the only exceptions were the priests and Levites (pp. 77 f.). Knowing this old sociological system of life, it is understandable that mixed marriages were common and that therefore Ezra was faced with an almost unsolvable problem. His main weapons became the *torah* and the theory of the blood-relationship. Only these two phenomena could save and uphold the Jewish society and its cult.

CHAPTER SEVEN

COMPOSITION

As for its character, the first part of the Book of Joel (1:2-2:17) very much resembles a psalm of lament. However, it will not be advocated here that this passage, as far as its structure is concerned, is a complete lamentation; only that most of it is composed in the style of a lament.[1] The typical introduction for a lament is missing in Joel. Such an introduction should begin with an invocation of the deity, which can sometimes take the form of a hymn.[2] Instead of the typical invocation of the lamentation style, Joel begins in v. 2 with an oracle formula, the so-called *šimʿū* oracle,[3] שמעו־זאת, directed to a certain group, here, the elders, זקנים, and the inhabitants of the country.[4] Verse 3 announces the uniqueness of what will be heard. Here, the call to listen is extended to the coming generations. Then, in verse 4, there occurs a lamentation motif—the beginning of a description of the disaster combined with a call to the people to awaken and to lament, verse 5.[5] The picture of the disaster and the desolation of the country continues in vv. 6 ff., and the style of the lament is adhered to. Then in v. 13, the prophet summons the priests to lamentation and mourning which is to be done in the sanctuary.[6] They have to wail and lament because the sacrifices are cut off from the temple of Yahweh. Joel also asks them to call the elders and the people together for a fast, v. 14. In v. 15, the cry for penance occurs in connection with the *Leitmotiv* of the book, the day of Yahweh, which has to be seen as one of the reasons for the penance. In the following verses, the motifs of destruction and loss return.

---

[1] For the structure of a lament, cf. W. Baumgartner, *BZAW* 34/20, pp. 11 ff., D. Cameron, *Songs of Sorrow and Praise. Studies in the Hebrew Psalter*, 1924, p. 126., E. Sellin—G. Fohrer, *Introduction to the O.T.*, pp. 267 f.

[2] Cf. Ps. 89.

[3] Cf. Isa. 1:2, which, however, does not have the זאת. See also Isa. 1:10, 28:3, 49:1, 51:1, Jer. 13:15, Am. 3:1, 4:1, 5:1, Mic. 1:2, 3:19. See A. S. Kapelrud, *Joel Studies*, p. 12. For the parallelism שמעו//האזינו, see, among others, H. W. Wolff, *Hosea* (BK XIV:1), p. 123.

[4] Cf. Hos. 5:1 and Ps. 49:2.

[5] Wolff, "Aufruf zur Volksklage", *Joel*, p. 5.

[6] Cf. H. Gunkel and J. Bergrich, *Einleitung in die Psalmen*, 1933, p. 117 ff., 137, H.-J. Kraus, *Psalmen* p. 514, H. Reventlow, *Liturgie und prophetisches Ich bei Jeremia*, pp. 118 f.

From this, it is clear that the prophet has not followed the stylistic pattern of a lamentation exactly, but he has used much of its form and content in building up his message. As far as the section 1:2-12 is concerned, one could agree with A. S. Kapelrud that "the description of the misfortune has all the emphasis".[1] Therefore, the style of a lament is proper. However, this section is not a liturgy in my opinion, because of the fact that the prophet calls upon the priests to lament and mourn and asks them to call the people together, v. 13.

The lamentation style returns in 1:19-20 [2] and is followed by a call to blow the shophar trumpet because the day of Yahweh is now coming, 2:1-11.[3] Wolff has labeled this part, which describes the disaster in greater detail than Ch. 1, as a proclamation of the eschatological catastrophe that will come over Jerusalem.[4] It is true that this is a description of a catastrophe, but it is not an eschatological one because it has already begun; because of this, the prophet is announcing more disaster. Perhaps one could say that it has some kind of an apocalyptic coloring, for in the apocalyptic literature, the events are to happen very soon also. The locusts of chapter one are to be seen as the portents of the imminent day of Yahweh which is presented in chapter two.[5]

The passage which follows, 2:12-17, expresses the demand for penance and the call to Yahweh for help.[6] This part does not end in the usual lamentation style with a promise about giving sacrifices or giving praise to Yahweh. Instead, the text relates that the prophet is calling upon the priests to take their usual position and wail, and in so doing, to ask Yahweh for help. Again, this is not a liturgy, but a prophetic text which uses liturgical style and motifs.

In summing up, one can say that 1:2-2:17 is not a lamentation but it shows an actual situation in which a lamentation should be heard and performed. Thus, instead of the promise to sacrifice or to give praise, the prophet orders the priests to liturgical actions of sorrow and fasting. The last verse of this part, v. 17, also concludes with a

---

[1] *Joel Studies*, p. 4.

[2] H.-P. Müller says that chapter one is a "prophetische Liturgie", "Prophetie und Apokalyptik bei Joel", *Theologia Viatorum* X, 1965/66, p. 234.

[3] H. W. Wolff characterizes 2:1 ff. as an eschatological alarm, *Joel*, p. 14.

[4] *Joel*, p. 6.

[5] Cf. E. Kutsch, "Heuschreckenplage und Tag Jahwes in Joel 1 und 2", *ThZ* 18/62, p. 87.

[6] Th. H. Robinson considers 2:12-14 to be a fragment of a penitential liturgy, *HAT*³ 14, p. 63.

prayer of the priests asking Yahweh to be compassionate and to spare his people, that the גוים may not rule over the people and triumphantly ask where their god now is. This ends that part of Joel that is patterned in the style which is associated with a mood of sorrow, reproach and lament.[1] As for its structure, it could be called liturgical, because the prophet has used the form of the lament—as well as the motifs and ideas that usually were heard in lamentations.[2] The text itself, however, is no actual lamentation or liturgy.

Verse 18 of the second chapter is the turning point of the book. It says that repentance is rewarded, and Yahweh's response in the oracle of vv. 19 ff. also shows that this is the case.[3] What has been said in negative terms prior to this point is put in the positive in the verses that follow. An analysis of the book shows that every motif mentioned in the first part of Joel, in terms of disaster for Judah or in terms of something which is missing, is turned into its opposite in 2:19 ff.[4] This is an argument for the unity of the book. Moreover, the key words are the same.[5] Here one ought especially note that the beginning of the oracle, v. 19, takes up again two important words from v. 17 according to the association principle; namely, חרפה and גוים. Thus the answer of Yahweh through the oracle promises immediately that what should happen according to v. 17 will never happen. Verse 19 and the verses which follow also promise that the corn and the wine and the oil will be restored again, as will be the leader of the cult congregation. The tone of the oracle and the vital content of the blessing which will come through the ṣĕdāqāh concern the sphere of material well-being.[6] The prayer has been heard, and Yahweh promises full restoration of what has been destroyed and also that he himself will be in the midst of the people from now on—which means that none other should be there.

---

[1] This weakens considerably A. Jepsen's theory that the many "Wieder-holungen", repetitions, that occur everywhere in this book disturb the context and are to be seen as the work of a later revision, "Kleine Beiträge zum Zwölf-prophetenbuch", ZAW 56/38, pp. 85 f.

[2] H.-P. Müller characterizes 1:5-2:17, 19-27 as representing "eine vorlitear-rische Sprache; hinter ihr wird die Institution eines öffentlichen Fastens sichtbar", Theologia Viatorum X, 1965/66, p. 241.

[3] Cf. Ezek. 18:30 ff., 2 Chr. 30:6 ff.

[4] Cf. A. S. Kapelrud, Joel Studies, pp. 6 f., Th. Chary, Les prophètes et le culte, p. 210. See also J. Bourke: "Les deux sections se complètent comme les deux tables d'un diptyque", "Le jour de Yahvé dans Joël", RB 66/59, p. 11, cf. Wolff, Joel, pp. 6 f.

[5] See Wolff, Joel, p. 7.

[6] Cf. M. Bič, Das Buch Joel, p. 67.

Thus far, the discussion has been concerned with 1:1-2:27; how-ever, as has been maintained, the following chapters are also to be seen as an integral part of the composition of the book of Joel. Chapter 3 cannot be separated from the preceeding oracle in 2:19-27.[1] It is, in fact, a continuation of it. This is shown by the phrase והיה אחרי־כן. Yahweh is still speaking. This oracle tells what will happen according to what has been said in 2:19-27. It concerns the idea that the day of Yahweh will inaugurate a new time for the people of Yahweh. As has been stated above, Joel is composed in a sym-metrical way. What is mentioned in the first part of the book as lacking, or what is mentioned in terms of disaster, is turned into its opposite in the second part of the book. In chapter 3, the day of Yahweh is mentioned as an experience of blessing for his people, vv. 1, 2, 5,— the opposite of disaster.[2] Another correspondence is to be found between 2:10 and 3:3-4a.[3]

Also in 4:1 ff., Yahweh speaks and the day of Yahweh is pictured again, but in contrasting nature from its description in 2:1-11. Instead of coming with defeat and disaster for Judah, it is coming with defeat and disaster for the גוים and with blessing for Judah and Jerusalem. In 4:12 the גוים are coming to meet their own destruction in the valley of Jehoshaphat, cf. 4:2, but in 1:6 the peoples were coming to cause the destruction of Yahweh's people. 2:11 describes the strength of Yahweh's army and how terrible his day will be for the people that should be his. In 4:9 ff. war terminology is used again, but here it is used against the enemies. Just as Yahweh in 2:11 utters his voice in front of his army to terrify his people, so he in 4:16 roars fom Zion terrifying heaven and earth, cf. 2:10. In the case of Yahweh's use of his voice in the fourht chapter, he is the refuge for his people. In 1:11 the prophet mentions that wheat and barley are no more, the harvest has perished. The tillers of the soil (*'ikkārim*) and the vinedressers have to lament. The opposite picture, combined with the motif of the judgment of the גוים, is given in 4:13. In 1:11, the lack of harvest was due to the גוים, and 1:5 mentions the wine being cut off. In 2:22 and 4:18, the wine will give its full yield. The mountains and the hills will flow with wine and milk, 4:18.[4] One

---

[1] Cf. Kapelrud, *Joel Studies*, p. 7, Wolff, *Joel*, p. 9, cf. p. 7 and 71, H.-P. Müller in *Theologia Viatorum* X, 1965-66, p. 248.

[2] Cf. Ezek. 39:29.

[3] Wolff says that "Überhaupt ist der Stil von Kap. 3 grundsätzlich nicht anderes als der Mischstil der vorigen Abschnitt", *Joel*, p. 70.

[4] Cf. Am. 9:13.

should also notice that the blessings of the vats, which will overflow, 2:24, is a motif that comes back in its opposite in 4:13. There the wine press will be full and the vats overflow because of the wickedness of the גוים.

Chapter 4 is structured out of four units which are all closely knitted together. The first part, vv. 1-3, can be said to announce the theme of the whole chapter: [1] the שוב שבות for Judah and Jerusalem "at that time", v. 1,[2] and the destruction of the enemies, vv. 2-3. Verses 4-8 contain the utterance of promise, in prose. It is negative toward the enemies, but positive toward Yahweh's own people. This section of prose deals with some particular foreign nations. The third unit, vv. 9-17, is similar in content to the unit preceeding it. It is an oracle of judgment that ends with a promise to Judah. Here, the prophet returns to the motif of the day of Yahweh. Yahweh is pictured here as the war lord who defeats end destroys the enemies; thus, he guarantees an ideal time in which strangers will profane his holy city no more. The final section, vv. 18-21, repeats and develops the promise of the ideal future and Yahweh's elimination of the enemies.[3] As mentioned before, this section is given a chiastic structure.[4]

A few words ought to be said about Joel 4:4-8, which has been considered a secondary section by most interpreters.[5] In dealing with this part I have followed the hypothesis that a prophet can interrupt his oracular poetic speech and switch to a narrative prompted by some phenomenon or word—a narrative which would seem an interruption to the logical, western mind, but which comes to the mind of the prophet due to mere mention or association of a particular

---

[1] A. S. Kapelrud, *Joel Studies*, p. 7.

[2] H. Gressmann, among others, sees the expressions בעת ההיא in v. 1 and ביום ההוא in v. 18 as very old eschatological phrases, *Der Messias*, pp. 83 ff., cf. P. A. Munch, "a temporal adverb", *The Expression bajjôm bāhū*, Oslo 1936, pp. 56 f., see also Kapelrud, *op. cit.*, p. 167, H.-M. Lutz follows Munch in seeing the latter phrase as an adverb not referring to the day of Yahweh, *Jahwe, Jerusalem und die Völker* (WMANT 27), 1968, p. 130, n. 2. That this should be the case in Joel is challenged by the investigation in this book.

[3] It is not necessary to elaborate from a logical and historical point of view with a thesis of two quite different days of Yahweh in the book of Joel, as has been advocated, for instance, by M. Vernes, *Mélanges de critique religieuse*, 1880, pp. 221 ff., and J. Bourke, *RB* 76/59, pp. 5 ff., 191 ff. Joel has used the common liturgical pattern of disaster—restoration for his message.

[4] Cf. above p. 96.

[5] Cf. Th. H. Robinson, *HAT*[3] 14, p. 67, C. Kuhl, *Die Entstehung des Alten Testaments*, 1953, p. 222, E. Sellin—G. Fohrer, *Introduction to the Old Testament*, 1968, p. 428.

word, phenomenon. An example for this kind of stylistic "interruption"—even if it is not an exact parallel—is Amos 7:10 ff. In Amos 7 there are three visions: vv. 1-3, 5-6, 7-9. Verse 9 gives the motivation for telling the story about Amos' clash with the chief priest at Bethel, Amaṣiah.[1] After this narrative, the book of Amos resumes the string of visions.[2] In the same way, Joel 4:4-8 may be considered an integral part of the book. 4:2-3 has led the prophet's associations of thought to the historical facts about his people having been sold as slaves (note the verb מכר in vv. 3, 6, 7, 8), and thus, as verse 2 puts it, they have been spread out, פזרו, among the nations. Once Joel has promised to the peoples mentioned in 4:4-8 that they will be sold in their turn to the Sabeans as slaves, Joel then resumes the oracle form and the motif of the day of Yahweh, complete with utterances about the judgment of the enemies. Thus, 4:4-8 can be seen as a part of the original message of Joel.[3] From the point of view of "Sitz im Literatur", this section is at the right place.[4]

Thus the conclusion can be drawn that the structure of the book of Joel could be called a correlative one. What is said in the negative for Judah and Jerusalem in the first part is said in the positive in the second part of the book. The same contrast is also to be noticed in the way the book deals with the enemies of Judah. The book of Joel is therefore a meaningful composition.[5] One could say that it has been composed from the viewpoint of reestablishing the right order, צדקה, for Yahweh's own people. This is the goal of the book. It is, of course, impossible to put forth as an indisputable fact whether or not this means that the book has been used as a liturgy at a special

---

[1] As matter of fact, this is a clash between two Israelite religious traditions, cf. Ahlström, in *Transitions in Biblical Scholarship*, pp. 117 f.

[2] The reference to Amos' confrontation with Amaṣiah was not written by the prophet. This incident was related by someone else, a fact which speaks for the book as having been written by someone who has known Amos and has learned from Amos himself the oracles and experience of Amos as a *nābīʾ*. After his return to Judah, Amos may have memorized (cf. Jer. 36) his oracles and taught them to some of his fellow *nōqdīm* or some *famulus* who may later have written them down, cf. Ahlström, "Oral and Written Transmission", *HTR* 59/66, pp. 78 ff.

[3] Cf. A. S. Kapelrud, *Joel Studies*, p. 159. I do not agree, however, with Kapelrud's notion that the section 4:4-8 has "been subjected to change during the process of transmission" and that, therefore, "the rythmic form was lost and substituted for prose", p. 159. For the reasons mentioned above, I do not believe that there ever was a rhythmic form of this passage.

[4] For the phrase "Sitz im Literatur", see L. Alonso-Schökel, "Die stilistische Analyse bei den Propheten", *SVT* 7/60, p. 162.

[5] J. Bourke, *RB* 66/59, p. 11, cf. Wolff, *Joel*, p. 7, and S. R. Driver, *The Books of Joel and Amos*, 1915, pp. 35 f.

festival, as some scholars have advocated.[1] However, it is beyond doubt that Joel has made use of liturgical forms, phrases and formulas. One should note that Joel addresses not only the elders and the people, 1:2, but also the priests, 1:13, 2:17, a fact which cannot be in support of the theory that the text is a liturgy. However, one could surmise that Joel delivered his message at a time when the people came together for one of the festivals at the temple. Joel 2:18 may then indicate that a day of penance was held, and after that day—or on one of the following days of the same festival—2:19-4:21 may have been delivered.[2]

What then can be said about the transmission and the writing down of the oracles of this prophet? Nothing factual is known concerning this problem. Thus, there is no other possibility than to resort to some hypothesis as a means to figure out what could have been a probable process. From the viewpoint of tradition history, there are two probabilities that can be considered. The first is that the prophet himself, of course, wrote down his prophecy as a com-

---

[1] In his book *Psalmenstudien* III, 1923, S. Mowinckel saw Joel 1-2 as being a liturgy "bei einer grossen Heuschreckenplage aufgeführt", p. 29. He was followed by, among others, H. Gunkel, "Psalmen 4", *RGG* IV², col. 1614, (K. Galling, *RGG* V³, col. 677). Cf. H. Reventlow, who characterizes Joel 1 as a "Klageliturgie", which he compares with Jer. 14:1-15:9, *Liturgie und prophetisches Ich bei Jeremia*, 1963, pp. 154 f. Also, he considers Ch. 2 to be a liturgy, some kind of parallel to Ch. 1, p. 115. See also J. Gray, *I & II Kings*, p. 200. Mowinckel has later on revised his opinion somewhat by saying that Joel gives "evidence of strong influences from the forms of psalms and cultic liturgy", *Psalms in Israel's Worship* II, p. 93, cf. C. A. Keller, *Osée, Joël, Amos, Abdias, Jonas*, 1965, p. 105. I. Engnell characterized the whole book of Joel as "a liturgical type", understanding the word "liturgical" as a "purely form-literary term", *The Call of Isaiah* (UUÅ 1949:4), p. 60, cf. G. von Rad, who sees Joel as a liturgical compostion, *Old Testament Theology* II, p. 122 (Germ. ed., p. 135). Johs. Lindblom sees in Joel "a mixture of liturgical elements and other prophetic sayings [a somewhat peculiar statement because it implies that liturgical elements are prophetic sayings!] for the most part with an eschatological context". Ch. 3 and 4 he sees as "purely eschatological prophecies" having "no direct connection with the foregoing", *Prophecy in Ancient Israel*, pp. 276 f. According to E. Sellin—G. Fohrer, Joel is a cult prophet who composed a liturgy "to be recited in the cult", *Introduction to the Old Testament*, p. 271, cf. p. 429. For Wolff, the book of Joel is "ein kunstvolles literarisches Gebilde" which has taken its basic forms from "einer grossen Klageliturgie", *Joel*, pp. 8 f., cf. Kapelrud, *Joel Studies*, p. 179, who also says that the whole book has a "liturgical structure", p. 191. See also the discussion by Th. Chary, *Les prophètes et le culte à partir de l'exil*, pp. 209 ff.

[2] Cf. W. Baumgartner, *BZAW* 34/20, p. 19. Before the covenant could be reestablished, one had to perform a rite of penance, cf. N. Lohfink, "Die Bundesurkunde des Königs Josias", *Biblica* 44/63, p. 477, n. 3, cf. p. 284, n. 1. It is this that Joel asks for in 2:15 ff.

position that he never gave as an oral message; or, secondly, that he spoke these oracles to the people of Jerusalem and later on, he or someone else wrote them down. Because of the character of the message, I believe that the latter is the case. It is the most natural to assume. In this case, one has to reckon with a period of oral transmission. This period I consider to be mostly a period of the prophet's own memorization of his utterances.[1] In this case, there again are two possibilities concerning the writing down of this prophecy. In the first alternative, Joel himself may have written it down, or he could have dictated it to somebody, which does not differ from writing it himself. Being a cult prophet, his ability to memorize was probably highly developed and he may also have been familiar with writing. From this point of view, everything in the book can be ascribed to Joel. The second alternative is that some other cult prophet, or a disciple of Joel for the office of prophet, learned the message. Such prophets and disciples were trained in memorizing oracles. Joel may have taught such a person his utterances, which was not uncommon in the Near East. Perhaps several persons learned them, and one of those who had learned the message perfectly took the pains to write it down.[2] This may have been done with the prophet's permission or authorization. Also, in this case, there is no reason to advocate that any verse be considered as secondary.

---

[1] For this phenomenon, cf. G. Widengren, *Literary and Psychological Aspects of the Hebrew Prophets* (UUÅ 1948:10), p. 73.

[2] For this problem, see my article "Oral and Written Transmission", *HTR* 59/66, pp. 78 ff. Dt. 6:7 gives a notion about the importance of the oral teaching. The father has to teach his sons the words of Yahweh's *tōrāh*: "You shall repeat them to your sons, and you shall talk about them when you sit in your house, and when you walk on the way, and when you lie down, and when you arise". Could one not assume that a prophet used this kind of technique, and that he did it more intensely than the common man? Thus, one could also assume that the way of teaching described in Dt. 6:7 reveals something of the prophetic system of teaching and learning, which, in Deuteronomy, has been extended as a principle for the entire population. However, from Dt. 6:8 and 9 it is clear that one cannot speak of oral technique only.

INDEX OF PASSAGES

INDEX OF AUTHORS